# The Health of Women
## A Global Perspective

Published in association with the
National Council for International Health

# The Health of Women

## A Global Perspective

EDITED BY

## Marge Koblinsky
## Judith Timyan
## and Jill Gay

**Westview Press**
BOULDER, SAN FRANCISCO, & OXFORD

Published in 1993 in the United States of America by Westview Press, Inc., 5500 Central Avenue, Boulder, Colorado 80301-2877, and in the United Kingdom by Westview Press, 36 Lonsdale Road, Summertown, Oxford OX2 7EW


Library of Congress Cataloging-in-Publication Data
The Health of women : a global perspective / edited by Marge
    Koblinsky, Judith Timyan, and Jill Gay.
        p.   cm.
    Includes bibliographical references and index.
    ISBN 0-8133-8500-8 (HC) — ISBN 0-8133-1608-1 (PB)
    1. Women—Health and hygiene.    2. Women—Health and hygiene—
Social aspects.    I. Koblinsky, Marjorie A.    II. Timyan, Judith.
III. Gay, Jill.
    [DNLM: 1. Women's Health.    WA 300 H433859]
RA564.85.H4324    1993
362.1'082—dc20
DNLM/DLC
for Library of Congress                                                     92-49573
                                                                                 CIP


Printed and bound in the United States of America

The paper used in this publication meets the requirements
(∞) of the American National Standard for Permanence of Paper
for Printed Library Materials Z39.48-1984.

10     9     8     7     6     5     4     3     2

# Contents

*v*

# Foreword

This monograph is the result of the unique combination of enthusiasm, teamwork, and dedication which characterized the planning and presentation of the NCIH 1991 International Health Conference on Women's Health.

More than sixty international health and development professionals actively participated in the planning process as part of the Conference Advisory Committee, under the able leadership of Peggy Curlin and Anne Tinker and supported by the NCIH staff led by Frank Lostumbo and Francesca Dixon. Ann Van Dusen, of the U.S. Agency for International Development Office of Health, provided vital assistance to NCIH in distributing the Call for Abstracts to international health professionals through the AID network of health officers overseas. Many committee members also served in the ranks of the more than thirty rapporteurs who followed the conference events, led the discussions, and incorporated the ideas into the development of the Action Agenda, a process brilliantly facilitated by Jill Sheffield.

Neither the conference nor the Action Agenda would have been possible if it were not for generous grants from the MacArthur Foundation, the Rockefeller Foundation, and the United States Agency for International Development. Of the more than 200 presenters and forty-five speakers who provided the base of material for this book, many from abroad were able to participate only because of a generous grant from the Ford Foundation made possible by Jose Barzelatto, who also provided critical assistance in developing the program.

The conceptualization and design of this book were the result of the extraordinary efforts of the chapter authors themselves and the three editors, Marge Koblinsky, Judith Timyan, and Jill Gay. And the entire endeavor was reinforced at every turn by the commitment and leadership of former NCIH president Russell Morgan.

The heart of an organization such as NCIH is the commitment of its members. This book is a tribute to the cooperative efforts that were so generously and voluntarily contributed by all involved.

*Eliot T. Putnam, Jr.*                                            *Janet Gottschalk*
President, NCIH                                                      *Linda Vogel*
                                              Governing Board Co-Chairs

## The 1991 Conference Advisory Committee

John Alden, Mary Ann Anderson, Raj Arole, Michele Andina, Jose Barzelatto, Naomi Baumslag, Rogers Beasley, Gretchen Berggren, Irene Boostrom, Judith Bruce, Roxanna Carillo, Paulette Chapponniere, Elayne Clift, Susan Cochrane, Francine Coeytaux, Sally Coghlan, Peggy Curlin, Nick Danforth, Frances R. Davidson, Francisco Di Blasi, Joan Dunlop, Veronica Elliott, Gayle Gibbons, Geeta Rao Gupta, Muhiuddin Haider, Polly Harrison, Judith Helzner, Pat Hutar, Pamela Johnson, Marge Koblinsky, Adetokunbo Lucas, Subhi Mehdi, Alvaro Monroy, Melanie Marlett, Martita Marx, Chloe O'Gara, Willa Pressman, Pam Putney, Rebeca de los Rios, Allan Rosenfield, Judith Senderowitz, James R. Sheffield, Jill Sheffield, Margaret Snyder, Adwoa Steele, Patience Stephens, Jeanne Betsock Stillman, Norma Swenson, Judith Timyan, Anne Tinker, Peggy Valentine, Linda Valleroy, George Varkey, Anvar Velji, Linda Vogel, Soon Young Yoon, and Margot L. Zimmerman.

# Introduction

*Peggy Curlin and Anne Tinker*

This book is the product of the 1991 National Council for International Health's (NCIH) Conference on "Women's Health: The Action Agenda." The conference was launched on a note of both rage and hope—rage at the inequities and neglect of the past and signs of hope for the growing recognition of the need for improvements in women's health and the prospects for change. The Conference celebrates twenty years of the alliance of international health practitioners and policy makers concerned with global health issues. In these two decades great strides were made in providing preventive health. Today, 80 percent of the world's children are immunized against infectious diseases. Progress has also been made in providing children with life saving treatment of diarrheal diseases. In this decade the child survival initiative has been an effective strategy to mobilize resources, advocacy and action to save children from needless death.

However, as we look back over the past twenty years of international health we are struck by the paucity of attention that the creators and sustainers of children have received. Every year millions of women suffer preventable illness and five hundred thousand of them die from pregnancy-related complications. Too many suffer and die because they lack the information and resources to care for themselves.

As our distinguished authors point out, factors such as the status of women and their work confound women's ability to access health care. This book addresses the information and services women need to improve their health and the context in which they live their lives.

The findings in this book reflect highlights from the papers presented and the formal and informal discussions during the conference. We feel they do considerable justice in representing the rich mixture of viewpoints of the 1,400 participants and speakers who represented seventy-four coun-

1

tries. This document attempts to gather together the major threads of experience in providing women of all ages with health care. Most importantly, it suggests concrete ways to redress international inattention to women's health. It also sets realistic targets for moving from concern to action.

The loom on which the threads of this experience will be woven into a new tapestry for women's health is made of guiding principles, clearly brought forth in the conference.

- Gender-specific data are essential, not only to assure that women are being reached, but to assure that resources are equitably and effectively shared.
- Health providers, planners and advocates must confront gender discrimination. Women don't want or deserve less, but society, culture and tradition often block their access to what is rightfully theirs. This must change.
- Women's health begins in infancy. Policies and programs must include attention to the adequate nutrition, health care and education of girls and young women as well as mothers.
- Although female mortality and morbidity are the gross indicators of women's health, the quality of their lives is an indicator of their ability to develop and maximize their potential. Women must be empowered by training, education and participation to seek prevention and treatment of diseases which maim and kill them. They must determine for themselves how many children they will have because it is they who take the risks of fertility and the responsibilities of motherhood.

Finally, who will weave the tapestry which will tell the tale and show the picture of a new world for women? Women themselves must determine what that picture will be. We, as health and development advocates, must sit by the artist and her work, listen carefully and thoughtfully to what she is saying and see the world through her eyes as she weaves this cloth with strength and beauty.

# 1

## Women's Health: The Price of Poverty

*Jodi L. Jacobson*

Two out of three women around the world presently suffer from the most debilitating disease known to humanity.[1] Common symptoms of this fast-spreading ailment include chronic anemia, malnutrition, and severe fatigue. Sufferers exhibit an increased susceptibility to infections of the respiratory and reproductive tracts. And premature death is a frequent outcome. In the absence of direct intervention, the disease is often communicated from mother to child, with markedly higher transmission rates among females than males. Yet, while studies confirm the efficacy of numerous prevention and treatment strategies, to date few have been vigorously pursued.

The disease is poverty. After four decades of conventional economic development strategies aimed at improving the human prospect, the number of people living in poverty continues to grow in nation after nation. More than one billion people worldwide live in "absolute poverty."[2] At least two billion others have incomes insufficient to meet more than their most basic immediate needs (Durning 1989; UNDIESA 1991b).[3] That women are disproportionately represented among these numbers makes poverty the leading cause of death and illness in females in more than just a figurative sense.

Measured in dollar terms alone, poor people have less income to spend on nutritious food, clean water, and adequate clothing and shelter, assets requisite to a minimum level of health and well-being. Engaged in a daily struggle to meet basic needs, the poor often can not avail themselves of preventive health care, or save for the exigencies of unexpected illness. And they have less access to the social tools, such as education and political clout, needed to improve and safeguard health.

But the health risks of poverty are nevertheless far greater for females than for males. Indeed, women lag behind men on virtually every indicator of social and economic status. In every country and at every socioeconomic level, women control fewer productive assets than do men. Women everywhere work longer hours but earn less income despite the fact that they are responsible for meeting 40 to 100 percent of a family's basic needs (UNDIESA 1991b). And, lacking alternatives, women are more often compelled to resort to jobs that are seasonal, labor-intensive, and carry considerable occupational risk. As a result, poverty among females is more intractable than among males, and their health even more vulnerable to adverse changes in social and environmental conditions.

Women also face unique reproductive health threats. High rates of preventable illness and death from complications in pregnancy and childbirth, from unsafe abortion, and from sexually transmitted diseases and reproductive cancers are commonplace wherever women are poor and lack access to comprehensive reproductive health care. At least one million women will die of reproductive causes this year, and more than 100 million others will suffer disabling illnesses (Jacobson 1991). In many countries—such as Bangladesh, Brazil, Nigeria, and Uganda—reproductive causes now account for more than 50 percent of deaths among women in their childbearing years (Jacobson 1991).

Finally, women are frequently deprived of their human right to self-determination. The legal codes and customary practices still adhered to in many cultures prevent women from making and carrying out independent decisions on such fundamental personal matters as when to seek health care or practice family planning, even when the resources are available. This "powerlessness," noted Dr. Carmen Barroso of the MacArthur Foundation in her keynote address to the 18th Annual Conference of the National Council on International Health (NCIH) held in June 1991, "is itself a serious health hazard," forcing women to struggle harder to break the cycle of poverty for themselves and their families.

## The Social and Political Dimensions

The impact of poverty and social status on women's health is a universal issue. In the United States, lack of access to income and education has had a proven adverse impact on reproductive health. Nearly 40 percent of African American women and one-fourth of all women in the United States do not receive prenatal care in the first trimester of pregnancy (Children's Defense Fund 1988). Race and economic distinctions are primary determinants of breast cancer mortality rates: In her work with the U.S.-based National Women's Health Network, Olivia Cousins found that in the

United States during the eighties "although . . . women of color did not contract breast cancer at rates similar to Euro-American women, they died at higher rates" (Cousins 1991). In New York City, AIDS is now the leading killer of women ages 25 to 40 (Jacobson 1991).

Women's health needs are paid little heed because their voices are rarely heard in policy circles. Women rarely can shape the answers to questions of relevance to their health in large part because they are underrepresented in politics and in the national and international bodies charged with safeguarding health. The overall share of women holding seats in the world's parliaments actually fell from 14.6 percent in January 1988 to 11 percent in September 1991, the lowest point in 16 years (Interparliamentary Union 1991). Only 3.6 percent of the top management positions of the United Nations are filled by women.

Consequently, few public policies have as a main goal improving the health and well-being of women. In fact, government policies and priorities that do not account for their diverse health needs often affect women adversely. In several industrial countries, for example, women have been neglected in programs aimed at the prevention and treatment of heart disease, cancer, and AIDS among other illnesses.

On the other hand, women's reproductive roles have been overemphasized, especially where fertility rates are high. "Because of the 'invisible' nature of women's productive contribution, their reproductive role receives the most attention," states Bangladeshi women's health advocate Meherun Nessa Islam. "As a result, the only health care women often get is family planning and even this is focused on controlling their fertility rather than improving their health "(Islam 1991). Other health concerns—such as unsafe working conditions and long hours at difficult labor that pose innumerable occupational hazards and the impact on women of inadequate sanitation and deteriorating environmental conditions—garner little attention.

But even in the sphere of reproductive health, religion and politics have taken precedence over public health concerns. For much of the past three decades, for example, women in the Soviet Union and much of Eastern Europe have relied heavily on unsafe abortion because of the enforced scarcity of suitable contraceptives and safe abortion services—a scarcity originally created to shore up birth rates (Jacobson 1991). Similarly, in the United States and elsewhere, women's legal right to safe abortion services is now threatened.

Some progress has recently been made on the part of international agencies in calling attention to women's health needs. But real improvements in the availability and acceptability to individual women of basic services are not occurring quickly enough. Unless concerted action is taken immediately, long-established problems of maternal illness and death, coupled with growing threats—such as occupational illnesses, domestic violence, the mounting reliance on unsafe abortion, the spread of AIDS and other STDs and the rise in breast and cervical cancer—will claim an ever-greater share of women in their prime.

Recognizing this, women throughout the world are taking direct action, empowering themselves in the struggle to reduce poverty, improve health, and realize a better quality of life for all people. Asked "What do women want?" participants in the NCIH conference put forward an international agenda that includes a broad range of social, economic, and health care reforms aimed at political empowerment and increased access to resources (See Table 1.1).

## Women and the Global Economic Crisis

In the Third World, the impact of structural-adjustment programs on women's health has been dramatic. Throughout the 1980s, a worsening global economic crisis brought into sharp relief the social, economic, and political dimensions of women's health. A decline in per-capita income caused by global recession, together with balance-of-payments problems,

TABLE 1.1 "What We Want—Voices from the South"

- Durable arrangements for the transfer of resources; reductions in, if not cancellations of, the debt burden; and direct investment to meet capital requirements.
- Favorable trading terms and better prices for primary commodities like coffee, tea, and cocoa.
- Access to credit and training; programs for awareness-and confidence-building.
- Joint ventures small and medium scale to create jobs; investments in sustainable economic growth.
- Investments in the development and dissemination of appropriate technology to reduce women's work burdens.
- Access to nutritious good food, safe water, and education for both girls and boys.
- Sustainable strategies for the use of natural resources.
- Reallocation of financial resources to critical health care areas like disease control, maternal and child health and family planning, and development of appropriate health systems.
- Cooperation to establish, expand, and strengthen community based approaches for promotional and educational activities of family planning and family life education.
- Access to information concerning women's bodies, and the right to choose the number of children born as well as to plan families without government interference.
- Access to human resources as well as to vaccines, medicines, and equipment.
- Universal access to contraceptives for both men and women.

*Source*: "What We Want—Voices from the South", a forum discussion held at the 18th Annual National Council on International Health Conference, "Women's Health: The Action Agenda for the Nineties," June 23-26, 1991, Arlington, Virginia.

deteriorating terms of trade, and heavy debt burdens carried by Third World countries, left a growing number of households unable to meet their basic needs. While the government investments vital to women have dwindled, the number of female-headed households has multiplied in the urban and rural areas of both industrial and developing countries.

Debt and interest payments owed by developing countries now equal three times as much as all aid received from industrialized countries in 1988 (Barroso 1991). Efforts to meet their obligations have forced these countries to reduce domestic investment at the cost of household income. In the 1980s, for example, per-capita incomes in sub-Saharan Africa and Latin America—the two most heavily indebted regions—fell by one-fourth and one-sixth respectively (Agarwal et al. 1990).

Meanwhile, fiscal crises have forced drastic reductions in vital services. Structural-adjustment programs required massive cuts in already tight health budgets. Real per-capita spending on health care fell in three-fourths of the nations of Africa and Latin America between 1980 and 1990 (Barroso 1991; Moser 1991).

The combination of increased family responsibilities and diminished economic prospects together force women to engage in a perilous balancing act in the struggle to support themselves and their families. Female-headed households in every country are swelling the ranks of the poor. Estimates indicate women are the sole breadwinners in one-fourth to one-third of the world's households (Agarwal et al. 1990). What is more, at least one-fourth of other households rely on female earnings for more than 50 percent of total income (Agarwal et al. 1990). Yet three-fourths of the world's women live in countries where per-capita gross domestic product either declined or increased only by an average of less than $10 annually during the eighties (UNDIESA 1991b).

In the Dominican Republic, the number of female-headed families has doubled to 21 percent over the last decade (Cottam 1991). Ninety-six percent of these households live below the poverty line (Cottam 1991). In rural Bangladesh, 25 percent of landless rural households are headed by females, compared to 15 percent in the total rural population (Agarwal et al. 1990). In some other countries—rural Ghana, Kenya, and Zambia, for example—the proportion now exceeds 30 percent (Agarwal et al. 1990).

Women cope with crises by putting their own needs last. The increasing scarcity of public resources means that more and more women sacrifice their own health by devoting an increasing proportion of personal resources—time, physical energy, and tangible goods—to support their families, and care for the sick and elderly (Moser 1991).

Reductions in food subsidies, real wages, and public sector employment force women to work longer hours to ensure their families' survival. Nutritional levels decline quickly: World Bank consultant Caroline Moser notes that as prices rise, "women are forced to shift to less expensive, often less nutritious foods in order to feed their families"(Moser 1991). Cuts in health and childcare along with those in family planning and education not only increase women's work burden, they virtually ensure that women's health needs go unmet. Working harder, eating less, and supported by fewer social services, poor women are increasingly susceptible to falling ill.

Adjustment programs, according to the report of an expert group on women and structural adjustment, "were designed without consideration of their impact on human conditions .... As a result, they have damaged the human and capital resource base available to society" (Agarwal et al. 1990). In large part, such programs are the product of development strategies based on "indicators of progress" that systematically fail to account for women's social and economic contributions to society.

## A Statistical Purdah

Unfortunately, many of the yardsticks used to guide international development over the past four decades are either incomplete or based on mistaken assumptions, and therefore reveal little about the quality of human life in general, and about women's lives in particular. Higher aggregate levels of agricultural production, for example, do not necessarily imply lower levels of malnutrition. A rising gross national product (GNP) does not necessarily produce a decline in the incidence of poverty or an improvement in equity. And a real increase in the health budget of one country does not automatically lead to better access to primary health care among those most in need of it.

Without the appropriate tools, it is impossible to answer critical questions regarding the impact of development policies and practices on women. For example, are women living longer *and* better? How much do they contribute to family income? Do they have more opportunities now than in the past? Do they have greater access to education, food, shelter, health care? How close are they to achieving parity with men? The failure of available measures to answer these questions underscores the need for collecting, disaggregating, and analyzing data by gender.

From the 1950s through the early 1980s, for example, standards of living as measured by widely used basic indicators—including life expectancy, per-capita income, and primary-school enrollment—rose dramatically. These gains notwithstanding, women never achieved parity with men. (See Table1.2). Perhaps more important, real socioeconomic gains among women have been far less substantive than statistics themselves might imply.

Consider life expectancy. Global average life expectancy among females rose from forty-nine years in the period 1950-55 to sixty-six years in 1985-

1990 (UNDIESA 1991a). Distressingly, indications are that even where women are living longer they may be suffering more. Much of the gain in life expectancy among both males and females over the past four decades can be attributed to dramatic reductions in infant mortality, as well as improvements in nutrition, sanitation, and access to primary health care services along with prevention of disease. But the vast majority of women worldwide continue to suffer the effects of chronic overwork, inadequate nutrition, frequent childbearing, and emotional stress.

Widespread regional differences in female life expectancy reflect a variety of socioeconomic and health conditions. For example, the average woman in Japan will live to about eighty years of age (UNDIESA 1991b). The life expectancy of women in most other Asian countries is sharply lower, reaching only fifty years in India and Pakistan (UNDIESA 1991b). Cancers and heart disease have replaced complications of pregnancy as leading causes of illness and death among the generally older, relatively wealthier female populations of the United States and Germany, while the latter remain critically important to the health of poor women throughout the Third World (UNDIESA 1991b; Asian and Pacific Women's Resource Collection Network 1989).

All other things being equal, global averages reveal women live longer than men for a number of reasons having to do with biology and lifestyle. In developed regions, female life expectancy is nearly seven years longer than for males. In Africa, Asia, and Latin America, women outlive men by three to five years on average (UNDIESA 1991b).

But aggregate statistics mask important qualitative differences in life expectancy between males and females. Mortality rates for young girls, for example, have been found to be markedly higher than those for males in a number of countries throughout the Middle East, North Africa, and the Indian subcontinent (Acsadi and Acsadi 1990; Kamel 1983). Such patterns are the product of, among other things, gender discrimination in the allocation of food and health care, coupled with high rates of death from complications of pregnancy and childbirth, all of which reflect the low socioeconomic status of women in these regions.

In India, for example, basic indicators of caloric intake and life expectancy measured by the government's 1991 census reveal marked declines among females relative to males in several states since 1980, despite an overall increase in the availability of food and health care (Crossette 1991; Ghosh 1991; Ram 1991). With the exception of girls aged ten to fourteen, Indian females die from preventable causes at higher rates than males from infancy through age thirty-five (Chatterjee 1991a).

Indian health scientist and World Bank consultant Meera Chatterjee estimates that, for India as a whole, deaths of girls under age five exceed those of boys by nearly 330,000 annually (Chatterjee 1991a). Every sixth infant death is attributable to gender bias (Chatterjee 1991a). Data confirm that women aged fifteen and older die from the common major diseases—such as tuberculosis, typhoid, and gastroenteric infections—at consistently higher rates than for males (Chatterjee 1991a).

As a result, contrary to patterns found in the majority of countries, the ratio of women to men in India has actually been declining since the early part of the century. (See Figure 1.1). There are now only 929 women for every 1,000 men compared to 972 in 1901 (Government of India 1991). Dr. Veena Mazumdar, director of the Delhi-based Centre for Women's Development Studies, notes that "the declining sex ratio is the final indicator that registers . . . women are losing out on all fronts—on the job market, in health and nutrition and economic prosperity" (Ram 1991).

Deeper exploration of other measures of progress reveal similar gender biases. In 1985, 60 percent of the adult population worldwide was literate, compared to about 46 percent in 1970, clearly a significant improvement

TABLE 1.2  Gender Disparities in the Human Development Index, Selected Countries, 1991

| Country | Overall Human Development Index (percent of 100) | Index for Females as a Share of Males |
|---|---|---|
| Finland | 96 | 93.7 |
| Sweden | 98 | 90.2 |
| France | 97 | 86.4 |
| United States | 98 | 82.8 |
| Canada | 98 | 82.7 |
| United Kingdom | 97 | 81.0 |
| Italy | 95 | 78.5 |
| El Salvador | 52 | 75.4 |
| Philippines | 61 | 77.5 |
| Japan | 99 | 77.0 |
| Portugal | 88 | 76.6 |
| Paraguay | 67 | 72.9 |
| Sri Lanka | 66 | 72.8 |
| Ireland | 94 | 72.8 |
| Costa Rica | 88 | 69.8 |
| South Korea | 88 | 67.9 |
| Kenya | 40 | 51.5 |

The "Human Development Index" (HDI) is an attempt to gauge development by the degree to which people have the options to enable them to "lead a long and healthy life, to be knowledgeable and to find access to the assets, employment and income needed for a decent standard of living." The measures used in this table reveal the female HDI as a share of that for males. The data needed to make these comparisons were available for only thirty countries in total; seventeen of those appear here.

*Source:* United Nations Development Programme, 1991. *Human Development Report 1991.* New York: Oxford University Press.

(UNDIESA 1991b). Literacy among men rose faster than that among women, however, meaning that the gender gap in literacy actually widened. Between 1970 and 1985, the number of illiterate women rose from 543 million to 597 million, while that of men increased by four million to 352 million (UNDIESA 1991b).

Today, only 15 percent of all women in Africa are literate, as opposed to 33 percent of all men (Starrs 1987). In Asia, one-third of all women can read, compared with more than one-half of all men (Starrs 1987). Without opportunities to learn and acquire skills, adult women cannot participate fully in the increasingly market-oriented economies of the world—a situation that reinforces their marginalization.

Moreover, while primary school enrollments for both boys and girls are roughly equal in Latin America and the Caribbean, as well as in industrial countries, female enrollments in sub-Saharan Africa and in southern Asia still lag far behind those for boys (UNDIESA 1991b; UNDP 1991). In some countries, even though girls and boys enter school at the same or similar rates, boys are much more likely to finish. A survey from India, for example, showed that while about 60 percent of rural boys and girls are enrolled in school, only 15 percent of girls remained in school after five years, as opposed to 35 percent of boys (UNDP 1991).

In Africa, "more and more girls are dropping out of both primary and secondary school or just missing school altogether due to increasing poverty," states Madame Phoebe Asiyo of the United Nations Fund for Women. "Increasing poverty combined with the cost-sharing programs some countries have implemented are having very negative effects on girls' education" (Asiyo 1991).

## The Invisible Workforce

In every society, women provide critical economic support to their families, alone or in conjunction with spouses, by earning income in agriculture, in informal and formal labor markets, and in emerging international industries. Nevertheless, virtually every country invests far less in its women workers—and they receive a considerably smaller share of what society produces—than their male counterparts. The lack of public investment to increase female productivity coupled with persistent occupational and wage discrimination prevents women from achieving parity with men in terms of jobs and income.

Data indicate women work longer hours than men in every country except Australia, Canada, and the United States (UNDIESA 1991b). Hours worked earning wages or producing subsistence goods are rarely offset by a reduction of duties at home. Time allocation studies support the contention that women throughout the world maintain almost exclusive responsibility for childcare and housework (Agarwal et al. 1990). Moreover, gender disparities in total hours worked are greatest among the poor. In most developing countries women work an average of twelve to eighteen hours per day—as opposed to ten to twelve for men—in their multiple roles within families as caretakers, educators, health promoters, and income earners (Agarwal et al. 1990).

The notion that females do not contribute to family income is a tragic fallacy that both international agencies and national governments have failed to combat. Most of women's economic activity takes place in the non-wage subsistence economy for the purpose of household consumption. Although "income generation" of this type is critically important, especially to the poorest households, it is typically underestimated or ignored. In one study of Nepalese villages, for example, estimates to household income based on wages earned put the value of female contributions at 20 percent (UNDIESA 1991b). Taking account of subsistence production, however, brought this contribution to 53 percent of total household consumption. Similarly, estimates from the Philippines of women's "full

FIGURE 1.1 Number of Women Per 1000 Men, India

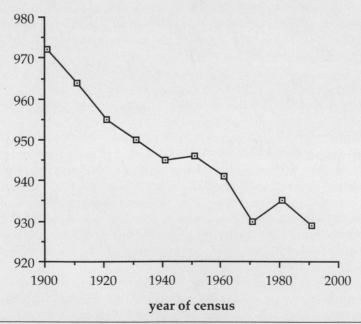

year of census

*Source*: *New Delhi, India, Government Census*, 1991.

income" contribution were twice as high as marketed income (UNDIESA 1991b).

Likewise, women's contributions to food production are rarely measured adequately in official statistics because many work without pay on family farms or earn wages only on a seasonal basis. This oversight implies that innumerable opportunities to increase production and improve nutrition are foregone daily. In Africa, for example, women produce 80 percent of the food consumed domestically and at least 50 percent of export crops (UNDIESA 1991b; UNDP 1991). But the United Nations Food and Agriculture Organization finds that only 2 to 10 percent of contacts made by agricultural extension agents in Africa involved women farmers (UNDIESA 1991b).

Throughout Southeast Asia and the Indian subcontinent at least 70 percent of the female labor force is engaged in agriculture (UNDIESA 1991b). Yet fewer than 10 percent of women farmers in India, Nepal, and Thailand are land owners (UNDIESA 1991b; Bennett 1989). Some studies show the role of women in agricultural production as measured by labor inputs is increasing in these regions as more and more men migrate to cities and towns (UNDIESA 1991b). But without access to information and credit, and in the absence of meaningful legal reform regarding land tenure, the potential of women farmers to improve their prospects will remain unrealized.

Nearly 40 percent of India's economy, for example, is based on agriculture. Few resources reach women, although they comprise a large share of both paid and unpaid (family) agricultural labor (Chatterjee 1991a; Bennett 1989). National survey data on which investment decisions are based imply women make up 46 percent of the agricultural labor force (Chatterjee 1991a; Bennett 1989). A study by the United Nations International Labor Organization detailing the way rural women spend their time indicates that up to 90 percent of rural women in central India participate in agriculture (Chatterjee 1991a).

Yet government attempts to enhance productivity have largely benefited men. The failure to pass and enforce laws ensuring women equal access to productive resources such as land and credit grants them an economic future that is abysmal at best. The agricultural extension system mostly bypasses the 40 percent of India's self-employed cultivators that are women (Bennett 1989; Chatterjee 1991a). The distribution of irrigation outlets, skewed in favor of large landholders, discriminates against the small family farms on which women work and produce food for domestic consumption. And the credit needed to enhance on-farm crop and labor productivity remains out of reach of women largely because they lack ownership of land as collateral. Recent findings reveal that as the plight of female farmers has worsened, nutritional gaps between females and males have become more pronounced, even in areas where overall food production is increasing (Bennett 1989; Chatterjee 1991a).

As with measures of life expectancy and education, an upward swing in the share of the female labor force working in the "formal sector" seems unarguably positive. Females now make up over one-third of the global workforce (UNDIESA 1991b). But this, too, has proved to be a mixed blessing. In every country with data available, women's non-agricultural wage rates remain substantially lower than those for men. On average, women earn between 60 and 70 percent of the income garnered by men for the same or similar work (UNDIESA 1991b). In parts of Africa and Asia, the wage gap in male-female earnings reaches 50 percent (UNDIESA 1991b).

## Hazardous Endeavors

Because government investments in the training and education of women lag far behind those for men, even when women do enter the formal labor force, they can usually obtain only the lowest-skilled, lowest-paying jobs. Not coincidentally, in developing countries these are more often than not in unregulated industries. New occupational health risks have arisen as increasing numbers of women take jobs in factories in rapidly developing economies.

"In Thailand," according to Blair Brooke of the Population Council, "reproductive problems are still the leading cause of illness and death among women aged fifteen to forty-nine. But occupational risks are becoming increasingly important as young women move into industries where they are forced to work long hours at low pay rates under hazardous conditions" (Brooke 1991).

Walter K. Patrick, Chair of the Department of Community Health Development at the University of Hawaii, echoed these sentiments on the increase in both economic participation and occupational hazards among women in Free Trade Zones. In his presentation, he stated:

Multinational corporations are seen to have lower standards of health protection in manufacturing and marketing in the developing countries than in home-country operations. Women who represent the majority of the labor force in such multinational industries are often the victims of inadequate health protection policies. Various health problems including those that affect reproductive health, such as the teratogenic effects of toxic-chemical exposure, spontaneous abortion, miscarriage, and cancer are being increasingly recognized (Patrick 1991).

Even less well-recognized are the occupational hazards faced by women in carrying out their traditional roles. Female agricultural workers are subject to hazards that affect men as well, such as poisoning from pesticides and chemical fertilizers. But they also face additional hazards. Where women do most of the transplanting and weeding for rice cultivation, they are at high risk for backaches, postural defects, and infectious and parasitic diseases (Chatterjee 1991a).

Girls who begin carrying heavy loads of water at a young age are at risk for scoliosis, for example (Chatterjee 1991a). Even cooking has specific hazards: A study of four villages in rural Gujarat found that women who cooked in poorly ventilated huts were exposed to, on average, 100 times the level of suspended smoke particles deemed acceptable by the WHO, six times higher than other household members, and 15 times higher than a resident of Delhi (Chatterjee 1991a).

Low socioeconomic status may endanger women's health in other ways. Deepening poverty among women, a product both of their low status and general economic decline, is contributing to a rise in prostitution—and thus the spread of sexually transmitted reproductive-tract infections—in many urban areas worldwide. Researchers Mead Over and Peter Piot connect the lack of education among women, and the mushrooming growth of African cities (chiefly resulting from the increase in male migrants from rural areas), to a rise in prostitution and the further spread of infections (Over and Piot forthcoming).

Because of their multiple sexual contacts, prostitutes are more likely to contract and pass on reproductive-tract infections (Ngugi 1991). Chancroid, for example, is the most common cause of genital sores in Africa and is strongly linked to prostitution. A 1985 study found genital ulcers related to chancroid in 42 percent of prostitutes from a slum in Nairobi (Plummer and Ngugi 1989). Many male migrants have multiple sexual partners, including prostitutes, and therefore put themselves, and their wives and other partners at increased risk of disease (Over and Piot forthcoming).

In developing countries, prostitution is a recourse sometimes taken by infertile women rejected by their families and communities—or by countless others impoverished by continuing economic crises. The movement of abandoned or rejected barren women to urban prostitution has been noted in Niger, Uganda, and the Central African Republic (Over and Piot forthcoming). Equally insidious is the sale of women and girls into prostitution by their families, a practice documented in several countries in Asia (Barry 1984).

In her study of prostitutes and their role in preventing the spread of both STDs and HIV in Kenya, Dr. Elizabeth Ngugi found that "the majority are single girls who dropped out of school due to pregnancy . . . [who were] either chased away by parents or guardians or lacked financial support for themselves and their infants. The next largest category are divorcees, separated, widowed, and a few married women" (Ngugi 1991). This latter group cited lack of support from their husbands and unemployment as the major factor driving them into prostitution. "The basic reason—economics— remains the same no matter the group," stated Ngugi (Ngugi 1991).

Economics may drive young girls to increase their risks of infection and HIV in other ways. In Zaire, for example, J. Convisser and several colleagues found that young girls hoping to complete secondary school face few options when they "are told there is no money in the house for school fees" (Convisser et al. 1991). One option is to drop out of school and hope to get married. "A second option for the young woman is to stay in school by accepting a 'sugar daddy'—a [usually older] man who offers some sort of regular financial support in exchange for sexual favors" (Convisser et al. 1991).

Also common in Zaire is the practice whereby men take a second wife (Convisser et al. 1991). This leaves women in a position of extreme economic vulnerability. Although men are often unable to support two households and leave their wives to fend for themselves, social mores put the burden of "keeping the man at home" on women. "In short," states Convisser, "women are succumbing to economic and social pressures that expose them to potential HIV [and other] infection" (Convisser et al. 1991).

Many of the same factors—women's status, poverty, social disintegrations, prostitution—along with a growing trend of exchanging sex for drugs, are responsible for the disproportionately high rates of sexually transmitted diseases among women in some low-income populations in the United States (Aral and Holmes 1991). Chlamydia infections are believed to be rising rapidly among U.S. minorities. From 10 to 30 percent of sexually active adolescent women in the inner cities of the United States are now infected with chlamydia (Aral and Holmes 1991).

## Environmental Degradation and the Status of Women

Environmental degradation, too, often hits women first and hardest. Rural women are constantly occupied in the collection of natural resources. Reductions in fresh water supplies through overuse or pollution, deforestation of fuelwood stocks, and depletion of soil fertility through erosion are trends common to most countries and are most acute in developing regions. As these resources are depleted, the time and labor women expend to meet basic needs increases dramatically, further compromising their health (Ofosu-Amaah 1991).

At least one billion people worldwide lack access to safe water supplies. The burden of providing water for family needs falls to women and girls; small-scale surveys from Africa and Asia reveal females spend from five to seventeen hours per week collecting water from distant sources (UNDIESA

1991b). In allocating scarce time and resources, most women opt to protect their families, not their health. "One wonders what choices these women have," reflected Madame Phoebe Asiyo of the United Nations Fund for Women. "Do they walk the ten to fifteen kilometers to fetch water and fuelwood in order to cook meals for their families or do they walk the same distance to the nearest health center to have their tummies touched or to queue for family planning services? Where a woman does not perceive her own health needs, she will of course opt for the former" (Asiyo 1991).

Studies undertaken in some of the poorest countries are beginning to reflect the impact of environmental degradation on the health of both women and children. In rural Namibia, some 40 percent of households are headed by women. These households, according to a Namibian govern- ment report, are encountering a "high and rising propensity to [become ill], and [face chronic] income and basic food shortages due to drought and the depletion of natural resources" (Ithana et al. 1990). These constraints, combined with "lack of access to agricultural services, including basic input supply, processing, and marketing facilities . . . and a probable tendency for remittances from husbands and sons to grow less reliable over time," make the economic and health prospects for women and their children grave indeed (Ithana et al. 1990).

Malawi's population growth rate, at 3.3 percent, is one of the highest in Africa. There, too, natural resource constraints are impeding progress. "The demand for fuelwood far outstrips the supply," states a government report, "and with the increasing population density, the gap between demand and supply is expected to continue [widening]. As such, women have serious problems fetching firewood from distant and dwindling forests" (Govern- ment of Malawi 1990).

Unpredictable rainfall, shortages of surface water, and a drought-prone environment are characteristic of countries throughout sub-Saharan Africa. In Malawi, "there is still a problem of safe water supply for 46 percent of the rural population, [a problem which] mostly affects women, who are respon- sible for fetching water" (Government of Malawi 1990).

An additional problem faced by many countries is the large and growing flow of refugees from civil and international conflict. Women and children now represent nearly 80 percent of the fourteen million refugees displaced by war and political conflict worldwide (UNDIESA 1991b). Rarely are these refugees provided with sufficient levels of education or health care.

Malawi, for example, is currently host to more than eighty thousand refugees from Mozambique, a number equivalent to a 10 percent increase in the country's population. Nearly 65 percent of these refugees are women and children in dire need of health care and nutritional assistance, which the Malawian government is hard-pressed to provide for its own people (Government of Malawi 1990).

Mozambique, too, faces a health crisis aggravated by vast numbers of internally displaced peoples. It is estimated that two to three million people have been displaced within the country due to internal strife. Often they migrate to the periphery of urban centers, which, according to a country status report, "do not have the infrastructure to absorb this new and large human horde. As a result, many end up living in sub-human conditions, in a situation of extreme poverty, famine, and disease" (Cecatti 1990).

## A Dubious Birthright

At the household level, gender bias in the allocation of resources usually begins at birth. Poverty and cultural beliefs about the value of women's work conspire to deprive females from infancy of the very resources they need be productive members of society throughout their lives.

A number of social and cultural traditions limit girls' access to education. In Africa, for example, is the practice of bride price, whereby a prospective husband gives money or goods to the bride's family in acknowledgment of the value of her labor and offspring. A report from Tanzania points out that when parents anticipate marrying their daughters early and obtaining a good bride price, they view "education for girls as a waste of time and resources" (Government of Tanzania 1990).

Similar obstacles face girls in parts of Asia. According to tradition in many agrarian societies, only males inherit their parents' property. Where land is the primary form of wealth, having at least one surviving son may be the only sure way of keeping it in the family. Sons are also responsible for providing their parents, particularly their mothers, with a secure future; widowed or divorced women without adult male sons to support them invariably face destitution (Acsadi and Acsadi 1990).

Daughters are viewed as a drain on household income. Not only is the work they do not valued by society, when they marry they take with them a dowry their parents may be forced into debt to provide. Parents are apt to invest in educating girls only when they perceive long-term gains will outweigh immediate costs. The outlays faced by individual families—such as the need to pay for uniforms, books, and even bribes to take advantage of a "free" education—raise the opportunity costs of sending girls to school when they are needed at home or in the fields. Parents hold little hope for recouping these expenses, since sex-discrimination combined with low levels of access to education and training prevent females from earning wages equal to men later in life (Acsadi and Acsadi 1990).

Nutrition and health care can also be marked by gender bias. Both girls and boys in Third World countries are far more likely to be nutritionally disadvantaged from the start. Data compiled by the United Nations

Children's Fund, for example, indicate that the daily per-capita calorie supply for all citizens, measured as a percentage of minimum nutritional needs, exceeds 100 percent in only 79 out of 131 countries (UNICEF 1989).

But malnutrition is far more prevalent among females than males in developing countries for reasons that have more to do with gender than geography. Males in some cultures take precedence over females in the allocation of food, a practice that may extend to the youngest children. Girls almost inevitably receive insufficient nourishment for the energy they expend in daily chores, not to mention for proper growth and development. Thus a nutritional gender gap often develops in early childhood.

Gender discrimination in the allocation of food—as well as health care and education—is a widespread and well-documented practice in much of South Asia, where strong preferences for male children diminish the "value" of females (Acsadi and Acsadi 1990). Studies from Bangladesh, India, Nepal, and Pakistan indicate that boys consistently receive more and better food than their sisters, although the nutritional needs of prepubescent boys and girls are virtually identical. According to a report from Uttar Pradesh, India, women breast-fed boys for an extended period with "the conscious view to providing them with a good start in life, whereas girls were not given this consideration" (Acsadi and Acsadi 1990).

Evidence of similar patterns of discrimination in the allocation of household resources from an early age has been found throughout the Middle East and North Africa, as well as in parts of sub-Saharan Africa. A maternal health status report from Lesotho asserts that the major contributor to the poor nutritional status of women is "the tradition of feeding men and boys before women and girls, [where] the nutritious foods are served to male members of the families and females would then have the leftovers" (Government of Lesotho 1990).

These gender disparities may result in far higher death rates among females than males in the critical period between infancy and age five. The United Nations Population Fund states that in the early eighties, deaths of children aged one to five were higher for females than males in Bangladesh, Egypt, India, Jordan, Mauritania, Morocco, Nepal, Sudan, Turkey, and a number of countries in Latin America (Sadik 1989). More recent data show these higher mortality rates still prevail in several countries in South Asia (Acsadi and Acsadi 1990; Chatterjee 1990a).

As girls grow into adulthood, their nutritional status often worsens due to the combined demands of childbearing, an increasingly heavy workload, and loss of iron stores through menstruation. A study conducted in the early 1980s, for example, showed that 20 to 45 percent of women of childbearing age in sub-Saharan Africa received inadequate calories daily (Mhloyi 1990). These nutritional deficits contribute to what may become lifelong handicaps, such as stunted growth and chronic anemia, two of the main factors behind complications of pregnancy and childbirth (World Health Organization forthcoming).

Myths restricting food consumption may further deplete a woman's strength at a time when she urgently needs an adequate and balanced diet. Pregnant women throughout Africa, Asia, and the Middle East are barred by taboo from eating a variety of foods including eggs, milk, and sometimes even fruits and vegetables (Acsadi and Acsadi 1990; Kamel 1983). Another contributor to inadequate food intake by women is the diversion of household income by their husbands to non-food purchases, most significantly alcohol (Mhloyi 1990).

From one-fifth to one-quarter of the women in most developing countries are now aged fifteen to forty-nine (UNDIESA 1991a). For a large majority of these women, the surest route to status and security is to bear many children, preferably sons. In many settings, even girls in their teens are under pressure to marry and bear their first child as soon as possible. In Zaria, Nigeria, for example, 83 percent of girls have been married by 14 years of age (Usman 1991). Consequently, many young women become both wives and mothers well before their eighteenth birthday, initiating a pattern of childbearing often referred to in health care circles as the "four toos"—too early, too close, too often, too late.

Ironically, women's needs—for adequate rest, good nutrition, and health care—are often ignored even when they are engaged in the one activity in which they have an undisputed monopoly: pregnancy. Poverty pressures both rural women and those in the informal urban economies to work through the final stages of pregnancy, putting enormous demands on their physical energy and allowing them little time for the rest they so badly need. Even those women employed in the formal sector have little job security. Maternity leave and benefits schemes are rare.

The lifelong drain on physical stamina experienced by women and girls is magnified during pregnancy, further compromising the health of both mother and child. The United Nations Children's Fund (UNICEF) has found that many African women gain minimal weight even in the last trimester of pregnancy, which, coupled with anemia, increases the chances of premature birth and a low-birth-weight baby (UNICEF 1989).

Despite these connections, until recently maternal health has not received much attention even in those programs ostensibly aimed at improving the health of both mothers and children. In a paper presented at the June 1991 NCIH conference, for example, Hilary Cottam of CARE revealed the failure of a U.S. food distribution program to account for maternal nutritional needs. "Generally speaking," Cottam asserted, "the priority for the P.L. 480 Title II project food-aid has been Maternal and Child Health (MCH) projects. The subject of women and appropriate food use, both in terms of nutritional status and general developmental impact has, however, been largely ignored both in official guidelines and practical implementation" (Cottam 1991).

CARE's data show the deepening effects of economic crisis have left the majority of Dominican families unable to buy enough food to meet basic needs. Today, 28 percent of women are malnourished and 43 percent are anemic (Cottam 1991). The U.S. program has focused on improving child malnutrition by providing direct intervention to children despite the fact that the three most common causal factors of poor nutrition among children—low birth weight, maternal illiteracy, and the absence of exclusive breast-feeding—are directly related to women's health status (Cottam 1991).

From one pregnancy to another, a women may never receive medical care. Lack of access to timely and effective basic maternal health care is a critical problem for Third World women and contributes mightily to maternal health problems. Indeed, the health care systems of most developing countries might be characterized by a different set of "four toos"—too far from home, too few trained birth-attendants, too poorly equipped to identify or handle complications, and too deficient in quality of care.

Even the existence of prenatal care facilities does not always translate into effective care. In Zimbabwe, for example, where at least 90 percent of pregnant women receive at least one prenatal checkup, most women are not checked until well into their third trimester (Government of Zimbabwe 1990). One study from Zimbabwe concluded that "motivation to come to prenatal care is high [but] most women book late" (Government of Zimbabwe 1990). Less than 20 percent of the women surveyed presented themselves for care before 20 weeks' gestation, making "interventions for treatment of anemia [and other problems], and administration of . . . immunizations difficult," according to the study (Government of Zimbabwe 1990).

There are myriad reasons why women are unable to make use of care that is theoretically "accessible" to them. One is lack of access to education on the importance of prenatal care. Lack of freedom is another—and often critical—factor. Other influences on the decision to seek health care are the strength of traditional beliefs and practices regarding pregnancy and delivery, distances, costs, and the real or perceived quality of services.

According to various studies, long distances to health facilities (made worse by poor roads and transportation networks) are obstacles to prenatal care. For example, 96 percent of mothers in two Nigerian villages who had not used a health facility to give birth cited distance as the reason (Thaddeus and Maine 1990). Surveys in South Asia, Central America, and among Navajo Indians in the state of New Mexico found similar results on the influence of distance to health-care-seeking behavior (Thaddeus and Maine 1990).

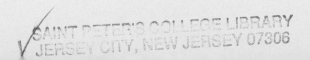

Poverty plays a major role in transportation and other costs, even when health services themselves are free. (See Chapter 7). Quality of care is another vital determinant of the share of women who seek medical treatment. Poor relationships between health care professionals and their clients, long waits, and administrative red tape are but a few of the problems cited by women seeking care (Thaddeus and Maine 1990). Studies show that well-staffed and well-equipped facilities—more the exception than the rule—attract a higher proportion of people in surrounding communities (Thaddeus and Maine 1990). And women from many developing countries cite other factors—the lack of emotional support and privacy, differences in language and culture between health professionals and their clients, a rude medical staff, and the often-expected "gift" for medical attention—as reasons why they do not make more use of available facilities (Thaddeus and Maine 1990).

Lacking prenatal care, the majority of women then face the prospect of giving birth without trained medical assistance. Only about one-third of all births are assisted by trained attendants in Africa and South Asia, as opposed to 64 percent in Latin America, 93 percent in East Asia, and virtually 100 percent in North America (Starrs 1987). In many Third World communities, traditional birth attendants—usually village-based women untrained in modern medicine—are the only source of maternal health care or the only affordable alternative to clinics (WHO and FIGO 1985). Because relatively few countries have put resources into training traditional attendants, their potential for reducing illness and deaths related to pregnancy remains untapped (WHO and FIGO 1985; Maglacas and Simons 1986).

Vast potential also exists for family planning—the use of contraceptive methods or other pregnancy prevention strategies—to improve women's reproductive health. Employing family planning methods to space or limit births improves the health of both mothers and children. Used correctly, several contraceptive methods—such as condoms, diaphragms, and hormonal pills—can assist women and their partners in preventing transmission of reproductive-tract infections. Perhaps most importantly, access to good-quality family planning services enables individuals to exercise a basic human right—to decide freely the number and spacing of offspring.

Contraceptive services alone are inadequate for safeguarding women's reproductive health. Unfortunately, these services invariably are offered to the exclusion of, rather than in addition to, assistance with a broader spectrum of reproductive health issues. Such issues include unwanted pregnancy, reproductive-tract infections, and infertility—conditions that a majority of women worldwide face one or more times during their lives.

Moreover, rather than meeting women's varied needs, governments and policy makers have devised programs that are often extremely limited in scope (Jacobson 1991). Too few programs provide a wide-enough array of contraceptive methods to insure women may both achieve an acceptable balance of personal risks and preferences in using contraception and switch methods as reproductive needs change. Too few offer adequate counseling services; too few provide follow-up care to combat the high rates at which women who express the need for birth control abandon contraceptive methods they are currently using.

In a number of countries high contraceptive prevalence rates exist against a backdrop of deteriorating reproductive health. In Brazil, for example, a recent study by the World Bank concludes that women's reproductive health needs are "poorly met," in part because government policies limit access to reversible contraceptives, such as condoms, diaphragms, and IUDs (Saxenian 1989). The major types of contraceptive pills available in Brazil—some of which have been taken off the market in other countries because of suspected health risks—are sold over-the-counter (Saxenian 1989).

More than 90 percent of all pill users obtain their supplies at private pharmacies, 40 percent of them without medical supervision; the World Bank notes that "medical contraindications [associated health risks] to pill use appear to be frequently ignored by (perhaps due to lack of alternative, effective, temporary methods) or unknown to the women who self-prescribe them" (Saxenian 1989).

And, notes Joselina da Silva, a Brazilian teacher and organizer, "about 46 percent of sexually active women between sixteen and fifty-four are now sterilized; the great majority of them are between sixteen and twenty-four years old" (da Silva 1991). In effect, many women are being sterilized who might otherwise opt not to if there were more reversible methods available. Moreover, da Silva claims a disproportionate share of black Brazilian women are being sterilized; 78 percent of black women aged sixteen to fifty-four are sterilized in states with a black majority as opposed to about 22 percent of whites (da Silva 1991).

There are similar findings in other countries. Despite considerable reductions in Mexico's birth rates since the early seventies, for example, a report on that country from a conference on women's reproductive health concluded that, "women and girls suffer from 'traditional' health problems such as anemia, infection, malnutrition, maternal mortality, and cancer of the cervix, as well as 'modern' illnesses such as depression, obesity, and STDs. Health services for most, regardless of income, are very poor, failing to provide information, counseling, or appropriate medical care" (Germaine and Antrobus 1989).[4] Adrienne Germaine, Vice President of the International Women's Health Coalition, and Peggy Antrobus, Director of Development Alternatives for Women in a New Era, argue that "policy makers still ask why women's health should occupy a special place despite the evidence of low contraceptive prevalence, rising rates of adolescent pregnancy, septic abortions, and high rates of sexually transmitted diseases and pelvic infection" (Germain and Antrobus 1989).

## Empowerment and Health

The difficulties inherent in improving women's health prospects lie not in the need for undiscovered medical techniques or the creation of vast and costly new health establishments. What is required is commitment and leadership on the part of national and international bodies to reorient health care strategies to meet women's needs and expand the populations of women they seek to reach.

Much of the money needed for a comprehensive health care strategy could be raised by reordering priorities and improving the efficiency with which health resources are now used. Health care budgets are inadequate everywhere and need desperately to be increased. But currently available funds are often poorly allocated. Even the least developed countries typically spend 60 to 80 percent of their public health budgets on urban hospitals, although only a small share of their populations will ever seek hospital services (Griffin 1991). Charles C. Griffin, a health economics researcher at the U.S.-based Urban Institute, finds "in some African countries . . . a single national hospital may consume 75 percent of the government health budget" (Griffin 1991).

More fundamentally, however, real improvements in women's health status will require far-reaching socioeconomic and cultural change extending beyond the health care system. Because women's health is a direct reflection of their status, no strategy can be successful in the long-term unless women become equal partners in social development. Systematic and fundamental changes in the nature of policies toward and allocation of resources to women will have to be addressed as part of a long-term strategy of change. (See Table 1.3). In the words of Olivia Cousins, "There can be no true and valid discussion of women's health until we first address the issue of empowerment" (Cousins 1991).

Indeed, this is already happening: Throughout Africa, Asia, and Latin America, community-based women's groups are bringing women together to share problems and find solutions on issues ranging from sexuality and reproductive-tract infections to domestic violence and the availability of credit. And women in every region have begun to effect change by *educating* themselves and others, *organizing* to achieve common goals, and *lobbying* to change discriminatory policies and practices. Women representing three organizations involved in various stages of this process presented their strategies at the NCIH conference.

*Isis International.* An information and communications service for women from all over the world, Isis International disseminates information about women's health. All the information collected presents a gender perspective with a permanent focus on women's reproductive health. "In Latin America particularly," notes Amparo Claro, director of Isis

TABLE 1.3 Agenda for Empowerment

- **Enforce or enact where needed legislation** to improve women's status. Launch education campaigns to alert women to their rights; develop legal assistance programs to aid enforcement. The Convention on the Elimination of All Forms of Discrimination Against Women should be ratified by all countries that have not done so to date; those that have should enforce its provisions—regarding inheritance laws, property rights, marriage contracts, divorce laws—to empower women, enhance their self-determination, and enable them to become economically, socially, and politically independent.
- **Promote efforts to expand female education** and reduce female illiteracy, addressing such obstacles as inadequate infrastructure for formal and informal education, the lack of female teachers, the practice of keeping girls out of school to work at household tasks, gender biases in education, and all other factors that limit women's knowledge, potential earning power, and political participation.
- **Address women's specific needs in employment and economic development** by promoting women's savings schemes, and providing no or low-collateral credit, extension services, training and material inputs.
- **Increase food security** by investing in women farmers; implement policies that improve the nutritional status of women and girls, and expand nutrition education.
- **Promote the development, extension, and popularization of appropriate labor-saving technologies** to ease women's work burdens. Ensure women's access to water and other essential resources. Develop information and education programs to encourage key family members, such as husbands and in-laws, to assist with household and other chores.
- **Encourage consistent monitoring of the impact of structural-adjustment policies on social and economic welfare;** devise programs to ameliorate the adverse impact of such programs and policies on women's health and socioeconomic status.
- **Require the collection and publication of gender-disaggregated data on socioeconomic indicators by all governments and international bodies.**
- **Establish baselines for vital indicators of women's health and well-being, and use these to measure progress within five-year intervals,** including measures of female literacy, numbers of women in the formal employment sector, and the share of women decision makers.
- **Encourage research** on the socioeconomic factors influencing health care-seeking behavior, compliance rates, attitudes, and women's decision-making processes, their perceptions and views.

International, "articles published by Isis regarding access to health care, contraceptives and information have served as an important basis for demanding massive education campaigns in several countries" (Claro 1991).

Isis represents a wide variety of groups "the most visible of which are those whose objectives are collective or direct action and use of the media to promote education," says Claro (Claro 1991). Among the most successful campaigns organized by Isis was the 1991 maternal mortality campaign which serves to increase the size of the movement demanding better access to health services and quality care, as well as to safe abortion and contraceptives. Pushing governments and agencies to improve the collection of data on women's health is also a major focus (Claro 1991).

*Self-Employed Women's Organization (SEWA).* SEWA is a registered trade union of self-employed women workers whose long-term goals are to "create a society where there is full employment, security of income, food security, and also social security, particularly in the area of health care," according to Meera Chatterjee, the group's health director (Chatterjee 1991b). Another, more immediate goal is to increase women's self-reliance. SEWA's strategy is to mobilize women workers in the informal sector using a three-stage process that includes grass roots organizing, law enforcement, and policy changes (Chatterjee 1991b).

Among the first groups to be organized by SEWA was the home-based Workers of Ahemedabad. This group—women who produce goods and services from their homes—is the largest trade union in SEWA. Thirty percent of the home-based workers are sole supporters of their families and another 50 percent are substantial contributors. Nevertheless, because they worked at home and were "invisible" they were not considered workers by the government (Chatterjee 1991b).

The first step undertaken by SEWA was to organize the women in order to get them out of their homes, recognize each other as workers, and educate the public about their existence. Next, SEWA assisted the women in taking their case to the courts to exercise their rights under laws that at least theoretically protect them from exploitation by middlemen or unfair government practices and policies. Third, SEWA took its case to the International Labor Organization, mounting a campaign to have home-based workers—the numbers of which are on the increase in many countries—recognized and protected under the law (Chatterjee 1991b).

In this process, Chatterjee explained, "credit was a very important issue, especially because poor women find it hard to go on strike when there is no cushion to support themselves and their families" (Chatterjee 1991b). In response, a women's cooperative bank was formed, encouraging women to save, and in turn providing small loans so that women could have increased income security during strikes, or make purchases to enhance their productivity. SEWA also established a cooperative of sixty trained health workers providing preventive, curative, and promotive primary health care, and as always, stressing self-reliance (Chatterjee 1991b).

Chatterjee observed that "when poor women are organized, initially they may feel they are weak, but they eventually become strong and self-assured. Women who could not at first stand up and say their names in public were soon able to confront an unfair policeman, contractor, or employer. Through collective action women can solve problems and confront issues more effectively" (Chatterjee 1991b).

*National Women's Health Network* ."Health is a birthright, not a privilege," stated Olivia Cousins, "and this is the vision of the National Women's Health Network." NWHN organizes and lobbies for changes in women's health care policies in the United States. On the subject of breast cancer, for example, NWHN devised a three-year strategy to make the public aware of breast cancer, and organized women for action. Their next step was to lobby for change by "confronting and talking with those in power, in order to make policy that brings women's perspectives to what is important and viable" (Cousins 1991).

In a similar vein, NWHN took on the issue of AIDS, seeking to find out what happens to women with AIDS—"the kinds of things," Cousins reflected, "that bespeak what happens to women when we are in the lowest of power positions" (Cousins 1991). What NWHN found was that not only were women excluded from most of the trials and studies that had an impact on policy, but that the services and programs for women were "sadly lacking" (Cousins 1991). In reaching a consensus that AIDS is a common problem, NWHN started by looking at research at the state level, and undertook a survey of state agencies involved in some type of AIDS work. Armed with information, NWHN has been lobbying to make policies and programs more responsive to women with AIDS; doing speak-outs; and working with other organizations like the Congressional Caucus on Women and the Food and Drug Administration (Cousins 1991).

The common themes of this session were the importance of self-reliance, collective action, consciousness-raising, and the inclusion of women's diverse experiences and voices. But, as Meera Chatterjee pointed out, "organizing is a process in which each phase leads to a new phase; there is no question of success or failure. Instead, we face a series of small victories and 'compromises.'" These examples are but a few of the many ways women are working together to effect change.

Alleviating women's poverty—and empowering women to change discriminatory practices on their own terms—is, in essence, the most fundamental of all development challenges.

## Notes

1. Sixty-two percent of the world's women live in countries classified by the Untied Nations as having "very low GDP [gross domestic product]," calculated at less than U.S. $1,000 per-capita. Another 13 percent live in countries where per-capita income is, by UN definitions, "low"—ranging from $1,000 to $3,000 per-capita annually. Per-capita averages themselves disguise wide disparities between rich and poor in every society, including industrial countries.

2. Absolute poverty is defined by the World Bank as "a condition of life so limited by malnutrition, illiteracy, disease, squalid surroundings, high infant mortality, and low life expectancy as to be beneath any reasonable definition of human decency." Approximately 1.2 billion people are estimated to live in "absolute poverty."

3. Between 60 and 70 percent of people in most countries earn less than their nation's average income and have little if any social safety net. See Durning 1989 and UNDIESA 1991b.

4. For further discussions on women's reproductive health see Adrienne Germaine, "Reproductive Health and Dignity," paper presented for the International Conference on Better Health for Women and Children Through Family Planning, Nairobi, Kenya, October 1987, available from the International Women's Health Coalition, New York.

## References

Acsadi, George and Gwendolyn Johnson-Acsadi. 1990. "Safe Motherhood in South Asia: Sociocultural and Demographic Aspects of Maternal Health." Background paper prepared for the Safe Motherhood-South Asia Conference. Lahore, Pakistan.

Agarwal, Bina, Bare, T.D., Henriques, M.L., Mathews, I., Chainery-Hesse, M., Ariffin, J., Ghaid, D., Jolly, R., McAskie, C., and F. Stewart. 1990. *Engendering Adjustment for the 1990s: Report of a Commonwealth Expert Groups on Women and Structural Adjustment*. London: Commonwealth Secretariat.

Aral, Sevgi O. and King K. Holmes. 1991. "Sexually Transmitted Diseases in the AIDS Era." *Scientific American* 264:2.

Asian and Pacific Women's Resource Collection Network. 1989. *Women's Resource and Action Series: Health*. Kuala Lumpur: Asian and Pacific Development Centre.

Asiyo, Phoebe. 1991. "What We Want: Voices from the South," presentation to the 18th Annual National Council on International Health Conference. Arlington, Virginia.

Barroso, Carmen. 1991. "Women's Health: Towards an Agenda for the Nineties." Keynote presentation to the 18th Annual National Council on International Health Conference. Arlington, Virginia.

Barry, Kathleen, 1984. *Female Sexual Slavery*. New York: New York University Press.

Bennett, Lynn. 1989. *Gender and Poverty in India: Issues and Opportunities Concerning Women in the Indian Economy*. World Bank internal document.

Brooke, Blair L. 1991. "Women's Health in Southeast Asia." Presentation to the 18th Annual National Council on International Health Conference. Arlington, Virginia.

Cecatti, Jose Guilherme. 1990. "Strategy for a National Programme of Safe Motherhood in the People's Republic of Mozambique." Paper presented to the Conference on Safe Motherhood for the Southern African Development Coordinating Conference (SADCC) Countries. Harare, Zimbabwe.

Center for Population Options (CPO). 1990a. "The Facts: Teenage Pregnancy and Sexually Transmitted Diseases in Latin America." Washington, D.C.: CPO.

Center for Population Options. 1990b. "The Facts: Teenage Pregnancy in Africa." Washington, D.C.: CPO.

Chatterjee, Meera. 1991a. *Indian Women: Their Health and Productivity.* World Bank Discussion Paper 109. Washington, D.C.: World Bank.

Chatterjee, Mirai. 1991b. "Women Organizing." Presentation to the 18th Annual National Council on International Health Conference. Arlington, Virginia.

Claro, Amparo. 1991. "Women Organizing." Presentation to the 18th Annual National Council on International Health Conference. Arlington, Virginia.

Convisser, J., Momat, K., Ami, K.S., and E. Liebow. 1991. "Focusing on Women and AIDS: Using Television Drama in Zaire to Promote Safe Behaviors." Paper presented to the 18th Annual National Council on International Health Conference. Arlington, Virginia.

Cottam, Hillary. 1991. "Food Aid and Women's Health: A New Approach in the Dominican Republic." Paper presented to the 18th Annual National Council on International Health Conference. Arlington, Virginia.

Cousins, Olivia. 1991. "Women Organizing." Presentation to the 18th Annual National Council on International Health Conference. Arlington, Virginia.

Crossette, Barbara, 1991. "India's Population Put At 844 Million." *The New York Times,* March 26.

Da Silva, Joselina. 1991a. "What Do We Want—Voices of the South?" Presentation to the 18th Annual Conference of the National Council on International Health. Arlington, Virginia.

Da Silva, Joselina. 1991b. "Women Organizing." Presentation to the 18th Annual Conference of the National Council on International Health. Arlington, Virginia.

Durning, Alan B. 1989. *Poverty and the Environment: Reversing the Downward Spiral.* Washington, D.C.: Worldwatch Institute.

Germaine, Adrienne and Peggy Antrobus. 1989. "New Partners in Reproductive Care." *Populi* 16:4.

Ghosh, Arun, 1991. "Eighth Plan: Challenges and Opportunities—XII. Health Maternity and Child Care: Key to Restraining Population Growth." *Economic and Political Weekly,* April 20.

Griffin, Charles C. 1991. "The Need to Change Health Care Priorities in LDCs." *Finance and Development* 28:1.

Government of India. 1991. Census Commissioner, Registrar General. *Census of India. Provisional Population Totals, Paper One of 1991.*

Government of Lesotho, Health Ministry. 1990. "Lesotho Country Paper." Paper presented at the Conference on Safe Motherhood for the Southern African Development Coordinating Council (SADCC) countries. Harare, Zimbabwe.

Government of Malawi. 1990. "Malawi Country Paper." Paper presented to the Conference on Safe Motherhood for the Southern African Development Coordinating Conference (SADCC) Countries. Harare, Zimbabwe.

Government of Tanzania. 1990. "Tanzania Safe Motherhood Strategy." Paper presented to the Conference on Safe Motherhood for the Southern African Development Coordinating Conference (SADCC) Countries. Harare, Zimbabwe.

Government of Zimbabwe. 1990. "Zimbabwe Country Paper." Paper presented at the conference on Safe Motherhood for the SADCC countries. Harare, Zimbabwe.

Interparliamentary Union, 1991. "Women in Parliament: Numbers Continue to Decline," press release, Geneva, September 27.

Islam, Mehrun Nessa. 1991. "Present Health Status of Women, Policy Initiatives, Health Movements and Issues for Action." Presentation to the 18th Annual National Council on International Health Conference. Arlington, Virginia.

Ithana, P., Tjongarero, A., Katjiongua, B., Marenga, M., and Kate Burling. 1990. "The Republic of Namibia Country Paper." Paper presented to the Conference on Safe Motherhood for the Southern African Development Coordinating Conference (SADCC) Countries. Harare, Zimbabwe.

Jacobson, Jodi L. 1990. *The Global Politics of Abortion*. Worldwatch Paper 97. Washington, D.C.: Worldwatch Institute.

Jacobson, Jodi L. 1991. *Women's Reproductive Health: The Silent Emergency*. Worldwatch Paper 102. Washington, D.C.: Worldwatch Institute.

Jain, Anrudh K. 1989. "Fertility Reduction and the Quality of Family Planning Services." *Studies in Family Planning* 20:1, pp. 1-16.

Kamel, Nahid M. 1983. "Determinants and Patterns of Female Mortality Associated with Women's Reproductive Role." In Alan D. Lopez and Lado T. Ruzicka, eds., *Sex Differentials in Mortality*. Canberra, Australia: Australian National University.

Maglacas, A. Mangay and John Simons, eds. 1986. *The Potential of the Traditional Birth Attendant*. Geneva: World Health Organization.

McNamara, Robert S. 1981. *The McNamara Years at the World Bank: Major Policy Addresses of Robert S. McNamara, 1968-1981*. Baltimore, Maryland: Johns Hopkins University Press.

Mhloyi, Marvelous. 1990. "Maternal Mortality in the SADCC Region." Background paper for the Conference on Safe Motherhood for the Southern African Development Coordinating Conference (SADCC) Countries. Harare, Zimbabwe

Moser, Caroline. 1991. "Women's Health is More than Just a Medical Issue." Presentation to the 18th Annual National Council on International Health Conference. Arlington, Virginia.

Ngugi, Elizabeth N. 1991. "Education and Counselling Interventions." Paper presented at the 18th Annual National Council on International Health Conference. Arlington, Virginia.

Ofosu-Amaah, Waafas. 1991. "Environmental Impacts on Women's Health." Presentation to the 18th Annual National Council on International Health Conference. Arlington, Virginia.

Over, Mead and Peter Piot. Forthcoming. "HIV and Other Sexually Transmitted Diseases." Draft chapter in Dean T. Jamison and W. Henry Mosley, eds., *Disease Control Priorities in Developing Countries*. Washington, D.C.: World Bank.

Patrick, Walter K. 1991. "The Impact of Manufacturing Industries on the Status and Health of Women." Presentation to the 18th Annual National Council on International Health Conference. Arlington, Virginia.

Plummer, Francis A. and Elizabeth N. Ngugi. 1989. "Prostitutes and Their Clients in the Epidemiology and Control of Sexually Transmitted Diseases." In King K. Holmes et al. eds., *Sexually Transmitted Diseases* (second edition). New York: McGraw Hill.

Ram, Aisha, 1991. "Women's Health: the Cost of Development in India." Status report from Rajasthan to Panos Institute, Washington, D.C.

Rosenbaum, S., Layton, C., and J. Liu. 1991. *The Health of America's Children*. Washington, D.C.: Children's Defense Fund.

Sadik, Nafis. 1989. *The State of the World's Population 1989*. New York: United Nations Population Fund.

Saxenian, Helen, 1989. "Brazil: Women's Reproductive Health." Unpublished draft, World Bank, December 29.

Singh, Shusheela and Deidre Wulf. 1990. *Today's Adolescents, Tommorow's Parents: A Portrait of the Americas*. New York: The Alan Guttmacher Institute.

Starrs, Ann. 1987. *Preventing the Tragedy of Maternal Deaths: A Report on the International Safe Motherhood Conference*. Nairobi, Kenya: World Health Organization.

Thaddeus, Sereen and Deborah Maine. 1990. *Too Far To Walk: Maternal Mortality in Context*. New York: Columbia University Center for Population and Family Health.

United Nations Children's Fund (UNICEF). 1989. *State of the World's Children 1989*. New York: Oxford University Press.

United Nations Department of International Economic and Social Affairs (UNDIESA). 1991a. *World Population Prospects 1990*. New York: United Nations.

United Nations Department of International Economic and Social Affairs (UNDIESA). 1991b. *The World's Women: Trends and Statistics 1970-1990*. New York: United Nations.

United Nations Development Program (UNDP). 1991. *Human Development Report 1991* New York: Oxford University Press.

Usman, Hajara. 1991. "The Socioeconomic Factors Affecting the Health of Women in Zaria and Environs." Paper presented to the 18th Annual National Council for International Health Conference. Arlington, Virginia.

Wasserheit, Judith H. 1989. "The Significance and Scope of Reproductive Tract Infections Among Third World Women." *International Journal of Gynecology and Obstetrics*. Supplement 3.

World Bank. 1990. *World Development Report: Poverty*. New York: Oxford University Press.

World Health Organization (WHO) and the International Federation of Gynaecology and Obstetrics (FIGO). 1985. "Traditional Birth Attendants: A Resource for the Health of Women." *International Journal of Gynaecology and Obstetrics*, Volume 23.

World Health Organization (WHO). Forthcoming. *Maternal Mortality: A Global Factbook*. Geneva: WHO.

# 2

# Mother and More: A Broader Perspective on Women's Health

*M.A. Koblinsky, Oona M.R. Campbell, and Siobán D. Harlow* [1]

Women's health is ill-defined. Over the past few decades, our under-standing of women's health has been driven by a focus on fertility regula-tion. While this focus has been eminently beneficial, it has left us with a narrow conceptualization of women's health bounded by the ages fifteen to forty-five and the reproductive system. Recently, the emphasis has broad-ened from fertility to include maternal health, reproductive-tract infections, and to a lesser extent cancers of the reproductive organs, but many aspects of women's health remain neglected.[2]

The dominance of reproductive functioning in our conceptualization of women's health becomes obvious when one looks for a definition of women's health. As noted by Graham and Campbell (1990), there are comparatively few explicit statements in the literature of what is meant by women's health. Those that exist reveal a high degree of overlap with definitions of reproductive health and maternal health (Table 2.1). One definition of women's health that goes beyond the reproductive functions to include many social aspects of women's lives that may impact on health is the following:

> A woman's health is her total well-being, not determined solely by biological factors and reproduction, but also by effects of work load, nutrition, stress, war and migration, among others (van der Kwaak 1991).

On either side of the reproductive years, huge gaps continue to exist in our understanding of women's health. Adolescence marks a time in a woman's life when improved health status and adequate growth could help buffer the future demands of such energy-intensive activities as heavy manual labor or childbearing. Studies on the nutritional status of adolescent girls are now beginning, and descriptive studies of adolescent pregnancy are underway in several parts of the world. However, most health problems experienced by adolescent girls are still under-investigated. Awareness of the problems of the mature woman—the menopausal and aging woman— has also begun to grow, particularly as the populations of many countries begin to age. This awareness has not yet solidified into a research or program agenda. Similarly, nonmaternal, nonreproductive health needs during the reproductive years have received scant attention.

Defining and measuring a problem is the first step toward action. For women's health, we are still at this early stage: What does women's health include, and how do we measure it? This chapter aims to extend the boundaries of our understanding of women's health in four areas described at the 1991 NCIH Conference: maternal health, menstruation and its effect on nonreproductive functioning, and the neglected areas of occupational health and aging.

## Maternal Health: What's the Problem?

News that 500,000 women die each year in childbirth, 99 percent of whom are in developing countries, shocked participants at the Safe Motherhood Conference in Nairobi in 1987. Researchers in several developing countries around the world have since shown that the major causes of maternal death—hemorrhage, obstructed labor, infection, hypertensive disorders of pregnancy, and septic abortion—are not only similar throughout the world, but are, for the most part, preventable. What is not so well-appreciated is that millions of women suffer morbidities and long-term disabilities related to their pregnancy. Based on the findings of one small study in rural India (Datta et al. 1980), it is often stated that for every maternal death, there are 16.5 illnesses resulting from childbirth, yielding 8.25 million maternal morbidities each year worldwide. A literature review presented here shows that this is a gross underestimate: There are over one hundred acute morbidity episodes for every maternal death—an estimated sixty-two million women suffer maternal problems annually. None of the studies reviewed, however, reports the full spectrum of maternal health problems, as only acute morbidities—those occurring during pregnancy, delivery or in the postpartum period—are reported.

Maternal morbidity also includes chronic problems, such as uterine prolapse or vesico-vaginal fistula, which generally become obvious only some time after childbirth. Information on the prevalence of chronic maternal problems are typically available only from hospital-based studies which

TABLE 2.1 Selected Examples of Definitions of Women's Reproductive and Mental Health

| Definitions | Source |
| --- | --- |
| **Women's Health** | |
| "Reproduction and nutrition dominate women's special health concerns...[but]... in the long run, it is clear that women's health status...cannot be significantly improved without additional action to uplift women's overall social and economic conditions." | World Federation of Public Health Associations 1986, p.8,10. Orr 1987, p.3 |
| "Women's health... while recognizing the reality of women's reproductive and nurturing functions takes a broader view of women's lives and makes legitimate demands for services which meet the needs of the 'whole woman' irrespective of age or social status." | |
| "...as Lewin and Oleson state, 'the entire range of issues which touch on illness, sickness, disease, wellness, wellbeing as well as those activities of prevention, diagnosing, healing, caring, and curing.' Health in this sense is a way of total wellbeing, which is not only determined by biological factors and reproduction, but also by effects of work load, nutrition, stress, war and migration, among others." | van der Kwaak 1991, p.2. |
| **Reproductive** | |
| "...the ability of women to live from adolescence or marriage, whichever comes first, to death, with reproductive choice, dignity and successful childbearing and to be reasonably free of gynecological disease and risk." | Evans et al. 1987 (quoted in El Mouelhy et al., 1988, p.5). |
| "Reproductive health means a) that people have the ability to reproduce as well as to regulate their fertility with the fullest possible knowledge of the personal and social consequences of their decisions, and with access to the means of implementing them; b) that women are able to go through childbirth safely; and c) that the outcome of pregnancy is successful in terms of maternal and infant survival, and well–being. In addition, couples should be able to have sexual relationships free of the fear of unwanted pregnancy and of contracting disease." | Fathalla 1988 (paraphrased from Barzelatto 1990, p.30). |
| "The ability to enjoy sexual relations without fear of infection, unwanted pregnancy, or coercion; to regulate fertility without risk of unpleasant or dangerous side effects; to go safely through pregnancy and childbirth; and to bear and raise healthy children." | Germain and Antrobus 1989, p.18. |
| **Maternal Health** | |
| "Safe motherhood...should be to promote good health, not merely to avoid death...[including] the quality of life for women during and after the reproductive period." | Paraphrased from Walsh et al. In press, p.56 |
| "Safe motherhood [encompasses] more than...the causes and consequences of maternal illness and death...improvements [are also needed] in women's overall status and improvements in the health services that are a key component of primary health care and that women—particularly pregnant women—need." | Paraphrased from Starrs 1987, p.22. |
| "Maternal health encompasses positive or negative outcomes—physical, social or mental, in a woman from any cause related to childbearing or its management." | Graham and Campbell 1990, p.14. |

may over- or underestimate the actual extent of suffering. In community-based studies, such as the WHO Studies on Family Formation Patterns and Health, the levels of uterine prolapse were found to be high—affecting up to 19, 25, 9 and 10 percent of women under forty-five years of age in Columbia, Pakistan, the Philippines, and Syria respectively (Dahman et al. 1981). Since prevalence increases with parity (women with seven or more children were two to seven times more likely to experience uterine prolapse as women with one or two children), prolapse is likely to affect younger women in countries where marriage and childbearing begin at an early age and fertility is high. Mild and moderate cases typically go unreported, as women are most likely to report prolapse only when it is severe enough for the cervix or uterus to actually protrude from the vagina. In most cases, the WHO investigators found women's reports of prolapse to be far lower than those detected in the medical exam.

Tables 2.2, 2.3, and 2.4 present data on acute maternal morbidities that occur during pregnancy, labor and delivery, and in the postpartum period respectively. Data from the Maternity Care Project in Bangladesh, as reported at the NCIH Conference (Stewart and Whittaker 1991), are compared with ten population-based studies in developing countries identified through a literature review. Most of these studies are in Asia—the SEARO Multicenter Study of Low Birth Weight and Perinatal Mortality conducted in Burma, Thailand, Indonesia, and India (Perera and Lwin 1984; Alisjahbana et al. 1983), two Chinese studies (Li et al. 1982; Yan et al. 1989) and two Indian studies (Datta et al. 1980; Gordon et al. 1965). Data from Africa are drawn from one study on postpartum hemorrhage in Malawi (Bullough et al. 1989). In the Western Hemisphere, data are used from a national retrospective study of all pregnancies in Jamaica (Department of Child Health 1989). Two studies from North America, one from Canada (Montquin et al. 1987), the other from the United States (Rooks et al. 1989) of low-risk women, women who had no preexisting medical problems as determined by themselves or their provider, are included for comparative purposes.

Drawing conclusions from these data on the levels of acute maternal morbidities is difficult; few studies define the terms used, and there are variations in the data collection instruments, the type of information obtained, and the personnel collecting it. Validation of women's self-reports was not always carried out and completeness of data drawn from medical records is questionable. In the Matlab Maternity Care Project, for example, data were drawn from the records of professionally trained nurse-midwives posted at field level. The midwives saw 60 percent of the pregnant women in the study area (2,672 women), attended the birth of 9 percent (396 women) and visited 37 percent (1,669 women) in the postpartum period. The main focus of their visits was to provide services, not to study morbidities. Hence the data derive from visits that are not necessarily

TABLE 2.2 Medical Problems During Pregnancy (% of births)

| Medical Problems | Developing Countries Range (9)* | | Matlab, Bangladesh | Canada–Low-Risk Women | U.S.–Low-Risk Women |
|---|---|---|---|---|---|
| Antepartum Hemorrhage | 0.20-1.2 | | 1.0 | 1.6 | NA |
| | 9.0 | Jamaica | | | |
| Sepsis | | | | | NA |
| PROM | 0.8 | India | | 0.8 | |
| Maternal Infection | | | | | |
| Fever | 8.6 | India | 3.0 | | |
| Hypertension | 0.1-2.8 | (5) | | 9.6 | NA |
| | 10.4 | Jamaica | | | |
| | 15.0 | China | | | |
| Pre-eclampsia | 1.3-11.0 | (3) | 30.0*** | [3.7]** | |
| Severe/Eclampsia | 0.1-3.5 | (3) | 6.0*** | [0.4] | |
| Anemia | | | | NA | NA |
| Mild | 1.1-20.0 | (3) | 91.0 | | |
| Moderate/Severe | | | 3.0 | | |
| Problems During Pregnancy | 3.0-37.0 | (3) | NA | 23.0 | 29.0 |

* Numbers in parentheses refer to number of population-based studies which provided information.
** Percentages in brackets are included in percentage given for "Hypertention."
*** According to index developed in Matlab.

systematic; in fact, only 18 percent of women saw a midwife more than once during pregnancy in Matlab.

*Problems During Pregnancy.* Given the limitations of the data available on acute maternal morbidities, the degree of consistency across studies is somewhat surprising. One might conclude from Table 2.2 that pregnancy is relatively problem-free, given the low levels of life-threatening problems reported in these studies. For example, in nine projects, only approximately 1 percent of pregnant women suffered antepartum hemorrhage. Jamaica was the exception with 9 percent of women reporting this condition. Sepsis, a rather poorly defined entity with fever as its most easily diagnosable sign, occurred in 3 percent of pregnancies in Matlab and nearly 9 percent in rural India.

Hypertension and the related conditions, pre-eclampsia and eclampsia, exhibited more marked variation between countries, perhaps because measuring blood pressure and diagnosing pre-eclampsia in a field situation are difficult (Villar et al. 1989), or because there may be ethnic differences in baseline hypertension (WHO 1987). Relatively high levels of hypertension during pregnancy (10 to 15 percent of pregnant women) were noted in the Chinese studies, and in Jamaica. These estimated levels are still low, however, when compared with population-based studies that focused specifically on blood pressure during pregnancy. Two such studies in the United Kingdom (Butler and Bonham 1963; Chamberlain et al. 1978), and a third in Cuba (Ochoa Rojas 1981) studied every birth in their respective countries over one week. In both 1958 and 1970, more than a quarter of the pregnant women in the UK had diastolic pressures equal to or greater than 90 mm Hg (29 and 27 percent respectively), while 22 percent of pregnant Cuban women suffered the same. On the other hand, a recent review stated that pregnancy-induced hypertension and pre-eclampsia occurs in 6 to 8 percent of all pregnancies in American women (Henderson and Little 1991) (see "Definitions of Maternal Problems" for further discussion of the hypertensive disorders of pregnancy).

Anemia causes weakness, fatigue, and leads to lowered work output but is not life-threatening in pregnant women, unless severe (<7 gm/dl). In such cases, even a small blood loss may cause death. Anemia is very prevalent among pregnant women in developing countries: In 1982, WHO estimated 60 percent of these women suffered some level of anemia (<11 gm/dl) (DeMaeyer and Adiels-Tegman 1985). A recent update of this information (Jordan and Sloan 1991) continues to find a prevalence of 60 to 70 percent, suggesting that there has been no reduction in the levels of anemia in pregnant women in developing countries over the past decade. By contrast, the levels of anemia as estimated in the studies reviewed, one of several health problems measured, were much lower (1 to 20 percent) (Table 2.2). An exception is the Matlab project, which reports mild anemia in 91 percent of pregnant women and moderate to severe anemia in 3 percent. Again, the explanation for these discrepancies probably lies in the means of diagnosing anemia. For example, anemia was diagnosed in Matlab by midwives examining and grading the conjunctival and buccal mucosa for pallor. The accuracy of this method is unknown in the Matlab setting, but a validation study is underway. Obviously this area requires further refinements in field-measurement.

While these data provide a picture of the percentage of pregnant women suffering one specific problem, how many total women suffer any acute problem during pregnancy? The range in three studies reporting total women suffering during pregnancy is broad. In Indonesia, Alisjahbana and her colleagues state that only 3 percent of all pregnant women had any problem (1983), whereas the two Chinese studies show 18 and 37 percent respectively, primarily hypertension and anemia (Yan et al. 1989; Li et al. 1982). In the American and Canadian studies of low risk pregnant women, 29 and 23 percent suffered problems during pregnancy respectively, mostly urinary-tract infections, anemia and transient hypertension in the U.S. (Rooks et al. 1989), and hypertension in Canada (Montquin et al. 1987). That women in developing countries suffer fewer problems during pregnancy than well-nourished, healthy American and Canadian women is highly unlikely. These data deficiencies for developing country studies probably reflect the problems of definition and measurement alluded to above.

*Problems During Labor and Delivery.* Labor and delivery are typically thought to present the greatest risk for the woman and her infant. Prolonged labor, cephalo-pelvic disproportion or obstructed labor are among the most common medical problems reported in this period by population-based studies (see Table 2.3). Reports do not always distinguish between these three entities. Studies in India (Datta et al. 1980), Burma (Perera and Lwin 1984), Jamaica (Department of Child Health 1989), and China (Yan et al. 1989) give prevalences of between 0.3–1.3 percent, while another Indian study (Gordon et al. 1965) and the Matlab project in Bangladesh (Stewart and Whittaker 1991) showed that 11 and 13 percent of pregnant women respectively had prolonged or obstructed labor. Young age, primiparity and short stature are often cited as risk factors for obstructed labor and may explain the high levels of obstructed labor seen in India and Bangladesh.

Malpresentations or "unstable lie" are seen relatively frequently and account for poor infant outcomes more often than for maternal demise (Table 2.3). The exception is transverse lie, a relatively rare phenomenon reported to affect 0.1–0.2 percent of women, which necessitates a Cesarian section in order to avoid uterine rupture and death of the woman.

Hypertensive disorders of pregnancy continue to present themselves as problems during labor and delivery—particularly eclampsia, which requires immediate delivery. In Matlab, pre-eclampsia was present in 10

TABLE 2.3 Medical and Management Problems During Labor and Delivery (% of births)

| Medical Problems | Developing Countries Range | | Matlab, Bangladesh | Canada–Low-Risk Women | U.S.–Low-Risk Women |
|---|---|---|---|---|---|
| | | (4)* India | | | |
| Problonged labor/CPD/ Obstructed Labor | 0.3-1.3 11.0 (>24 hours) | India | 13.0 | NA | NA |
| Hypertension | 7.7 | China | | NA | NA |
| Pre-eclampsia | 1.7 | China | 10.0 | | |
| Eclampsia | 0.2 | China | | | |
| Management Problems | | | | NA | |
| Unstable Lie | | | | | |
| Breech | 0.8-4.0 | (6) | | | |
| Transverse/shoulder dystocia | 0.1-0.2 | (3) | | | 0.15 |
| Multiple Pregnancies | 0.2-1.4 | (5) | 3.0 | | 0.04 (diagnosed at birth) |
| Mode of Delivery | | | | | |
| Cesarian Section | 4.0-9.5 | (3) | | 10.0 | 4.4 |
| Forceps | 0.1-3.8 | (3) | | | 0.2 |
| Vacuum | 0.2-6.3 | (3) | | | 0.4 |
| Normal | 78.0 | China | | | |
| Problems During Labor and Delivery | 5.9-21.0 | (4) | 4% referred to hospital | NA | 21.3 (15.8% transferred to hospital) |

*Numbers in parentheses refer to number of population-based studies which provided information.

percent of the women attended by midwives at birth, but none progressed to eclampsia. Where it does progress, eclampsia is seen in less than 1 percent of women during labor or delivery.

Viewing labor and delivery by each complication presents a fragmented picture of the overall problem, but reports of the proportion of women suffering any complication during this period vary widely. One study in China reported 11.4 percent of women experience a problem during labor and delivery (Yan et al. 1989) while the other showed 21 percent (Li et al. 1982.). Settings as diverse as rural India (Shah et al. 1984) and Jamaica (Department of Child Health 1989) showed levels of 6 and 7 percent respectively. The U.S. study of low-risk women concluded that 21 percent of women had "somewhat" serious complications during labor and delivery, such as maternal temperature above 37.8° C, retained placenta, hypertension, birth weight greater than 4499g, and moderate shoulder dystocia (Rooks et al. 1989). Again, it appears that women in developing countries are having fewer problems than healthy women in developed countries; obviously the problems of definition and measurement are legion.

*Problems During the Postpartum Period.* Having passed safely through pregnancy and delivery, women remain at risk and, in fact, are at highest risk of death from postpartum morbidities. Identifying and managing these morbidities is especially problematic as this is the time women are least likely to retain contact with service providers, especially if the problem emerges sometime after delivery. The postpartum complication causing the majority of maternal deaths, hemorrhage, often happens immediately following delivery and can rapidly lead to death, especially within the home setting, where the majority of developing-country deliveries occur. Five population-based studies (see Table 2.4) found that postpartum hemorrhage plagued between 2 to 5 percent of delivery women, while a study in Malawi that focused solely on postpartum hemorrhage found 8 percent of women suffering this problem (Bullough et al. 1989). In Matlab, 6 percent of women suffered retained placenta, a frequent cause of postpartum hemorrhage (Stewart and Whittaker 1991). Taken together, these studies suggest that postpartum hemorrhage follows 2 to 8 percent of deliveries, a figure lower than the findings of a Technical Working Group of WHO which recently concluded that in the absence of oxytocics at delivery, the frequency of postpartum hemorrhage varies between 10 and 20 percent (WHO 1990).

Postpartum sepsis is documented in 1 percent of women in India (Datta et al. 1980) and China (Li et al. 1982), but another Indian study showed 8 percent (Gordon et al. 1965) and the Matlab project registered 5 percent (Stewart and Whittaker 1991). Since women rarely receive postpartum care and may fail to present their problems as related to pregnancy, the levels of postpartum sepsis are probably underreported.

TABLE 2.4 Postpartum Complications (% of births)

| Complications | Developing Countries Range | | Matlab, Bangladesh | Canada–Low-Risk Women | U.S.–Low-Risk Women |
|---|---|---|---|---|---|
| Postpartum Hemorrhage | 1.9-5.0 8.0 | (5)* Malawi | NA | NA | 0.50 |
| Retained Placenta | | | 6.0 | NA | NA |
| Sepsis | 1.0 | (2) | 5.0 | NA | NA |
| Fever | 8.0 | India | | | |
| Eclampsia | | | <1.0 | NA | 0.01 |
| Other | 1.9 | China | 5.0 | NA | NA |
| Women With Postpartum Complications | 6.0 | China | NA | NA | NA |

*Numbers in parentheses refer to number of population-based studies which provided information.

What is the proportion of total women giving birth who suffer postpartum complications? Only one study in China (Li et al. 1982) reported overall levels of postpartum complications, stating that 6 percent of all women delivering in their program had postpartum complications.

*Summary of Maternal Health Problems.* Unfortunately, none of the population-based studies state the percentage of total pregnant women who suffer any problem during the forty-six weeks encompassing pregnancy, labor and delivery, and the puerperium. The U.S. data on low-risk women show 29 percent of women with problems during pregnancy and 21 percent during labor and delivery but provide no figure for the postpartum period. These percentages reflect the minimum level of problems expected during pregnancy and delivery since the population was well-nourished, relatively healthy and of low risk (Rooks et al. 1989). On the other hand, this study included a broader range of morbidities than most other population-based studies. The Chinese study (Li et al. 1982) shows that 37 percent of women had problems during pregnancy, 21 percent during labor and delivery, and 6 percent during the postpartum period. Assuming that problems during pregnancy continue during labor and delivery, but that women experiencing postpartum complications may be different, this study suggests that approximately 40 percent of women may suffer an acute problem in the process of bearing a child. This figure seems plausible when compared with the U.S. figures, and with the fact that approximately 9 to 15 percent of deliveries require higher-level care for serious complications in the woman or her baby. Even without taking into account many underlying morbidities which may be aggravated by pregnancy (e.g. tuberculosis), or chronic conditions emerging after the puerperium (e.g. vesico-vaginal fistulas), this 40 percent translates into 61.8 million pregnant women with acute complications each year—and up to 23 million women needing higher level care for severe complications![2]

## Issues in Determining Maternal Morbidity

Given the magnitude of this problem, why haven't maternal health problems been well-studied? A myriad of responses to this question exist. Women's health has been neglected in general, a neglect which fuels, and is fueled by, a lack of information (Graham and Campbell 1990). As attention increasingly focuses on maternal health, the need to develop programs to prevent the appalling number of maternal deaths (the majority of which have known causes and means of prevention), together with a widespread assumption that the fundamentals of disease in women are already known, means that relatively low priority is given to basic epidemiological and methodological research in this area. Moreover, before the levels and determinants of either acute or chronic maternal health problems can be determined, formidable methodological obstacles must be overcome. These include listing the morbidities, defining them, conducting valid field measurements, and obtaining representative, population-based estimates (Campbell and Graham 1990). Two elements of these measurement-related problems were highlighted at the NCIH Conference: the difficulties of locating pregnant women in situations where they do not use services, and of defining problems in ways that can be understood by trained interviewers as well as by the women they interview (Utomo et al. 1991; Stewart and Whittaker 1991; Campbell and Graham 1991).

*Finding Pregnant Women.* In countries where women deliver on their own or with relatives or traditional birth attendants—and this is the norm for approximately 50 percent of the pregnant women in developing countries—identifying pregnant women to ascertain their morbidity status is no small matter. The ease of ascertaining pregnancy depends on whether laboratory tests, clinical examinations, or women's reports are used and on the gestational age of the pregnancy, with early pregnancies being the most difficult to detect (Campbell and Graham 1991).

Pragmatically, studies have to rely on women's knowledge of pregnancy and their willingness to speak about it; little is gained, for example, by using assays to detect early pregnancy unless women want their pregnancies detected. If substantial numbers of women do not know or are unwilling to state that they are pregnant, it becomes difficult to obtain a representative sample (Campbell and Graham 1991). A drug trial using ivermectin to cure river blindness in Liberia went to considerable lengths to identify and exclude pregnant women. They found that on average their questions had a specificity of 98 percent but a sensitivity of only 79 percent (Pacque et al. 1991). For very early pregnancies, sensitivity was as low as 26 percent. Similarly, Airey and Campbell (1988) found significant deficits in reports of early pregnancies in the Demographic and Health Surveys.

The difficulties which emerge when trying to obtain women's report of their last menstrual period (LMP) are illuminating. In rural Indonesia, interviewers go house to house periodically and ask questions about a woman's reproductive status; pregnancy is determined by the absence of menstruation within the previous 5 weeks (Utomo et al. 1991). If missed periods cannot be explained by a recent delivery, abortion or stillbirth, lactation, by the onset of menopause or by the use of an injectable or Norplant, and the woman "feels" she is pregnant, she enters the list of "suspected pregnancies." These are confirmed one month later when interviewers revisit the woman's house. This method confirmed 60 percent of suspected pregnancies in one site and 68 percent in another. Two months after the initial recording of pregnancy, this percentage declined further to

54 and 48 percent of those originally suspected to be pregnant. In the absence of urinary tests to confirm pregnancy, it is not possible to state whether this decline is due to false positives or early abortions. Unfortunately, false negatives were not reported.

As the data show, using the LMP is not a guaranteed basis for detecting early pregnancy. Women may not know the date of their last period reliably and may give interviewers different dates when asked a month later, even with the use of probing and local events to fix the date. The Indonesian project used both repeated interviews and a daily diary or calendar provided women to record the start of menstruation.

A second problem in detecting pregnancy through LMP is irregular menstruation. When this occurs, the interviewer looks for other signs or symptoms of pregnancy. In the absence of physical signs, pregnancy may be difficult to ascertain, as with women, for example, who become pregnant during lactational amenorrhea. Unmarried, very young, or older women with many children, may be ashamed to respond to questions about the date of their last menstrual period.

Given these problems in detecting pregnancy, the Indonesian interviewers are asked to err on the positive side—list *all* women suspected of pregnancies and confirm them the next month. Using this method, the mean gestational age of pregnancies when they are detected in the Indonesian project is four months; only at seven months are 100 percent of pregnant women known.

Given the expense of longitudinal surveillance techniques, as in the Indonesian and Matlab projects, a major question is whether there are alternative effective means of detecting pregnancies in areas where women deliver at home. Where home delivery is the norm in the ten population-based studies reviewed, most employed midwives to collect information on pregnancies through periodic visits to women's homes, or trained nonmedical health visitors to carry out interviews (as in the case of the Indonesian study reported here), with events followed up by medical staff. Other methods to detect pregnancy, such as cross-sectional surveys at six monthly intervals or a village informant system, may be possible, but there are as yet no published data on the use of such methods. There is an urgent need to determine other means of detecting pregnancies where women do not come for services as longitudinal surveillance does not appear to be cost-efficient.

*Defining Morbidities.* Not only is the definition of women's health still debated, but each of the morbidities affecting pregnant women also requires listing and defining. For some of these morbidities there are accepted or explicitly established criteria (see Table 2.5). The next step is to translate these into useful field terms—terms that can be understood by women and field interviewers.

TABLE 2.5 Definition of Morbidities

| | |
|---|---|
| Anemia (WHO, 1989) | 70-110 g/l hemoglobin |
| Moderate Anemia | below 70 g/l hemoglobin |
| Severe Anemia | 4069 g/l |
| Decompensated | below 40 g/l |
| High risk of congestive failure | |
| Antepartum hemorrhage | Any bleeding during pregnancy, prior to delivery |
| Postpartum Hemorrhage (WHO 1990) | Loss of 500 mls or more of blood from the genital tract after delivery of the baby |
| Retained Placenta (WHO 1990) | Placenta has not been delivered within one hour after the birth of the baby. |
| Gestational hypertension (WHO 1987) | Rise of diastolic blood pressure to 90 mm Hg (12.o.i. Pa) or above provided that the level is sustained during the second half of pregnancy and the rise has been caused or unmasked by pregnancy. No significant proteinuria (<0.3 g/l): a) after 20 weeks of gestation b) during labor and/or within 48 hours of delivery |
| Pre-eclampsia (WHO 1987) | Development of gestational hypertention and significant proteinuria (≥ 0.3 g/l) a) after 20 weeks of gestation b) during labor and/or within 48 hours of delivery |
| Eclampsia | Pre-eclampsia with convulsions and/or coma during the antepartum, intrapartum, or postpartum period. |

Underlining the need for clear field definitions is the syndrome of pregnancy-induced hypertension, pre-eclampsia, and eclampsia. Reviewing the literature highlights the confusion surrounding the definition, diagnosis, prevention, and treatment of this syndrome, which causes considerable maternal mortality and morbidity, along with fetal growth retardation, premature delivery and perinatal asphyxia. Maternal problems are principally associated with the ecamplsia component of the syndrome while fetal mortality and neonatal morbidity are mainly associated with severe pre-eclampsia remote from term, especially during the second trimester.

Even though pregnancy-induced hypertension, pre-eclampsia, and eclampsia are considered major maternal problems, there are few population-based studies on the hypertensive disorders of pregnancy. Those that exist are difficult to compare because of the lack of standardized definitions and the logistics for field studies. In developing countries, the WHO Collaborative Study on Hypertensive Disorders of Pregnancy (WHO International Collaborative Study of HDP 1988) and the Jamaica Perinatal Mortality Survey (Department of Child Health 1989) have definition and measurement procedures which make them relatively comparable. The WHO study obtained maternal blood pressure and proteinuria from all pregnant women living in one or more geographically defined areas in Burma, Thailand, Vietnam, and China. In Jamaica, measurements of maternal blood pressure were available for 85 percent of the over ten thousand women throughout the country who were pregnant in a two-month period in 1986, and measurements of proteinuria were available on 75 percent of these women. Because of the high proportion of primigravidae in the WHO studies, the comparisons of incidence figures are given for primiparae/primigravidae only. In Vietnam, Burma, Thailand, and China, the incidence of diastolic hypertension was 5.3 percent, 7.3 percent, 25.5 percent, and 33.2 percent respectively. The magnitude of the incidence for Jamaica (10.4 percent) falls among these. In Matlab, Bangladesh, nearly 90 percent of women seen during pregnancy by a midwife were measured at least once for blood pressure. Only 5.4 percent of all pregnant women had a blood pressure greater than, or equal to, 90mm Hg regardless of parity or gravidity status. As it is known that complications appear at lower blood-pressure levels when women are thin prior to pregnancy and have low weight gain during pregnancy (WHO 1984), as is the case with Bangladeshi women, the authors of the Matlab study explored using a cut-off point of 75mm Hg as an alternative to 90 mm Hg (Stewart and Whittaker 1991). This cut-off produced a level of 30 percent of women with pregnancy-induced hypertension, a level higher than any other population-based study has reported. What is appropriate in this case remains unknown.

In addition to its focus on defining pregnancy-induced hypertension, the Bangladesh study also gave examples of other maternal problems needing clear field-oriented definitions. For example, the definition of "prolonged labor" is problematic in settings where most labors and deliveries occur at home in the presence of untrained and nonliterate personnel; the time of onset of active labor or when the membrane is broken is unknown. How does one define "postpartum hemorrhage" when blood and discharge are not systematically collected, pads are not used, and perceptions of what is abnormal may vary widely among different cultures and depend greatly on past childbirth experience. In Bangladesh, for example, bleeding after delivery is sometimes viewed positively as a "cleansing of the womb" after many months of "accumulated blood" (Stewart and Whittaker 1991).

Beyond the problems of finding pregnant women and of defining morbidities in a way that is understandable, validating women's self-reporting of morbidities is yet a third major hurdle to overcome before measurement of maternal health is more frequently carried out. The discrepancy between women's perceptions of their problems, and problems detected through clinical examinations and laboratory tests, was noted in work presently underway in rural Egypt (Khattab et al. 1991). This discrepancy had also been seen in other studies which both interviewed women about gynecological problems and examined them clinically or with laboratory tests (Bang et al. 1989; Wasserheit et al. 1989).

## What We Do and Do Not Know About the Menstrual Cycle[3]

Despite the many limitations in our knowledge of morbidities during pregnancy and the puerperium, maternal health is presently at the center of our conceptualization of women's health due to the Safe Motherhood Initiative. By contrast, the fact that menstrual-cycle patterns may be a fundamental determinant of women's health status, and that alterations in menstrual function may influence many disease processes, has scarcely influenced the public health agenda for research on women.

A recent report in Lancet (Badwe et al. 1991), confirming previous findings that timing of surgery during the menstrual cycle strongly influences how long women with breast cancer survive (Hrushesky et al. 1989; Senie et al. 1990), provides a provocative illustration of the physiological significance of the menstrual cycle to women's health. Long-term survival was substantially greater when breast cancer surgery was done in the luteal as opposed to the follicular phase (ten-year survival 84 versus 54 percent). This finding suggests that cyclic change in a woman's internal endocrine environment alters her natural resistance to metastatic spread.

Despite the medical implications of women's cyclic physiology, however, scientific inquiry into the menstrual cycle has been limited and disjointed. Recognition of the relevance of menstrual function to women's health is not the same as assuming that women are totally defined by their reproductive hormones. Medical science has also been all too willing to accept that certain diseases—for example, premenstrual syndrome (Osofsky 1990; Schmidt et al. 1991)—are wholly caused by hormonal imbalances. Nonetheless, continued failure to perceive and investigate the linkages between the reproductive system and other aspects of women's health carries a great cost. In the case of timing of surgery for breast cancer, this cost may have been premature death for an untold number of women.

Whether in its presence or its absence, periodic bleeding is an integral part of a woman's life experience throughout much of her reproductive life. In addition to concern provoked by unexplained alterations in bleeding patterns, considerable clinical morbidity is directly attributable to menstrual disturbances. In the United States, for example, four million office visits, 20 percent of all visits for problems of the female genital tract, are made annually for disorders of menstruation (NCHS 1982a). Menstrual dysfunction and other abnormal vaginal bleeding are also the primary diagnoses for 350,000 hospitalizations per year (NCHS 1982b), and dysfunctional uterine bleeding is one of the three leading indications for hysterectomy. In Niue Island, 50 percent of all women over twenty years of age reported a history of excessive menstrual pain (Taylor et al. 1985).

Despite the magnitude of clinical morbidity associated with menstruation, neither the nature of variability in normal menstrual function nor the etiology of menstrual dysfunction are well understood. Although the distribution of menstrual-cycle lengths within the population of women and the gross changes which occur in the population from menarche to menopause have been described (e.g. Treloar et al. 1967), we have virtually no quantitative data on how cycle length varies from cycle to cycle *within a woman* as she ages or on how age-related changes may differ from woman to woman (Harlow and Zeger, forthcoming). Data on hormonal patterns that underlie variation in menstrual-cycle length are limited to a few studies on length of the follicular and luteal phases (e.g. Lenton et al. 1984a; Lenton et al. 1984b). How daily hormonal patterns might differ from woman to woman or how hormonal metabolism might differ, both of which are crucial to describing women's internal endocrine environments, has scarcely been investigated.

Knowledge of why menstrual cycles vary is even more sparse. Age of menarche varies considerably from country to country and seems to be highly dependent on nutritional status (Gray 1979). Age at menopause also differs somewhat (Gray 1979). With a few notable exceptions, data on regional differences in menstrual patterns during reproductive life scarcely exist (Belsey et al. 1988). Regional differences are of interest because they provide clues about how life and environmental conditions may influence the reproductive system. They can also suggest why health risks associated with variation in menstrual function, or with hormonal manipulation of the reproductive system, might differ among populations. Currently, potential risks can only be infrequently inferred because of our limited knowledge of environmental determinants of menstrual dysfunction.

To date, information is largely confined to data on the effect of weight, physical activity and stress on menstrual-cycle length, ovulation, and luteal function (Bullen et al. 1985; Dale et al. 1979; Drew 1961; Ellison 1990; Harlow and Matanoski 1991; Warren 1983), although our understanding of these factors also remains inadequate. Studies of weight have generally examined highly selected clinical populations or athletes, although some data exist from cultures which experience extreme seasonality in food availability (Ellison 1990). Detailed information about the influence of weight on endocrine metabolism is sorely lacking even though this relation may be critical to understanding the link between menstruation and other health outcomes (Schneider et al. 1983). The effect of exercise appears to be highly dependent on a woman's underlying biological susceptibility yet little is known about what determines susceptibility. Exercise data is derived mostly from western athletes and not from cultures where women typically are occupied in energy-intensive tasks such as farming. Studies of psychological stress, often considered the primary determinant of dysfunction, have basically only evaluated major life changes and catastrophic events.

However, the reproductive system is responsive to a multitude of environmental signals, and systematic exploration of alternative factors is clearly warranted. Although some data exist about the probable impact of dietary factors, drugs, pesticides, solvents, occupational strain, chronic stress, sound, light, social violence, and the presence of female or male companions, few epidemiological studies have been undertaken (Harlow 1986; Pirke et al. 1985; Preti et al. 1986; Cutler et al. 1986). Furthermore, previous research has generally focused on how these factors interfere with ovulation. Focusing on ovulation and pregnancy defines the relation between menstruation and women's health too narrowly. Evaluation of environmental determinants of hormonal patterns and endocrine metabolism is also needed. As far as the larger impact of menstrual function on women's health, evidence continues to accumulate suggesting that a woman's internal hormonal environment plays a critical role in determining her long-term risk of developing chronic diseases such as osteoporosis, cancer, and possibly cardiovascular disease (Gao et al. 1987; Henderson et al. 1985; La Vecchia et al. 1985; Olsson et al. 1983; Barret-Conner and Bush 1991; Sowers et al. 1990; La Vecchia et al. 1987). Age at first pregnancy has long been identified as a risk factor for breast cancer. Although the data are inconsistent, long menstrual cycles may be protective against breast cancer, and ovarian cancer and possibly even lung cancer (Gao et al. 1987; Henderson et al. 1985; LaVecchia et al. 1985; Olsson et al. 1983). Cessation of menstrual function at the time of menopause appears to alter women's health profile, increasing the risk of cardiovascular disease and osteoporosis. The menstrual cycle also appears to modulate several aspects of women's physiology. Though research is sparse, systematic differences have been demonstrated across the menstrual cycle in such diverse physiological parameters as glycogen storage (Hackney 1990; Nicklas et al. 1989) and immune function (Mathur et al. 1979; Kalo-Klein and Witkin 1989; Tumbo-Oeri 1985).

The relationship between menstrual function and women's health profile is not well-understood largely because well-designed and focused studies of the association between endocrine profiles and chronic disease or known physiological risk factors have not been conducted. No systematic investigation of the effect of the menstrual cycle on immune response, for example, has ever been undertaken and many studies which examine immune parameters suffer from such serious methodological flaws that they actually provide false information (Eichler and Keiling 1988; Coulam et al. 1983). Consequently, we have few clues about the optimal endocrine environment for promoting women's long term health. Systematic investigation of the physiological cycles engendered by the menstrual cycle is essential to building a better understanding of women's biological functioning and disease risk. Evaluation of the health consequences of steroid contraception and estrogen-replacement therapy will ultimately depend upon gaining a better understanding of the complex relationship between menstrual function and a women's health.

## More Neglected Areas: Women's Work

A further gap in our understanding of women's health concerns the association between a woman's occupation and her health status. Despite the growing sociological and economic literature describing 1) the number of hours spent doing household chores and the limited opportunity to rest, 2) women's double burden of household chores plus economically productive work, 3) the undercounting of women's contribution to agricultural production, and 4) the growing importance of employment in assembly-type production in export-processing zones (*maquilladora*), limited quantitative information is available about how women's daily work activities influence their health. Occupation has been viewed predominantly as an indicator or determinant of socioeconomic status. Four presentations at the

NCIH Conference highlighted the importance of beginning to consider how specific occupational characteristics—such as length of the working day, level of physical exertion, and exposure to pesticides and other chemicals—directly determine disease risk (Khan et al. 1991; Patrick 1991; Santana and Harlow 1991; Senapati 1991). Although most of the authors presented preliminary findings, they each raised provocative questions about how the relationship between health and women's activity is conceptualized and evaluated.

Khan discussed the potential association between long work days during harvest season and increased maternal and infant morbidity and mortality in rural Pakistan. As is true for housework, women did not tend to report their agricultural labor as work despite the fact that during harvest season they often labored as many as sixteen hours each day in the field. The level of physical exertion and lack of opportunity to rest during harvest time may be important risk factors for poor maternal and infant outcome (Khan et al. 1991).

Senapati examined the level of women's morbidity in housewives with and without paid employment. The women all lived in one of Calcutta's slums and women with paid employment generally worked as domestic workers. Women who worked outside the home had less time to care for their own needs and had worse nutritional status than women who did not work outside the home.

Santana and Harlow presented preliminary results on the association between women's occupation and the prevalence of minor psychological morbidity in a low-income urban neighborhood in Brazil. Whether paid or unpaid, housework as a principle occupation conferred the highest risk of psychological morbidity. Domestic work is the primary form of remunerated employment for Brazilian women. Women with more than one occupation had higher risk of morbidity than other women, a finding which supports the hypothesis that the *doble jornada* (double day) has a negative impact on women's health.

Patrick discussed the growing importance of the *maquilladora* and offshore assembly industry as a source of employment for women in developing countries. Although often touted as an important new source of paid employment for women, Patrick argued that the poor working and living conditions associated with employment in these industries can potentially have a negative impact on both women's health and social status. Despite the growing concern about the potential for adverse reproductive outcomes among women employed in the electronics industry in the United States (Huel et al. forthcoming; Pastides et al. 1988), for example, no comprehensive studies of reproductive outcomes in women employed in electronics *maquilladora* plants have been undertaken.

Three important themes emerge from these presentations which can serve as a guide to the development of an agenda for research and program-development in the area of occupation and women's health. First, focus should be placed upon those occupations of predominant importance to women including paid and unpaid domestic labor, agricultural labor, market activities and the *maquilladora* industry. Considerable effort will also need to be given to identifying the specific components of these occupations which influence disease risk. Activities which demand considerable physical exertion and contribute to long-term fatigue may be particularly important, and relevant health outcomes may be those most indicative of physical and mental strain. Popular workplace songs are suggested as a means of informing researchers of salient practices leading to health problems. Finally, research must explicitly incorporate women's unpaid housework in the conceptualization and measurement of women's work activities. Similarly, traditional occupations such as farming must also be explicitly defined as work activity. Given the importance of the informal economy, and therefore of informal jobs, consideration should also be given to the appropriate measurement and recognition of these activities. Further attention to the specific characteristics of women's work lives may substantially enhance our understanding of the nature of women's health complaints and of the distribution of disease in female populations.

## Beyond the Reproductive Years: Aging Women

If anything, policy makers' neglect of women increases as women age and their contribution to society, as either producers or reproducers, is considered to end. It is important therefore to emphasize that as populations age, older women form a growing proportion of the population and that their continuing contributions to society make it imperative that interest in their health is maintained. Moreover, health gains in this age group have been limited compared to improvements at younger ages.

One approach to understanding the health problems affecting older women is to research gender differences in the prevalence of various morbidities, as exemplified by the Baltimore Longitudinal Study on Aging's examination of the prevalence and treatment of hypertension, the number-one morbidity affecting older women in the United States (Metter 1991). A different, more holistic approach was taken in presentations by McGowan (1991) and Burdmen (1991) accenting four main areas which impinge on women as they age. These include nutrition, coping with stress, the negative effect of poverty, and the need for purposeful activity. The potential for all these factors to interact with women's health status at a time when women face an increasing burden of morbidity is readily apparent but was not directly addressed. Rather, it was stressed that successful aging universally allows for rumination at the end of life, putting one's affairs in order, and having a purposeful role.

## Conclusions and Recommendations

A definition of women's health must reflect the unique dimensions of our lives: The reproductive roles (childbirth), the biological reality (menstrual cycles), and the social context in which we live, work, and age. Each dimension impinges on our health and is in turn impacted by it. In this chapter we have tried to broaden and deepen our understanding of women's health, but we have obviously only begun.

Women die prematurely from several causes—many causes that also kill men. One cause that is gender-specific, however, is childbirth. Hemorrhage, infection, obstructed labor, hypertensive disorders of pregnancy, and complications of induced abortion are recognized as the major killers of women during pregnancy, labor and delivery and the puerperium. These same problems cause serious suffering in other women as well, but may not kill them. That approximately sixty-two million women are estimated to experience these and other serious morbidities associated with childbirth yearly, suggests that considerable efforts are needed to establish how common morbidities are in pregnancy. It is also imperative to recognize that there are other conditions, including indirect maternal morbidities (where pregnancy aggravates underlying morbidities) and long-term effects of pregnancy, about which little is known. A systematic listing of health problems known or thought to be associated with pregnancy and childbirth would provide an initial starting point to developing an epidemiological understanding of maternal morbidity.

Once morbidities of interest are identified, there remains a considerable need for methodological development. Definitions of the morbidities in question must be explicitly stated, and ways to measure them in field settings found. Where possible, studies are needed to validate, or at least examine the reliability of, information obtained from women. Care must also be given to the context in which research is carried out in terms of who sets the research agenda, of how morbidities are defined, and of how information is collected. Depending on whether clinical examinations, laboratory tests, or women's self-reports are used, it will be possible to gather various items of information. Interviews conducted by lay or medically trained interviewers are also likely to yield different results. Estimates of the levels of maternal morbidity should be population-based and preferably representative of a wider community. The biases associated with use of facility data in settings where health services are only accessible to, or used by, a small minority are clear. Such situations can lead to over- or underestimates of the prevalence of maternal health problems, depending on the selection biases present. As research into female morbidities is still in the early stages of development, publication of results should be careful to present data that are comparable to other studies.

We also need to start conceptualizing the effects of menstrual health and conducting population-based studies of the natural variability in menstrual cycles across the reproductive life course. This includes looking at cycle length, bleeding duration, hormonal patterns, and metabolic pathways. Once these patterns are established, epidemiological studies are needed to identify their host and environmental determinants. Basic research on the effect of hormones and variability in hormonal levels across the menstrual cycle on women's physiology is also needed, as is systematic research programs on the relationship between the endogenous endocrine environment and chronic disease. Finally, as with maternal morbidity, a research methodology needs to be developed which can address the study of menstrual cycles and of the endocrine environment including hormonal assays that are feasible for field use to facilitate investigation of metabolic pathways, and analytic methods for evaluating hormonal patterns and menstrual diary data.

The contribution of a women's biology (as exemplified by her reproductive role and her menstrual function) to her health is not the only component in gender-specific health problems. Consideration must also be given to how the social roles of women impinge on their health. These are often complex issues to research. With women's work, for example, consideration must be given not just to how work affects health, but also to how health affects work. The interaction of activity and health can also be seen in aging women, where part of the phenomenon of successful aging depends on purposeful activity. The specific characteristics of women's lives as they work and age may substantially enhance our understanding of the nature of women's health complaints and of the distribution of disease in female populations.

Achieving these ambitious recommendations necessary to understand female morbidities will involve work in conceptualizing and researching the problems. Perhaps more importantly, however, it involves an attitudinal change on the part of policy makers, funders, and researchers to allow for a broader definition of women's health which incorporates the full length of our lives, the full range of our activities, and all the discomforts and illnesses we face. This would be a first step towards a program that enhances women's health and quality of life—a program long overdue.

## Notes

1. The authors gratefully acknowledge the collaboration of Sally Coghlan, who joined them as rapporteur at the NCIH Conference for this topic.
2. The *UN Demographic Year Book* (1991) documents the world population to be 5.2 billion in 1989 with a crude birth rate (CBR) of 27 per thousand (1985–1990). Multiplying the population by the CBR and adding 10 percent to account for stillbirths and early abortions gives 154.4 million pregnancies per year worldwide. If 40 percent of these pregnancies are complicated, this gives 61.8 million pregnant women per year with an acute morbidity.
3. This section draws from the paper presented at the 1991 NCIH Conference by Siobán Harlow (1991).

## References

Airey, P. and O. Campbell. 1988. *Demographic and Health Surveys: A Critical Assessment of the Health Component Based on Six African Surveys.* London School of Hygiene and Tropical Medicine, Workshop on the Determinants of Health and Morality in Africa, September 1, 1988–October 26, 1988.

Alisjahbana, A., Suroto-Hamzah, Emelia, Tanuwidjaja, Suganda, Wiradisuria, Sambas, and Bakir Abisujak. 1983. "Perinatal Mortality and Morbidity Survey and Low birth Weight." *Final Report 5, The Pregnancy Outcome in Ujung-Berung, West-Java.* Fakultas Kedokteran Universitas Padjadjaran.

Badwe, R.A., Gregory, W.M., Chaudary, M.A., Richards, M.A., Bentley, A.E., Rubens R.D. and I.S. Fentiman. 1991. "Timing of Surgery During Menstrual Cycle and Survival of Premenopausal Women with Operable Breast Cancer." *Lancet* 337:1261-1264.

Balderrama-Guzman, V., Lim-de Mesa, T., and L.C. Somera. 1976. "Family formation and maternal health. D. Manila." In A.R. Omran and C.C. Stnadley, eds., *Family Formation Patterns and Health.* Geneva: World Health Organization. pp. 358-366.

Bang, R., Bang, A., Baitule, M., Choudhary, Y., Sarmukaddam, S. and O. Tale. 1989. "High prevalence of gynecological diseases in rural Indian women." *Lancet* 1:85-88.

Barrett-Connor, E. and T.L. Bush. 1991. "Estrogen and coronary heart disease in women." *JAMA*, 265(14):1861-1867.

Barzelatto, J. 1990. *Special Challenges in Third World Women's Health.* Presentations at the 117th annual meeting of the American Public Health Association. October 1989, Chicago, IL. New York: International Women's Health Coalition.

Belsey, E.M., d'Arcangues, C. and N. Carlson. 1988. "Determinants of menstrual bleeding patterns among women using natural and hormonal methods of contraception." *Contraception* 38(2):243-257.

Bullen, B.A., Skrinar, G.S., Beitins, I.Z., von Mering, G., Turnbull, B.A. and J.W. McArthur. 1985. "Induction of menstrual disorders by strenuous exercise in untrained women." *New England Journal of Med* 312:1349.

Bullough, Colin H.W., Msuku, Rose S. and Lucy Karonde. 1989. "Early suckling and postpartum hemorrhage: Controlled trial in deliveries by traditional birth attendants." *The Lancet* (September 2, 1989): 522-525.

Burdmen, Geri Marr. 1991. "Women, aging, and health promotions: An international perspective." Presentation at the 18th annual NCIH International Health Conference. Arlington, VA.

Butler, N.R. and D.G. Bonham. 1963. *Perinatal mortality: The first report of the 1958 British perinatal mortality survey*. Edinburgh: E. & S. Livingstone. Pp.86-100.

Campbell, O.M.R. and W.J. Graham. 1990. *Measuring maternal mortality and morbidity: Levels and trends*. Maternal and Child Epidemiology Unit Publication. London: London School of Hygiene and Tropical Medicine.

Campbell, O.M.R. and W.J. Graham. 1991. *Measuring the determinants of maternal morbidity and morality: Choosing outcomes and identifying determinants*. Maternal and Child Epidemiology Unit Publication. London: London School of Hygiene and Tropical Medicine.

Chamberlain, G. 1978. "British births 1971." *Obstetric care*. London: Heinemann Medical Books, Ltd. 2:80-107.

Coulam, Carolyn B., Silverfield, Joel C., Kazmar, Raymond E. and Garrison Fathman. 1983. "T-lymphocyte subsets during pregnancy and the menstrual cycle." *American Journal of Reproductive Immunology* 4:88-90.

Cutler, Winnifred, Berg, Preti, George, Krieger, Abba, George, R. Huggins, Garcia, Celso Ramon and Henry J. Lawley. 1986. "Human auxillary secretions influence women's menstrual cycles: The role of donor extract from men." *Hormones and Behavior* 20:463-473.

Dahman, A., Gharib, M., and A.R. Omran. 1981 "Family formation and maternal health. D. Syrian Arab Republic." In A.R. Omran and C.C. Standley, eds., *Further Studies on Family Formation Patterns and Health*. Geneva: World Health Organization. pp. 296-302.

Dale, E., Gerlach, D.H. and A.L. Wilhite. 1979. "Menstrual dysfunction in distance runners." *Obstet Gynecol* 54:47.

Datta, K.K., Sharma, R.S., Razack, P.M.A., Ghosh, T.K. and R.R. Arora. 1980. "Morbidity pattern amongst rural pregnant women in Alwar, Rajasthan— a cohort study." *Health and Population -Perspectives & Issues* 3(4):282-292.

DeMaeyer, D. and M. Adiels-Tegman. 1985. "The prevalence of anaemia in the world." *World health statistics quarterly* 38:302-316.

Department of Child Health. 1989. *The perinatal mortality and morbidity study, Jamaica, final report*. Mona, Jamaica: University of the West Indies.

Drew, F.L. 1961. "The epidemiology of secondary amenorrhea." *J Chronic Dis* 14:396.

Eichler, F. and R. Keiling. 1988. "Variations in the percentages of lymphocyte subtypes during the menstrual cycle in women." *Biomed. & Pharmacother* 42:285-288.

Ellison, P.T. 1990. "Human ovarian function and reproductive ecology: New hypotheses." *Am Anthropol* 92:993.

Evans, J.L., Lamb, G.A., Murthy, N. and Shorter, F.C. 1987. "Women and children in poverty: Reproductive health and child survival." Report to the trustees of the Ford Foundation for its middecade review of programs. New York: The Ford Foundation.

Fathalla, M.F. 1988. "Research needs in human reproduction." In E. Diczfalusy, P.D. Griffin and J. Khanna, eds., *Research in human reproduction: Biennial report 1986-1987*. Geneva: World Health Organization.

Gao, Y.T., Blot, W.J., Zheng, W., Ershow, A.G., Hsu, C.W., Levin, L.I., Zhang, R., and Jr. J.F. Fraumeni. 1987. "Lung cancer among Chinese women." *Int J Cancer* 40:604.

Germain, A. 1989. The Christopher Tietze International Symposium: an overview. In A. Rosenfield, M. Fathallo, A. Germain and C.L. Indriso, eds., *Women's Health in the Third World: The impact of unwanted pregnancy. Supplement to International Journal of Gynecology and Obstectrics*. Ireland: Elsevier Scientific Publishers. Pp. 1-8.

Gordon, John E., Gideon, Helen and John B. Wyon. 1965. "Complications of childbirth and illnesses during the puerperium." *The Journal of Obstetrics and Gynecology of India* 15(2):159-167.

Graham, Wendy J. and Oona M.R. Campbell. 1990. *Measuring maternal health: Defining the issues*. London: Maternal and Child Epidemiology Unit, London School of Hygiene and Tropical Medicine.

Gray R.H. 1979. "Biological factors, other than nutrition and lactation which may influence natural fertility: A review." In H. Leridon and J. Menken, eds., *Natural Fertility*. Liege: Ordina Editions. Pp. 217-251.

Hackney, A.C. 1990. "Effects of the menstrual cycle on resting muscle glycogen content." *Horm. metab. Res.* 22:647.

Harlow, S.D. 1986. "Function and dysfunction: A historical critique of the literature on menstruation and work." *Health Care Women Int* 7:39.

Harlow, S.D. 1991. "What we do and do not know about the menstrual cycle or questions scientists could be asking." Paper presented at the 18th annual NCIH International Health Conference. Arlington, Va.

Harlow, S.D. and G.M. Matanoski. 1991. "The association between weight, physical activity and stress and variation in the length of the menstrual cycle." *Am J Epidemiol* 133:38.

Harlow, S.D. and S.L. Zeger. "An application of longitudinal methods to the analysis of menstrual diary data." *Journal of Clinical Epidemiology*. Forthcoming.

Henderson, Perry and George A. Little. 1990. "The detection and prevention of pregnancy-induced hypertension and preeclampsia." In Irwin R. Merkatz and Joyce E. Thompson, eds., *New Perspectives on Prenatal Care*. New York: Elsevier Publishers. Pp. 479-500.

Henderson, B.E., Ross, R.K., Judd, H.L., Krailo, M.D. and M.C. Pike. 1985. "Do regular ovulatory cycles increase breast cancer risk?" *Cancer* 56:1206.

Hrushesky, W.J.M., Bluming, A.Z., Gruber, S.A. and R.B. Sothern. 1989. "Menstrual influence on surgical cure of breast cancer." *Lancet* 2:949-952.

Huel, G., Mergler, D. and R. Bowler. "Evidence of adverse reproductive outcomes among women microelectronic assembly workers." *British Journal of Industrial Medicine*. Forthcoming.

Jordan, Elizabeth A. and Nancy L. Sloan. 1991. "The prevalence of anemia in developing countries, 1979-1989 an annotated bibliography." *MotherCare Working Paper 7A*. Arlington, Va.: MotherCare.

Kalo-Klein, Aliza and Steven S. Witkin. 1989. "Candida albicans: Cellular immune system interactions during different stages of the menstrual cycle." *Am J Obstet Gynecol* 161:1132-6.

Khan, T. 1981. "Family formation and maternal health. C. Pakistan." In A.R. Omran and C.C. Standley, eds., *Further Studies on Family Formation Patterns and Health.* Geneva World Health Organization. pp. 287-295.

Khan, Zeenat H. and Farid Midhet. 1991. "Women's and infants' mortality and morbidity during and after harvest season in rural Pakistan." Paper presented at the 18th annual NCIH International Health Conference. Arlington VA.

Khattab, Hind. 1991. "Research methods to elicit information from women." Paper presented at the 18th annual NCIH International Health Conference. Arlington, VA.

La Vecchia, C., Decarli, A., Di Pietro, S., Franceschi, S., Negri, E. and F. Parazzini. 1985. "Menstrual cycle patterns and the risk of breast disease." *Eur J Cancer Clin Oncol* 21:417.

La Vecchia, C., Decarli, A., Franceschi, S., Gentile, A., Negri, E. and Fabio Parazzini. 1987. "Menstrual and reproductive factors and the risk of myocardial infarction in women under fifty-five years of age." *American Journal of Obstetrics and Gynecology* 157:1108-1112.

Lenton, E.A., Landgren, B.M., Sexton, L. and R. Harper. 1984a. "Normal variation in the length of the luteal phase of the menstrual cycle: Identification of the short luteal phase." *Br J Obstet Gynaecol* 91:685.

Lenton, E.A., Landgren, B.M., Sexton, L. and R. Harper. 1984b. "Normal variation in the length of the follicular phase of the menstrual cycle: Effect of chronological age." *Br J Obstet Gynaecol* 91:681.

Li Bo-ying, Dong Ai-Mei and Zhuo Jing-ru. 1982. "Outcomes of pregnancy in Hong-qiao and Qi-yi communes." *American Journal of Public Health* Supplement (September 1982) 72:30-32.

Mathur, Subbi, Mathur, Rajesh S., Goust, Jean Michell, Williamson, H. Oliver and H. Hugh Fudenberg. 1979. "Cyclic variations in white cell subpopulations in the human menstrual cycle: Correlations with progesterone and estradiol." *Clinical Immunology and Immunopathology* 13:246-253.

McGowan, Lisa. 1991. "Health concerns of aging women." Presentation at the 18th annual NCIH International Health Conference. Arlington, Va.

Metter, E. Jeffrey. 1991. "Gender differences in prevalence and treatment of hypertension and coronary heart disease." Presentation at the 18th annual NCIH International Health Conference. Arlington, Va.

Moutquin, J. M., Gagnon, Robert, Rainville, Carmen, Giroux, Luc, Amyot, Gilles, Bilodeau, Rolland and Pierre Raynauld. 1987. "Maternal and neonatal outcome in pregnancies with no risk factors." *CMAJ* 17:728-732.

NCHS. National Center for Health Statistics. 1982a. "Use of health services for disorders of the female reproductive system: United States 1977-1978." *Vital Health Stat* Ser. 13, No. 63. DHHS Pub. No. (PHS) 82.

NCHS. National Center for Health Statistics. 1982b. "Inpatient utilization of short stay hospitals by diagnosis: United States 1979." *Vital Health Stat* Ser. 13, No. 69. DHHS Pub. No. (PHS) 83.

Nicklas, B.J., Hackney, A.C. and R.L. Sharp. 1989. "The menstrual cycle and exercise: Performance, muscle glycogen, and substrate responses." *Int. J. Sports Med.* 10:264-269.

Ochoa, G. and A. Gil. 1981. "Family formation and maternal health. A. Columbia." In A.R. Omran and C.C. Standley, eds., *Further Studies on Family on Family Formation Pattern and Health.* Geneva: World Health Organization. pp. 273-282.

Ochoa Rojas, F.R. 1981. "Investigation perinatal (perinatal investigation.)" Havana: Instituto de Desarrollo de la Salud, Gentifico Tecnica.

Olsson, H., Landin-Olsson, M. and B. Gullberg. 1983. "Retrospective assessment of menstrual cycle length in patients with breast cancer, in patients with benign breast disease, and in women without breast disease." *JNCI* 70:17.

Orr, J. 1987. *Women's Health in the Community.* London: John Wiley.

Osofsky, Howard J. 1990. "Efficacious treatment of PMS: A need for further research." *JAMA* 264:387.

Pacque, M., Munoz, B., Poetschke, G., Foose, J., Gycore, B.M. and H.R. Taylor. 1990. "Pregnancy outcome after inadvertent ivermectin treatment during community-based distribution." *Lancet* 336:1486-1489.

Pastides, H., et al. 1988. "Spontaneous abortion and general illness symptoms among semiconductor manufacturers." *Journal of Occupational Medicine* 30(7):543-551.

Patrick, Walter K. 1991. "The impact of manufacturing industries on the status and health of women." Paper presented at the 18th annual NCIH International Health Conference. Arlington, VA.

Perera, Terence and Khing Maung Lwin. 1984. "Perinatal mortality and morbidity." *SEARO Regional Health Papers* 3:1-72.

Pirke, K.M., Schweiger, U., Lemmel, W., Krieg, J.C. and M. Berger. 1985. "The influence of dieting on the menstrual cycle of healthy young women." *J Clin Endocrinol Metab* 60:1174.

Preti, George, Cutler, Winnifred Berg, Garcia, Celso Ramon, Huggins, George R. and Henry J. Lawley. 1986. "Human axillary secretions influence women's menstrual cycles: The role of donor extract of females." *Hormones and Behavior* 20:474-482.

Rooks, Judith P., Weatherby, Norman L., Ernst, Eunice K.M., Stapleton, Susan, Rosen, David and Allan Rosenfield. 1989. "Outcomes of care in birth centers: The National Birth Center Study." *The New England Journal of Medicine* 321(26):1804-1811.

Santana, Vilma S. and S.D. Harlow. 1991. "Work and women's mental health in urban Brazil." Paper presented at the 18th annual NCIH International Health Conference. Arlington, VA.

Schmidt, Peter J., Nieman, Lynnette K., Grover, Gay N., Muller, Kari L., Merriam, George R. and David R. Rubinow. 1991. "Lack of effect of induced menses of symptoms in women with premenstrual syndrome." *The New England Journal of Medicine* 324:1208-1210.

Schneider, Jill, Bradlow, H. Leon, Strain, Gladys and Joseph Levin. 1983. "Effects of obesity on estradiol metabolism: Decreased formation of nonuterotropic metabolites." *Journal of Clinical Endocrinology and Metabolism* 56(5):973.

Senapati, Sisir Kumar. 1991. "Women's workload and its impact on their health and nutrition." Paper presented at the 18th annual NCIH International Health Conference. Arlington, VA.

Senie, R.T., Rosen, P.P., Rhodes, P, Lesser, M.L. 1990. "Prognosis of primary breast cancer patients in relation to time of diagnostic surgery during the menstrual cycle (abstract)." *Breast Cancer Res Treat* 16:146.

Shah, Usha., Pratinidhi, A.K. and P.V. Bhatlawande. 1984. "Perinatal mortality in rural India: A strategy for reduction through primary care. I Stillbirths." *Journal of Epidemiology and Community Health* 38:134-137.

Sowers, Mary Fran R., Shapiro, Brahm, Gilbraith, Miriam A. and Mary Jannausch. 1990. "Health and hormonal characteristics and premenopausal women with lower bone mass." *Calcif Tissue Int* 47:130-135.

Starrs, A. 1987. *Preventing The Tragedy of Maternal Deaths.* A report on the International Safe Motherhood Conference, Nairobi, Kenya, February 1987. New York: World Bank, World Health Organization and United Nations Fund For Populations Activities.

Stewart, Kate and Maxine Whittaker. 1991. "Methodological issues in defining female morbidity: A case study from the Maternity Care Project, Matlab, Bangladesh." Paper presented at the 18th annual NCIH International Health Conference. Arlington, Va.

Taylor, R., Whitmore, J., Robertson, S., Norton, R., Levy, S., Nemaia, H., Tukuitonga, C., Tongatule, T. and L. Siakimotu. 1985. "Niue women's health survey, 1983: Report." Technical Paper No. 187. Noumea, New Caledonia: South Pacific Commission.

Treloar, A.E., Boynton, R.E., Behn, B.G. and B.W. Brown. 1967. "Variation of the human menstrual cycle through reproductive life." *Int J Fertil* 12:77.

Tumbo-Oeri, A.G. 1985. "T and B lymphocyte populations in peripheral blood during the menstrual cycle in normal Kenya women." *East African Medical Journal* 62(2):90-91.

Utomo, Budi and Pandu Riono. 1991. "The use of the Indramayu sample registration system for the detection of early pregnancy and studying maternal morbidity." Paper presented at the 18th annual NCIH International Health Conference. Arlington, VA.

van der Kwaak, Anke, van den Engel, Marijke, Richters, Annemick, Bartels, Koos, Haaijer, Ineke, Mama, Amina, Veenhoff, Ann, Engelkes, Elly, Keysors, Loes and Ines Smith. 1991. "Women and health." *Vena Journal* 3(1): 2-33.

Villar, Jose, Repke, John, Markush, Linda, Calvert, William and George Rhoads. 1989. "The measuring of blood pressure during pregnancy." *American Journal of Obstetrics and Gynecology.* 161(4):1019-1024.

Walsh, J.A., Nashak, C.M., Measham, A.R. and P.J. Gertler. "Maternal and perinatal health problems." D.T. Jamison and H.W. Mosley, eds., *Evolving Health Sector Priorities in Developing Countries.* Washington: The World Bank. Forthcoming.

Warren, M.P. 1983. "Effects of Undernutrition on reproductive function in the human." *Endocr Rev* 4:363-377.

Wasserheit, J.N., Harris, J.R., Chakraborty, J., Kay, B. and K.J. Mason. 1989. "Reproductive tract infections in a family planning population in rural Bangladesh: An ignored opportunity to promote MCH-FP programs." *Stud Fam Plann* 20(2):69-80.

World Federation of Public Health Associations. 1986. *Women and Health.* Information for action issue paper. Geneva: World Federation of Public Health Associations.

World Health Organization. 1989. "African regional consultation on control of anemia in pregnancy." *WHO Report.* MCH/86.

World Health Organization. 1984. "Determining the causes of perinatal death." *WHO Report.* MCH/84.1

World Health Organization. 1988. "Geographic variation in the incidence of hypertension in pregnancy: World Health Organization international collaborative study of hypertensive disorders of pregnancy." *American Journal of Obstetrics and Gynecology* 158(1): 80-83.

World Health Organization. 1987. "The hypertensive disorders of pregnancy." *WHO Technical Report* Series 758. Geneva: WHO.

World Health Organization. 1990. "The prevention and management of postpartum haemorrhage." Report of a technical working group. *WHO Report* MCH/90.7

Yan, R.Y., McCarthy, Brian J., Ye, Hui-Fang, Qu, Chuan-Yan, Zhu, Li, Chen, Tong-Xiang and Deborah Kowal. 1989. "The risk approach in perinatal health Shunyi County, People's Republic of China." *U.S. Department of Health and Human Services, Publication* No. HHS 89-8412.

# 3

# Women's Nutrition Through the Life Cycle: Social and Biological Vulnerabilities

*Kathleen M. Merchant and Kathleen M. Kurz*

*She's thirty-five years old. When she was born her mother was malnourished and overworked. She was very small and low-weight at birth. She grew slowly. During childhood she had little good food to eat—even less than her brothers. She could not go to school as her brothers did, but remained at home with her mother to help with the housework and child-minding.*

*By adolescence, her pelvic bones were misshapen and she was shorter than she should have been. As was the tradition, she was married and had her first baby when she was only 14, even before she had fully developed. It was a difficult birth, but she survived it and many more, though once she had so much bleeding that everyone was afraid she would never recover. She's been anaemic ever since, a condition aggravated by the hookworm she carries. During another pregnancy she suffered a malarial fever and miscarried.*

*Like her mother before her, she never went to a health center when she was pregnant. It was too far away and too foreign. She used the same traditional midwife who delivered her and who helped her sisters. The midwife had no training in cleanliness, and she suffered serious infections after childbirth.*

*She had little time between pregnancies to regain her strength, and little enough food at any time. During later pregnancies her fatigue was draining her.*

*She had so much work in the house and the local brick factory she could not bear the thought of another pregnancy. When it came she went to a woman in the village for something to end it. She was very sick, but it worked.*

*Today she still feels dull pains and soreness in her belly which flare up from time to time. Also after so many pregnancies she probably has a partially prolapsed uterus, which often causes her discomfort, especially after a hard day's work carrying bricks.*

*She is a woman who cares desperately about her family and wants to limit her pregnancies. She heard about family planning from her sisters, but was always too afraid of her husband, who would never allow it . . . (UNFPA 1989; Hammer 1981).*

The nutritional problems of women and consequences for them are of increasing concern. Women's low status relative to men and their biological role in reproduction often puts them at higher risk than men for many nutritional problems. Although for several decades the priority of those concerned with international nutrition and health has been children, there is a growing recognition of another factor that puts half of the world's population at high risk for poor health and nutritional status: gender (Basta 1989; McGuire and Popkin 1989; Soysa 1987; UNFPA 1989).

For many females in the world, gender discrimination begins at birth with an overwhelming preference for male offspring. Unfortunately, discrimination often continues throughout their lives, resulting in lower education and employment opportunities and higher work loads, and possibly in reduced access to family food and community health care (Royston and Armstrong 1989).

Leslie (1991) reports that conservative estimates suggest that among the 1.1 billion women 15 years and older living in developing countries in 1985, over 500 million were stunted as a result of childhood protein-energy malnutrition, about 250 million suffered effects of iodine deficiency, and almost 2 million were blind due to deficiency of Vitamin A (DeMaeyer and Adiels-Tegman 1985; Galloway 1989; McGuire and Austin 1987; Hetzel 1988; Levin et al. 1991). Information specifically addressing prevalences among women is difficult to find for Vitamin A and iodine deficiencies, therefore the estimations are based on population prevalences, most likely leading to an underestimation of the deficiency among women alone. Additionally, conservative estimates suggest that more than 500 million of the world's people are chronically hungry, and that women are disproportionately represented among the hungry (Bread for the World 1990).

This chapter addresses the nutritional problems and consequences faced by women throughout the life cycle. The emphasis is on the nutritional problems of women living in a context of poverty. The most severe and urgent nutritional problems specific to women are found in this setting. However, two nutritional problems of significance to women in more affluent circumstances (osteoporosis and eating disorders) also are discussed.

Within a life cycle approach to discussing women's nutrition, four broad stages have been chosen: (1) infancy and childhood, (2) adolescence, (3) reproductive years, (4) later years of life. First, the social vulnerability of women, a product of their low status, is examined at each of the four life stages as well as the potential for general undernutrition. Next, the intergenerational implications of undernutrition and their role in perpetuating malnutrition is described. A simple but effective illustration of this has been produced by the UNFPA (1989) and is shown in a modified form in Figure 3.1. In the final section, the biological vulnerability that women face

FIGURE 3.1 The Vicious Cycle of Malnutrition

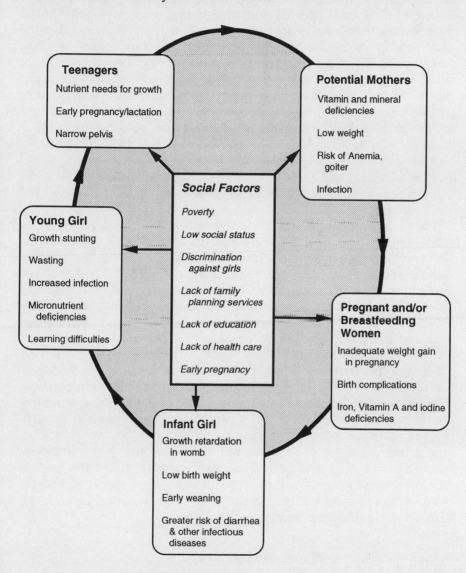

*Source:* Modified from UNFPA, 1989

due to their role in reproduction will be addressed with respect to two sources of stress (early pregnancy and frequent reproductive cycling) and three specific nutritional deficiencies (iron, vitamin A and iodine), as well as the problem of osteoporosis. The nutritional role in maternal morbidity and mortality is also discussed in this section. An attempt will be made to illustrate the problems using available data, and to identify both the major gaps in information and, hence, research needs. Priority actions to reduce the nutritional problems of women living in poverty in developing countries are discussed in the concluding section.

## Poverty and Social Vulnerability: The Potential for Undernutrition Through the Life Cycle

The focus of this section is the nutritional problems created through social relationships rather than biological effects of gender. Not all nutritional problems can be separated completely into either social or biological categories, but it is useful to trace the root cause of the nutritional "vulnerability" because it gives guidance when one is looking for a solution. The social context can reduce or increase the impact of the biological vulnerability. For example, in many cultures there is a traditional period following the birth of a child during which a woman is expected to reduce her usual activities, sometimes referred to as a "lying-in" period. This social practice *reduces* the impact of the biologically rooted high-energy cost of lactation. Conversely, a social practice of food taboos prohibiting the intake of a nutrient-rich food during childhood, pregnancy, or lactation *increases* the risk of a nutritional problem developing during these periods of high nutrient needs.

A major underlying cause of malnutrition is poverty, and it is within settings of poverty that the social vulnerability of females increases the risk for nutritional problems. For each of the four life stages, social vulnerabilities particular to women will be identified, and the cumulative consequence of undernutrition will be discussed.

### Infancy/Childhood — Preference for Males

Children are at risk for many nutritional deficiencies. Their high growth rates, small stomach capacities, and higher rates of illness due to less-developed immune systems, are partially responsible. During childhood, males and females have very similar energy and nutrient needs, as illustrated by the grouping of males with females for the U.S. Recommended Dietary Allowance up to the age of ten (FNB/NAS/NRC 1989a). Given that the nutrient needs are the same for the first ten years of life one might expect vulnerability to nutritional problems and their health consequences would be the same. Actually, girls have a biological advantage, and in optimal environments have an estimated advantage of 1.15-to-1 over boys in mortality rates (Royston and Armstrong 1989). In spite of this, many countries exhibit higher mortality rates for girls. For example, according to data from the World Fertility Survey (1983) reported by UNFPA (1989), among one–two year-olds in Turkey, the mortality rate of girls is 1.6 times that of boys; in Pakistan and Sri Lanka, it is 1.5 times higher; Bangladesh and Trinidad and Tobago, 1.4 times higher; and Colombia, 1.3 times higher. Among two–five year-olds in Costa Rica, the mortality rate of girls is reported to be 1.7 times higher; Syria, 1.6; and Thailand and Pakistan, 1.5 times higher.

The implication of this evidence is that discriminatory behavior on the part of caretakers shifts the balance. A belief exists in some regions that young boys require greater quantity and quality of food than young girls. In families where the resources are highly constrained, the choice may be made in some societies to conserve by giving girls less; although when food shortages become particularly extreme, the difference between the food intake of the girls and that of the boys may narrow (Payne and Lipton 1989). In many regions girls will become members of other families upon marriage and do not bear the social responsibility for supporting the parents in old age. In these cases they may be viewed as temporary and somewhat less valuable members of the family than the boys (Katona-Apte 1988; Chaudhury 1988).

Not only equal access to food, but equal access to health care and education are also key determinants of vulnerability to undernutrition. Specifically, frequent or severe episodes of illness can have an impact on nutritional status and, therefore, growth through anorexia (depressed appetite leading to a reduced intake) or increased need for certain nutrients. Additionally, nutritional deficiencies decrease resistance to infection. Education has an impact on the timing of childbearing and income-earning potential, both of which affect nutrition and health status. A dramatic difference in school-enrollment and literacy rates between girls and boys exists in many countries, particularly those countries with the highest infant mortality rates (UNICEF, 1990).

A preference for male children is expressed in many countries surveyed (Royston and Armstrong 1989), which may or may not lead to preferential care behavior for boys when resources are limited. In an effort to compile all available evidence of male preference in caretaking behavior, an annotated bibliography was produced by the World Health Organization (WHO 1986a). The following evidence is derived from brief descriptions of articles referenced in this source. Differential breast-feeding practices (a longer duration for boys) has been reported in Pakistan, India and the Philippines.

Evidence of unequal food allocation between male and female children has been recorded for communities in Bangladesh, Mexico and the Philippines. In the studies from Bangladesh and Pakistan the gender differential was also examined and observed in anthropometric data of the same children. Additional reports from some communities in Jordan, Colombia, Saudi Arabia, Iran, Bolivia, Kiribati, Jamaica and several reports from regions of India contain evidence of a gender differential in anthropometric data. Seeking health care for male children appears to be more common than for female children in some communities of India, Nigeria, Egypt, Bangladesh, and Korea. The evidence from Korea is particularly illustrative: It was found in the Kanghura Community Health Project that when measles immunizations were provided free of cost the proportions of boys and girls being immunized were almost equal; but when a small fee was charged, the proportion of girls fell to little above a quarter. Others also report that female children are taken less frequently to health centers for care (Holmboe-Ottesen et al. 1988; Chaudhury 1988). Despite widespread evidence of discriminatory behavior in indicators reported above, stunting was rarely more prevalent among girls within samples from the updated version of the WHO Anthropometry Data Bank (WHO 1989). But these samples are not necessarily representative of groups at high risk for discriminatory behavior, and corresponding data for six to ten years of age is not available; therefore conclusions cannot be easily drawn. Given worldwide and regional variation, both culturally and in terms of available resources, evidence of discriminatory practices must be examined locally (WHO 1986a; UNFPA 1989).

From available evidence, the disparity between girls and boys appears to be greatest for access to education, followed by access to medical care and food. It is possible that the discrimination in favor of boys decreases as the item or service is perceived as more necessary for survival. For example, food is an immediate need for survival, medical care may be regarded as less so, and education may be regarded as nonessential, particularly for girls.

The prevalence of stunting during the early years of life in developing countries is strikingly high. The causes and consequences of childhood stunting are undesirable (Martorell 1985; Martorell 1989). For example, stunting is usually caused by inadequate food, poor health and other deprivations, and stunting results in reduced work capacity and higher risk of compromised reproduction among women, such as difficult deliveries and lower birth weights.

The intention here has been to identify the potential sources of social vulnerability for females during childhood which may increase the nutritional problems they face during this stage and later. The importance of food, medical care and education for girls is obvious but may be an area for improvement in many settings. In parts of India this has been recognized, and television messages are stressing the equal food needs between girls and boys. Clearly, each specific setting should be examined for potential biases in allocation of food, health care and educational opportunities among household members.

## Adolescence — Early Reproductive Role

Developmentally, adolescence is a time of transition from external control (most often from parents) to internal control. It is recognized as a crucial and influential time for development of behavioral patterns, which include eating patterns and self-care. Sources of information beyond family, such as media (TV, radio) become more important. Therefore, adolescence is potentially a good time for educationally-based interventions.

There is limited information concerning the nutritional status of adolescents. Dietary intake and physical activity patterns are the major components of energy balance. The physical activities of work and play during this age period will vary tremendously. Illness plays less of a role at this time than earlier in life. Growth accelerates and then slows during this time period, resulting in significant nutritional needs for growth.

The potential to realize many of the opportunities of adolescence (such as continued education and growth) is reduced if girls assume adult roles at an early age, especially if they begin having children during adolescence (Kurz 1991). Although legislation often exists prohibiting it, early marriage is a common phenomenon in many societies. Some of the most striking statistics come from the World Fertility Survey, in which it was "found that 25 percent of fourteen-year-old girls in Bangladesh, and 34 percent of fifteen-year-old girls in Nepal were married, although the legal minimum age for marriage is sixteen in both countries" (WHO/UNFPA/UNICEF 1989). Formal education for the girl usually ends when she marries and there is pressure to conceive to gain social status. Early marriage is not the only reason for early pregnancy: "in certain societies, such as some Caribbean and African countries, adolescent pregnancy and childbirth are common outside marriage and regarded as a means of improving status, demonstrating fecundity, and attracting a new partner to provide support for each successive child" (WHO/UNFPA/UNICEF 1989). Early pregnancy is also a problem for adolescents in many industrialized societies, resulting from increased opportunities for sexual encounters and inadequate availability of contraceptive information and services easily accessible to the adolescent. In some cases accessibility is hindered because of taboos regarding adolescent sexuality.

Adolescent girls are particularly vulnerable to social pressure about body image, and this may lead to eating disorders that can have severe and sometimes irreversible nutritional consequences. Eating disorders such as anorexia nervosa (extreme self-imposed food restriction resulting in starvation) and bulimia (intentional purging of food already ingested) are nutritional problems of increasing concern in industrialized countries. In these settings awareness of the problem is growing, but in most societies the effects of social pressure and body image on nutritional intake are virtually unknown (Leslie et al. 1988).

### Reproductive Years — Multiple Roles

Women have multiple roles to fulfill within their family and community. They have the major biological role in the process of reproduction frequently spending a large proportion of their reproductive years pregnant and/or breast-feeding. For example, assuming that a woman is capable of reproducing for thirty-five years of her life, it has been estimated that on average, a woman in Bangladesh spends 21.1 years of these thirty-five years pregnant and/or lactating. Correspondingly, on average, women of Pakistan spend 17.5 years; of Senegal, 16.4 years; of Kenya, 16.2 years; of Thailand, 15.8 years; of Peru, 13.0 years; and women of Haiti spend 12.4 years pregnant and/or lactating. These estimates were calculated using proportions presented by McGuire and Popkin (1989).

Additionally, the social roles of women often result in very heavy work loads for women living in poverty. The frequent combination of these roles creates major challenges for women. The social roles of women generally include major responsibilities within the family, involving care for the other members, household management, food preparation, cleaning duties, use of health care, and education and supervision of children. In addition to this family role, they frequently have kin and community roles, and finally, paid or unpaid productive roles in agriculture, the marketplace, home production, and factory or other work activities. There is a growing recognition of the important role women play in food chain activities (Holmboe-Ottesen et al. 1989) and health maintenance. Time allocation studies have shown repeatedly that a woman's work day is longer than a man's and that women have less leisure or discretionary time available than men (Holmboe-Ottesen et al. 1989; McGuire and Popkin 1989). This also has been shown for girls who frequently spend more time in household maintenance activities than boys. The long hours and multiple roles of women create a social vulnerability to problems of malnutrition, particularly during the reproductive years. In two studies among Indian women, for example, their heavy work load was highly associated with their low weight (Anderson 1991; Senapati 1991).

Pregnancy, lactation, and menstruation increase women's requirements for various nutrients compared to their premenarcheal years. Heavy work loads also increase women's food requirements. The amount of physical labor performed daily by women varies tremendously worldwide, depending on a variety of environmental and familial factors. For example: Is firewood used for fuel?, Is it nearby?, Is the water source a well?, Is the well nearby?, Are there children, siblings, elders to help with the tasks? Too often the situation is similar to the following scenario.

### Burkina Faso: "The whole trip took almost four hours"

*Kalsaka's women used to get wood close to their compounds. The village committee had banned this, so now they walk for about five kilometers into the hills that form a backdrop to the village, where erosion, crusting and years of low rainfall have killed off many trees.*

*To see exactly what the job is like, we went out with the women on one expedition. We set out at 7:30. The women had already been to the wells twice for water. I used to imagine wood-gathering was merely a matter of picking up sticks lying around. In fact it is a complex and energy-consuming operation.*

*On arrival at their destination, the women split up in all directions. Branches are attacked with machetes and hoes. As these are not very sharp, it can take a long time to hack through a single branch. Stumps are too thick to cut through. Usually the women leave them till the following year, when they are rotted enough to be pried loose. This is done by flinging as big a stone as they can lift at the top of the stump, then shaking until it comes out of the soil.*

*The women work with energy and considerable courage. Small babies are carried along and shaken at every blow of the machete. Young girls come along to help. The fittest women climb up trees, scramble up steep slopes of sharp scree, often in bare feet, and wrestle with shrubs perched on the edge of cliffs. Falls and injuries from cutting tools and stones are common. The whole trip took almost four hours. The women do it two or three times a week. (P. Harrison 1988 quoted in UNFPA 1989).*

Time constraints may lead to infrequent meals, and exhaustion may lead to a reduced appetite. Given the low income, long hours worked, and multiple roles frequently fulfilled by women in settings of poverty, they are more likely to have trouble meeting their food needs and to be at risk for general undernutrition.

Although worldwide data describing the prevalence of undernourished adult women is lacking, the prevalence of low birth weight (< 2,500 g) is an indirect indicator, in so far as low birthweight is caused by poor maternal nutritional status (WHO Working Group 1986b). Based on WHO estimates of 1982, twenty million babies (16 percent of all births worldwide) are born each year with low birthweight, and eighteen million of these are born in developing countries (Kramer 1987). The relative importance of maternal nutritional status as a determinant of low birth weight obviously varies with differing circumstances, but its importance is well-established. It has been estimated that maternal nutritional factors (specifically, low caloric intake; low weight gain during pregnancy; low pre-pregnant weight; and short stature, an indicator of childhood undernutrition) account for close to half of the impact of established factors with direct causal impacts on intrauterine growth retardation in rural developing-country settings (Kramer 1987). Recent data suggest that fetal growth is initially protected at the expense of maternal fat stores when there is energetic stress during pregnancy (Merchant et al. 1990a,b). What degree of maternal malnutrition must occur before fetal growth is compromised is not known. The implication of this evidence is that the incidence of low birth weight attributable to maternal malnutrition would underestimate maternal malnutrition, indicating that maternal undernutrition is extremely common. Similarly, it appears that maternal undernutrition is underestimated by indicators of undernutrition in their children (Mock and Konde 1991).

## Later Years — Marginalization

By the time a poor woman reaches the later years of her life, she is experiencing the cumulative effect of social vulnerabilities that started earlier in her life: preference for males, early reproduction, and multiple roles, among others. Although the social position of women rises with age in some cultures, many older women may become more socially vulnerable as they become marginalized. The same may be true for an older man, but given the low status of women worldwide, an aged woman generally has less power than an aged man in the community. He may have been more able to acquire education, possessions or status within his community, which are assets for survival. This is particularly true of highly patriarchal societies in which financial responsibility for a female traditionally lies in the hands of a male throughout her life. One illustrative case is that of Bangladesh. If a woman is abandoned or widowed and destitute she falls out of the realm of traditional protection and is left to her own devices for survival. A recent article by Katona Apte (1988) addressed the "coping strategies of destitute women in Bangladesh." In this article she provides vivid descriptions of the factors that lead to destitution for women. Although widowhood or abandonment can happen during the reproductive years, it increases in occurrence during later years of life. Soysa (1987) reports that, "As a widow, a woman suffers much indignity. If a woman survives her husband, it is believed to be the results of 'karma'—her sins in a previous life. She is dependent upon the son's kindness for her support and she is often bereft of possessions, jewelry or fine clothes. More importantly, she eats sparingly, and fasts often because it is said to be unhealthy to eat much in this stage of life. In fact, widowhood in the lower socioeconomic groups condemns women to beg for their food."

It is not only the elderly women of developing countries who are vulnerable. The 1979 State of the World's Women paper reported, "that old

people—and particularly elderly women—are to be found in disproportionate numbers in the most run-down urban areas, in slums and squatter
settlements. In New York, for example, studies show that 40 percent of the
one million older residents live in slum areas." Clearly in some circumstances, the low status of women leaves them in a situation with high risks
in later years.

Although very little information is available, one would suspect that
chronic energy deficiency is an important problem for elderly women living
in circumstances of poverty. Although data on older women are limited,
research is increasingly demonstrating that the elderly, male and female,
have a tendency to have poorer intestinal absorption of some nutrients
(Morrison 1984). Food intake decreases and, when combined with problems
of decreased absorption, may make the elderly vulnerable to specific
nutrient deficiencies. Loneliness, isolation, poverty, depression, apathy
and debilitation may contribute to the lower food intake of the elderly. In
addition, the prevalence of chronic disease is much higher as age increases.
Evidence is accumulating that many chronic diseases have nutritional
causes and consequences. As in childhood, the factors that predispose
women to be discriminated against in the allocation of resources are the
factors that will increase their risk of undernutrition during old age. In
addition, the impact of frequent reproductive cycling on health in later
years remains to be elucidated. Long-term depletion or undernutrition is
likely to have health consequences in old age. But what these consequences
are specifically and how they might be measured are areas for future
research.

The most striking conclusion that can be drawn regarding women's
nutrition and this final stage of the life cycle is that almost no information
is available. This alone is a dramatic illustration of the invisibility of the
elderly in developing countries to nutrition and health care planners, policy
makers, and providers. In the case of women, this is partially a reflection of
the undervaluing of women beyond their reproductive years, and partially
a reflection of the all too often short life span of individuals exposed to all
the health risks of poverty.

## Intergenerational Effects of Undernutrition and Small Body Size

A nutritional problem is generally the consequence of earlier problems
and the cause of later problems. Therefore it can rarely be assigned to a
single stage of the life cycle, particularly as the consequences can be felt by
later generations. A cycle of suboptimal growth is perpetuated across
generations. Figure 3.1, adapted from the UNFPA's Population Report of
1989, illustrates this intergenerational cycle. Many social factors contribute

to the less-than-optimal growth from conception to puberty. Indirectly, factors such as poverty, low social status, and lack of health care, play a role, as listed in the figure. More directly, factors such as infrequent feeding (small stomach capacity), low energy density of food, high exposure to infection, reduced immunocompetence, and anorexia due to illness, both during pregnancy and early childhood, contribute to growth retardation. It is also important to recognize that behaviors are passed on intergenerationally, and therefore, behavioral patterns that contribute to growth retardation also will be passed on.

There is evidence that maternal size constrains fetal growth during the final stages of pregnancy. Therefore small maternal size resulting from stunting during early childhood and/or from very young maternal age will constrain fetal growth beyond what it would have been had optimal childhood growth and/or pregnancy timing for the mother occurred. Compromised growth at early stages (gestation to three years) is particularly difficult to make up for at later stages (Martorell et al. 1990), partially because growth is occurring at such an accelerated pace during this time period. In addition, due to the overwhelming environmental factors discussed previously, it is unlikely that an initially poor start will be entirely overcome, resulting in a small adult stature. The females will continue in the cycle by producing offspring with a greater probability of having intrauterine growth retardation, and so the process cycles on.

This cycle of undernutrition must be broken by optimizing growth through better nutrition and health. The major window of opportunity for growth is during gestation through three years of age (Martorell et al. 1990), although adolescent girls may also benefit from supplementation (Kulin et al. 1982; Satyanarayana et al. 1981).

## Biological Vulnerability (Reproductive Role)

Most nutrition and health research on women has been conducted with a focus on the effects of maternal nutrition and health status on the child. A crucial evolution in this area of research is the recognition of the importance of women's health and nutrition for women themselves. The reproductive years bring with them particular health risks for women.

A thorough nutrient-by-nutrient discussion of needs during the reproductive years is given elsewhere (Adair 1987; NAS 1990; NAS 1991). Six major nutritional challenges for women have been chosen for this discussion, each resulting from their biologically-determined reproductive role. In addition, the contribution of undernutrition to the major causes of maternal mortality are discussed. These nutrition-related problems were chosen because the consequences are relatively distinctive, commonly occurring and of a serious nature. Although severe deficiencies of micronutrients result in the most dramatic and easily assessed consequences, it is important to remember that milder forms of these deficiencies may also have consequences: "the severely deficient persons represent index cases, or the tip of the iceberg, in the spectrum of nutritional status within the population" (Buzina et al. 1989). Mild-to-moderate deficiencies of iron, iodine, vitamin A, and energy are also relevant and of concern in the following discussion.

## Early Pregnancy/Growth Competition

With the onset of puberty, early pregnancy poses an additional nutritional challenge to females, the other challenge being optimal growth. Although growth begins slowing for females by the age of approximately fourteen, gains in linear growth, particularly of the long bones, is not complete until the age of eighteen, and peak bone mass is not achieved until the age of twenty-five (FNB/NAS/NRC 1989b). In a study of growth of the birth canal in adolescent girls, it was revealed that before eighteen years of age, maternal height is less indicative of the size of the bony birth canal than after eighteen years of age (Moerman 1982). In particular, "the development of the bony birth canal is slower than that of height during the early teenage period and the canal does not reach mature size until about two to three years after growth in height has ceased" (Harrison et al. 1985). Therefore increased nutrient needs for growth are present throughout adolescence.

The nutrient needs of pregnancy and lactation will be in addition to nutrient needs of growth. Although the impact of the competing nutrient needs of pregnancy on the young mother's linear growth may be minimal (unless the mother is extremely young, less than thirteen years), there is little information on how bone formation and calcium deposition will be affected in a young mother. Fetal growth is likely to be affected. The incidence of low birth weight is higher among young mothers. Adolescent mothers have a higher risk of developing anemia (WHO/UNFPA/UNICEF 1989). In a supplementation trial using combinations of iron, folic acid, and antimalarial drugs, Nigerian primigravida teenagers showed benefits in maternal and fetal growth (Harrison et al. 1985). Increased food intake to cover needs of growth as well as pregnancy and lactation are clearly indicated in adolescent pregnancies. Reduced growth through the stress of early pregnancy may have lifelong deleterious consequences.

The magnitude of the problem can be partially described with the following statistics: Percentages of women giving birth by age eighteen are as follows: Africa, 28 percent; Latin America, 21 percent; and Asia, 18 percent (from the UN Demographic Yearbook). Percentage of first births to women ages fifteen to nineteen years are as follows: Costa Rica, 44 percent; Mexico, 41 percent; USA, 29 percent; Philippines, 24 percent; Malaysia, 19 percent; and Jordan, 18 percent (UN Population Division 1986).

## Frequent Cycling/Depletion

"Too young, too old, too many and too close." This statement from the UNFPA (1989) summarizes the problem of frequent pregnancies and periods of lactation that contribute to nutritional depletion of the mother. There is increasing evidence that when pregnancies are too frequent, intake too low, and work demands too high, women do not have adequate time to recuperate from the nutritional demands, and will show signs of nutritional stress such as loss of fat stores (Merchant et al. 1990a; Merchant et al. 1990b). Specific nutrient deficiencies may occur or chronic undernutrition may be the outcome of such reproductive stress. A weakness of most research addressing maternal depletion has been a failure to accurately quantify reproductive stress and women's nutritional status, instead using broad and misleading indicators such as parity and maternal weight (Merchant and Martorell 1988).

## Iron-Deficiency Anemia

Women have peak iron needs during the reproductive years. The consequences of iron-deficiency anemia are severe (DeMaeyer et al. 1989). Physical work capacity and resistance to fatigue and infection are decreased among anemic adults. The danger of death due to hemorrhage, a condition that is not unusual following labor and delivery, is greatly increased among anemic women. Pregnant anemic women also face an increased risk of getting infections. Evidence of lowered work capacity and reduced immunocompetence are seen even in mild iron deficiency defined as low serum ferritin and normal hemoglobin (Buzina et al. 1989). Conversely, an increased feeling of general well-being is reported following recovery from anemia. There are serious fetal consequences of iron-deficiency anemia in pregnant women, such as increased risk of miscarriage and of low birth weight (DeMaeyer et al. 1989). The estimated prevalences of anemia among all women and pregnant women, ages fifteen to forty-nine years, divided by regions of the world are given in Table 3.1. Iron-deficiency anemia results from inadequate intake of iron-rich foods (Aziz Karim and Midhet 1991), as well as from excessive blood loss during events such as childbirth, hemorrhage, menstruation, and various parasitic infections. Although provision of iron is probably the most common nutritional intervention during pregnancy, iron supplements do not reach many anemic women. A recent review of compliance with iron supplements suggested that the main reasons for lack of "compliance" were low accessibility of prenatal care, where supplements are distributed, and insufficient supply and distribution of supplements, but not side-effects experienced by women who consume them (Galloway 1991). Efforts to increase iron intake, through altered eating patterns and/or supplementation, should not be limited to pregnant women because iron needs are high for menstruating women also (Gopalan 1991).

## Vitamin A

The dietary intake of carotenoids and vitamin A is low among women in many regions of the world, although it varies tremendously (ACC/SCN 1987). Vitamin A has important roles in growth, vision and the health of the eye, and immune response. The additional fetal growth occurring during pregnancy contributes to an increased need for vitamin A during pregnancy, leaving women more susceptible to vitamin A deficiency at this time. Depletion of vitamin A stores is a possibility among women who, although not pregnant at the time, have had many pregnancies in rapid succession. Many aspects of the immune response may be depressed if vitamin A deficiency is present (IVACG 1979). Even mild-to-moderate vitamin A deficiencies impair immunocompetence (Buzina et al. 1989). A reduced

TABLE 3.1  Estimated Prevalence of Anemia of Women 15-49 Years by Region

|  | *Pregnant* | | | *All* | | |
|---|---|---|---|---|---|---|
|  | Anemic (%) | Anemic (million) | Total (million) | Anemic (%) | Anemic (million) | Total (million) |
| Africa | 63 | 11.3 | 17.9 | 44 | 46.8 | 106.4 |
| North America | – | – | 3.4 | 8 | 5.1 | 64.2 |
| Latin America | 30 | 3.0 | 9.9 | 17 | 14.7 | 86.5 |
| East Asia | 20 | 0.5 | 2.7 | 18 | 8.4 | 46.9 |
| South Asia | 65 | 27.1 | 41.7 | 58 | 191.0 | 329.4 |
| Europe | 14 | 0.8 | 5.7 | 12 | 14.1 | 117.5 |
| World | 51 | 43.9 | 85.7 | 35 | 288.4 | 825.0 |
| Developed | 14 | 2.0 | 14.8 | 11 | 32.7 | 285.5 |
| Developing | 59 | 41.9 | 71.0 | 47 | 255.7 | 539.5 |

*Source:* Based on DeMaeyer and Adiels-Tegman 1985.

FIGURE 3.2 The Geographical Distribution of Xeropthalmia in 1986

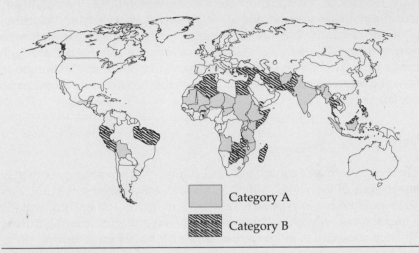

Category A

Category B

*Source:* DeMaeyer, 1986

resistance to infection is particularly hazardous to women after labor and delivery, when the potential for infection is high. Infection following birth is one of the major causes of maternal morbidity and mortality (Royston and Armstrong 1989).

Techniques for detection of mild-moderate vitamin A deficiency are needed. Clinical signs, such as xerophthalmia, are most commonly used, but these develop at the severe stages of deficiency. Therefore, it is clear that much undetected deficiency exists. Regional data for prevalences of vitamin A deficiency among adult women are not available as yet. But, because vitamin A needs are higher during pregnancy and some signs of deficiency such as night blindness occur more commonly among pregnant women, it can be postulated that in regions where there is a high prevalence of xerophthalmia, there is a high likelihood that pregnant women are at greater risk for deficiency than in regions with lower prevalence of xerophthalmia (Figure 3.2).

## *Iodine*

Iodine deficiency is the most common cause of endemic goiter. A goiter is the enlargement of the thyroid gland generally due to a deficiency of iodine, which is required for the production of thyroid hormone. Pregnant women are at high risk for developing goiter in regions with low iodine levels in the food supply because of their increased need for this hormone (and therefore iodine) during pregnancy. Iodine is required for adequate brain development at crucial stages during fetal development. Cretinism, a form of permanent mental retardation that affects a fetus during gestation, is the most severe consequence of iodine deficiency in women. A less debilitating consequence for adults is lethargy. Low iodine intake has generally been observed in populations living in regions where the soil is poor in iodine content. Frequently these are high mountainous regions (Matovinovic 1984). Although worldwide data on the prevalence of iodine-deficiency for adult women are not currently available, the iodine-deficient areas in developing countries provide the best indicators regarding the distribution of the problem among women (Figure 3.3).

## Osteoporosis

"Osteoporosis is defined as bone loss sufficient to bring about one or more symptomatic fracture(s) with minimal trauma" (Schuette and Linkswiler 1984). Although epidemiological studies have shown evidence for a series of risk factors, the etiology of osteoporosis is not well understood. Women are biologically vulnerable to developing osteoporosis because following menopause there is a dramatic loss in bone mass. This is believed to be due to the loss of estrogen production, although the role of estrogen in bone-mass maintenance is not yet well understood. Nutrition is believed to play a role in the prevention of osteoporosis and though

FIGURE 3.3 Distribution of Iodine-Deficient Areas in Developing Countries

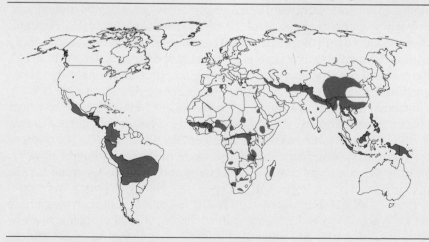

*Source:* ACC/SCN, 1987c

controversial, many believe that it plays a role in treatment (FNB/NAS/ NRC 1989b). Calcium and vitamin D are particularly important for bone formation and calcium loss is the main component of the loss in bone mass. Weight-bearing activity is also important for bone formation.

The prevalence of osteoporosis is very high in industrialized countries among postmenopausal women. There is very little information regarding its prevalence in developing countries. The following risk factors have been identified: female gender, white or oriental race, early menopause, advancing age, thin, small frame, immobilization, sedentary life-style, poor dietary calcium intake, family history of osteoporosis, cigarette smoking, alcohol abuse, high sodium diet, caffeine consumption, nulliparity, high protein intake, high phosphate intake, absence of breast-feeding (FNB/NAS/NRC 1989b). Although some of these risk factors would be less common among developing country populations, one might expect the incidence of some of the risk factors for this disease to increase as these countries continue on a trend of adopting "Western" life styles. At this point the best solution is prevention, and it appears that the best strategy for prevention is to maximize bone density and deposition, which may be facilitated by increasing calcium intake and weight-bearing activity where these are low.

## Maternal Mortality

A maternal death is defined by WHO as "the death of a woman who is or has been pregnant during the previous 42 days," although deaths attributable to pregnancy and childbirth also occur outside of this time frame. Besides difficulties of definition, there are many other obstacles to gaining an accurate estimate of the number of maternal deaths occurring in developing countries, most of which result in an underestimate. First and foremost, most deaths occur outside of hospitals in remote regions, partially because the women are unable to get to health care facilities. A thorough discussion of the challenges to estimating this problem accurately is contained in *Preventing Maternal Deaths* (Royston and Armstrong 1989).

Maternal mortality is a tragedy that shows one of the sharpest contrasts between developing and developed countries. The lifetime chance of maternal death in North America is 1:6,366 and in Africa is 1:21. The tremendous gap in this indicator of health is a result of the conditions of poverty. Not only are adequate health care services and facilities essential for the appropriate response to medical emergencies of labor, delivery, and recovery from childbirth, but maternal mortality is a problem of such magnitude that it is crucial to consider the ways in which nutritional problems cause or aggravate dangerous situations of childbirth complications. It is becoming increasingly clear that many problems could be reduced in severity or prevented through adequate nutrition at earlier stages (Merchant 1991).

Poor nutritional status contribute to at least three of the four major causes of maternal mortality: hemorrhage, infection, obstructed labor, and eclampsia, accounting for 20-35 percent, 5-15 percent, 5-10 percent, and 15-25 percent of maternal deaths, respectively. Women who die may have experienced several of these conditions. For example, obstructed labor can lead to the tearing of tissue causing blood loss (hemorrhage), and ultimately an infection could set in and be recorded as the cause of death.

Significant blood loss through hemorrhaging is much more serious in an anemic woman (Royston and Armstrong 1989). Given the estimated prevalence of 47 percent for iron-deficiency anemia among women of developing countries, the severity of hemorrhaging (the top cause of maternal mortality) could be reduced through reduction of anemia. Approximately 50 percent of maternal deaths in Indonesia and Egypt and over 30 percent of deaths in India are due to postpartum hemorrhage (UNFPA 1989).

Maternal infection is probably exacerbated by malnutrition. As previously discussed, even mild deficiencies of iron and vitamin A lead to reduced immunocompetence. Pregnant women are at increased risk for vitamin A deficiency. The potential hazards of micronutrient deficiencies to the immunocompetence of women should not be overlooked. Septic abortion is generally identified as the fifth major cause of maternal mortality. An undernourished woman undergoing abortion is less likely to be able to withstand hemorrhage or infection.

Small stature is a well-known risk factor for obstructed labor and contributes to the widespread preference for small newborns among women of many cultures (Gann et al. 1989; Brems and Berg 1989). This preference has important implications for interventions to increase birth size. The question arises, does maximizing fetal growth also increase the risk of maternal trauma and death at birth? Preliminary results indicate that when maternal and newborn risks are compared, the magnitude of increase in fetal growth due to maternal supplementation that will occur leads to a greater reduction in risk of morbidity for the newborn than the increase in risk of obstructed labor (cephalo-pelvic disproportion, in particular) for the mother (Merchant and Villar 1991). Additionally, intentional food restriction, which is commonly practiced in many regions, may not be able to reduce fetal growth adequately to reduce the risk of obstructed labor for the mother.

Clearly the long-term nutritional solution for reduction of risk for difficult delivery is to optimize female growth through adequate nutrition from gestation to early adulthood, when growth of the bony pelvis is completed (Moerman 1982). Likewise, improved maternal nutritional status before pregnancy, particularly with respect to iron, will reduce the risk of death from hemorrhaging or infection.

TABLE 3.2 Summary of Nutritional Problems and Potential Actions

| Period of the Life Cycle | Major Problem Leading to Undernutrition (in addition to poverty) | Priority Actions |
| --- | --- | --- |
| Infancy/ Childhood | Preference in Males | Public Awareness Campaign (regarding equal nutrional needs of young girls relative to young boys) |
| Adolescence | Early Reproductive Role | Teach Job Skills; Improve Access to Education; Take Actions (Through Legislation and Public Awareness) to Delay Early Marriage |
| Reproductive Years | Multiple Roles | Reduction of Women's Workload; Increase Men's Involvement in Care-taking at Household Level |
| | Frequent Cycling/ Depleting | Incress Access to Methods of Family Planning; Fund and Conduct Research for Safe, Healthy, Acceptable Contraceptive Options |
| Later Years | Marginalization | Increase Availability of Social Services and Support to Elderly |

## Conclusions

Women's nutritional status is crucial to their health, well-being, and productivity throughout their lives. Poor nutritional status arises from economic, political, social, cultural, and gender inequalities, as well as natural and human-made disasters. This chapter should alert the reader to the nutritional problems that are most likely to manifest themselves in women, particularly those women living in circumstances of poverty in developing countries. We have used a life cycle approach (infancy/childhood, adolescence, reproductive years, and later years) to examine women's nutrition under conditions of poverty, both to highlight that the social and biological circumstances of females change over the life cycle, and to illustrate that the effects of these circumstances on women's nutrition are cumulative. For example, a girl who is growth retarded in infancy and early childhood will be stunted during her adolescence, her reproductive years, and her older age. An anemic woman suffering severe hemorrhage in childbirth is more likely to contract a reproductive tract infection that causes her chronic pain through her reproductive years and later years of life.

The goal of improving women's nutrition will only be accomplished by working with women and their communities to define and act upon meeting their nutritional needs. Priority areas of need for action are briefly described below, and specific problems and potential actions are summarized in Tables 3.2 and 3.3.

*Enable women to meet food needs for consumption of adequate energy and nutrients.* Although the focus of sufficient food consumption has often been limited to childhood, pregnancy, and lactation, it is important at all times. It is important in infancy and childhood for the accelerated growth that occurs in this period, and results carry into adulthood (Rivera et al. 1991). It is important in adolescence because of a second period of accelerated growth, and also to prepare for adult roles. It is important in the reproductive years so that women can perform their multiple roles, and in older ages when many of these roles continue. Concentrating on short intervals within the life cycle is often not effective. For example, correction of iron-deficiency anemia, and thus diminution of its adverse effects on reproductive outcomes, cannot be expected by supplementing women for only nine months during their pregnancies (Gopalan 1991).

*Reduce women's work load.* Women's nutritional status will be compromised if their energy intake does not balance their energy expenditure. While one way to avoid imbalance is to ensure women's adequate food consumption, another way is to reduce their work load. Cost-effective technologies that reduce women's work load include wells or piped water

TABLE 3.3 Specific Nutrient Deficiencies and a Selection of Possible Actions

| Iron | Increase consumption of iron-rich foods and foods that enhance iron absorption. |
|---|---|
| | Supplement women and children in regions of high prevalence of deficiency at workplace, school, and/or health center. |
| | Increase parasitic control measures. |
| | Seek means of appropriate food fortification. |
| Vitamin A | Increase consumption of foods rich in vitamin A. |
| | Supplement women and children in regions of high prevalence of deficiency at workplace, school, and/or health center. |
| | Seek means of appropriate food fortification. |
| Iodine | Seek means of appropriate food fortification. |
| | Supplement women and children in regions of high prevalence of deficiency at workplace, school, and/or health center. |

near the residences, fuel-efficient stoves, grain hullers, bicycles, and ploughs (Leslie 1991).

*Increase girls' access to education.* Education of girls is positively associated with many factors important for their good nutritional status into adulthood. Women who are educated marry later, have their first child later, make greater use of health services, and are involved in work that generates more income for them and their families. While schooling is available worldwide, girls are often kept home because their help is needed for household work and care of younger siblings and/or school fees cannot be paid (or because the limited funds available in the family are used for their brothers' school fees). The benefits from girls' education are so great, however, that high priority should be given to overcome the forces that currently prevent them from obtaining it.

*Increase access to family planning and health care.* In the past several decades, women's access to family planning has increased considerably. This advance is applauded and further increases in access are encouraged for the future. Among future increases, we suggest that family-planning programs become accessible to and address the needs of younger women, those less than twenty-five years, and adolescents. Additional time between periods of pregnancy and lactation reduce the biological stress of reproduction and allow more time for repletion of nutrients such as iron and fat stores. Women's access to general health care has not increased as much as that of family planning, but the need for it has received greater attention since the high rates of maternal mortality worldwide became known. Greater utilization of health care improves women's nutrition because nutritional supplements and nutrition education are often delivered there, and because health problems that compromise nutritional status can be prevented or identified and treated.

*Enable women to share in the decisions of resource allocation at household, community, regional, national and international levels.* Increased food consumption and increased utilization of health care by women for themselves and their children, has often been shown to follow an increase in their control over household resources such as income. By increasing the role of women in resource-allocation decision making, several additional goals may be accomplished simultaneously. The need for equal access to education becomes immediately apparent. The benefit of women's knowledge and experience gained as primary caretakers and health care workers within households is made use of. And the recognition of women as competent partners is increased.

*Increase women's access to technical support in areas of agriculture and nutrition as well as financing, credit and management of cooperatives and market activities.* The opportunity for increasing their available resources, whether in food production, income generation, or simply time, must be improved. Activities such as directing agricultural extension efforts to women in settings where they are responsible for crops, so that they can grow foods rich in energy, iron, protein, vitamin A, and iodine, are needed. Training and support in community-organization techniques for activities such as childcare cooperatives, as well as training and support for women in obtaining credit and improving methods of business or marketing for those involved or wishing to become involved in marketplace activities, are needed. These are just some of the activities which can improve access to and acquisition of resources for women.

## Indicators

A comprehensive guide to nutritional assessment has been written by Gibson (1990). Yet, specific criteria for using anthropometric indicators to assess the nutritional status of adult women are lacking. The choice of an indicator will depend on the purposes of the assessment. Considerations of the woman's stage of the reproductive cycle should be incorporated into definitions of adequate nutritional status (Merchant and Martorell 1988). Otherwise, undernutrition in women may be underestimated. For example the weight measurement of a pregnant woman includes the weight of the baby, the placenta, and additional support tissues such as extra blood and breast tissue, in addition to her usual body weight. After giving birth, if a woman begins lactation, her fat stores not only support her own nutrient requirements, but will also be needed to support milk production during the early months of lactation. Therefore the range chosen to define adequate nutritional status for her may need to be higher because she is supporting this energetically costly process. There are difficulties in anthropometric assessment of adolescents, mainly due to the variation in maturation rates which affects the timing of the pubertal growth spurt (WHO Working Group 1986b).

*Body Mass Index (BMI).* A consensus is beginning to form regarding the usefulness of body mass index, which uses weight and height measures, for assessing chronic energy deficiency in adults; but the criteria established as yet do not differ by gender (James et al. 1988).

*Arm Circumference.* There is increasing support for the use of arm circumference as an indicator of women's current nutritional status because this measure appears to vary less by reproductive status (Shah 1991; Taggert 1967). It should be kept in mind, however, that arm circumference can be increased due to adequate fat stores (good nutritional status) or to big muscle mass from heavy physical work load. Therefore, it may be more useful for comparison within populations than between.

*Height.* Low height has been suggested as a useful indicator of women who may deliver low-birth-weight babies, as well as the risk for difficult delivery.

Recently an international forum reviewed current knowledge regarding the value of anthropometric indicators in predicting pregnancy outcomes (Krasovec and Anderson 1991). A final note regarding estimation of undernutrition among women, within their children, the prevalence of low birth weight attributable to nutritional causes and the prevalence of poor growth can be used as indirect indicators of poor maternal nutritional status for a deprived population when more specific information on women's nutritional status is lacking; however, these methods are likely to underestimate the prevalence of maternal undernutrition.

In conclusion, strengthening women through improvements in their nutrition and health status not only improves their own welfare but additionally is likely to be an effective avenue for promoting the health and welfare of those dependent on them. The intergenerational effects of malnutrition demonstrate that nutritional improvement throughout the life cycle is required to truly break "the vicious cycle of malnutrition."

## Note

Preparation of this chapter was partially funded by the United Nations Administrative Committee on Coordination/ Subcommittee on Nutrition (ACC/SCN).

## References

ACC/SCN. 1987. "First Report on the World Nutrition Situation." A report compiled from information available to the United Nations agencies of the ACC/SCN. Geneva: World Health Organization.

Adair, Linda S. 1987. "Nutrition in the Reproductive Years." In: F.E. Johnston, ed. *Nutritional Anthropology.* New York: Alan R. Liss, Inc.

Anderson, Mary Ann. 1991. "Undernutrition during Pregnancy and Lactation in India: Heavy Work and Eating Down as Determinants." Paper presented at the 18th Annual NCIH International Health Conference. Arlington, VA.

Aziz Karim, Saadiya and Farid Midhet. 1991. "Anemia in Pregnancy: a Continuing Problem in a Developing Country." Paper presented at the 18th Annual NCIH International Health Conference. Arlington, VA.

Basta, S.S. 1989. "Some trends and issues in international nutrition." *Food and Nutrition Bulletin* 11(1):29-31.

Bread for the World. 1990. "Hunger 1990: A Report on the State of the World's Hunger." Washington, DC.

Brems, Susan and Alan Berg. 1989. "Eating Down During Pregnancy: Nutritional, Obstetric and Cultural Considerations in the Third World." Paper presented for the UN Administrative Committee on Coordination - Subcommittee on Nutrition (ACC/SCN).

Buzina, R., Bates, C.J., van der Beek, J., Brubacher, G., Chandra, R.K., Hallberg, L., Heseker, J., Mertz, W., Pietrzik, K., Pollitt, E., Pradilla, A., Suboticanec, K., Sandstead, H.H., Schalch, W., Spurr, G.B. and J. Westenhofer. 1989. "Workshop on Functional Significance of Mild-to-Moderate Malnutrition." *American Journal of Clinical Nutrition* 50:172-176.

Chaudhury, R.H. 1988. "Adequacy of Child Dietary Intake Relative to that of other Family Members." *Food and Nutrition Bulletin* 10(2):26-34.

DeMaeyer, E. and Adiels-Tegman, M. 1985. "The Prevalence of Anaemia in the World." *World Health Statistics Quarterly* 38:302-316.

DeMaeyer, E.M., Dallman, P., Gurney, J.M., Hallberg, L., Sood, S.K. and S.G. Srikantia. 1989. "Preventing and Controlling Iron Deficiency Anaemia Through Primary Health Care: A Guide for Health Administrators and Programme Managers." Geneva: World Health Organization.

FNB/NAS/NRC. 1989a. Food and Nutrition Board/National Academy of Sciences/ National Research Council. *Recommended Dietary Allowances*, 10th Edition. Washington, D.C.: National Academy Press.

FNB/NAS/NRC. 1989b. Food and Nutrition Board/National Academy of Sciences/ National Research Council. "Osteoporosis" Ch. 23. In: *Diet and Health: Implications for Reducing Chronic Disease Risk*. Washington, D.C.: National Academy Press.

Galloway, Rae. 1991. "Determinants of Compliance with Iron Supplementation: Supplies, Side Effects, or Psychology?" Presentation at the 18th Annual NCIH International Health Conference. Arlington, VA.

Galloway, Rae. 1989. "The Prevalence of Malnutrition and Parasites in School-Age Children: an Annotated Bibliography." Washington, DC: The World Bank, Education and Employment Division.

Gann, P., Nghiem, L. and S. Warner. 1989. "Pregnancy Characteristics and Outcomes of Cambodian Refugees." *American Journal of Public Health* 79(9):1251-1257.

Gibson, Rosalind S. 1990. *Principles of Nutritional Assessment*. New York, NY: Oxford University Press.

Gopalan, C. 1991. "Women's Health and Nutrition: The Action Agenda for the 90's." Paper presented at the 18th Annual NCIH International Health Conference. Arlington, VA.

Hammer, V. 1981. "So Many Like Her." Geneva: World Health Organization.

Harrison, K.A., Rossiter, C.E. and H. Chong. 1985. "Relations between maternal height, fetal birthweight and cephalopelvic disproportion suggest that young Nigerian primigravidae grow during pregnancy." *British Journal of Obstetrics and Gynaecology supplement* 5:40-48.

Harrison, P. 1988. "Inside the Sahel: Report from Kalska." *Earthwatch*, No. 33. London: International Planned Parenthood Federation.

Hetzel, Basil S. 1988. "The Prevention and Control of Iodine Deficiency Disorders." ACC/SCN State-of-the-Art Series Nutrition Policy Discussion Paper No. 3. Rome, Italy: Food and Agriculture Organization.

Holmboe-Ottesen, G., Mascarenhas, O. and M. Wandel. 1989. "Women's Role in Food Chain Activities and the Implications for Nutrition." ACC/SCN State-of-the-Art Series Nutrition Policy Discussion Paper No. 4.

IVACG (International Vitamin A Consultative Group). 1979. "Recent Advances in the Metabolism and Function of Vitamin A and Their Relationship to Applied Nutrition." Washington, D.C.: The Nutrition Foundation, Inc.

James, W.P.T. , Ferro-Luzzi, H., and J.C. Waterloo. 1988. "Definition of chronic energy deficiency in adults: Report of a Working Party of the International Dietary Energy Consultative Group. *European Journal of Clinical Nutrition*. 42.

Katona-Apte, J. 1988. "Coping Strategies of Destitute Women in Bangladesh." *Food and Nutrition Bulletin* 10(3):42-47.

Krasovec, Katherine and Mary Ann Anderson, eds. 1991. *Maternal Nutrition and Pregnancy Outcome*. Washington, D.C.: Pan American Health Organization; Scientific Publication, No. 529.

Kramer, Michael S. 1987. "Determinants of Low Birth Weight: Methodological Assessment and Meta-Analysis." *Bulletin of the World Health Organization* 65(5):663-737.

Kulin, Howard E., Bwibo, Nimrod, Mutie, Dominic and Steven J. Santner. 1982. "The effect of chronic childhood malnutrition on pubertal growth and development." *American Journal of Clinical Nutrition* 36:527-536.

Kurz, Kathleen M. 1991. "Adolescent Girls: Nutritional Risks and Opportunities for Intervention." Presentation at the 18th Annual NCIH International Health Conference. Arlington, VA.

Leslie, Joanne. 1991. "Women's Nutrition: the Key to Improving Family Health in Developing Countries?" *Health Policy and Planning* 6:1-19.

Leslie, J., Pelto, G.H. and K.M. Rasmussen. 1988. "Nutrition of Women in Developing Countries." *Food and Nutrition Bulletin* 10(3):4-7.

Levin, Henry M., Pollitt, Ernesto, Galloway, Gae, and Judith McGuire. 1991 forthcoming. "Micronutrient Deficiency Disorders." In: Dean T. Jamison and W. Henry Mosley, eds. *Disease Control Priorities in Developing Countries*. New York: Oxford University Press for the World Bank.

Martorell, Reynaldo, Rivera, Juan and Haley K. Kaplowitz. 1990. "Consequences of stunting in early childhood for adult body size in rural Guatemala." *Annales Nestle* 48:85-92.

Martorell, Reynaldo. 1989. "Body Size, Adaptation and Function." *Human Organization* 48(1):15-20.

Martorell, Reynaldo. 1985. "Child Growth Retardation: a discussion of its causes and its relationship to health." In: Sir Kenneth Blaxter and JC Waterlow, eds. *Nutrition Adaptation in Man*. London and Paris: John Libbey.

Matovinovic, J. 1984. "Iodine," Ch. 41 In: R.E. Olson, ed. *Nutrition Reviews*. Washington, D.C.: The Nutrition Foundation, Inc.

McGuire, J. S. and Austin, J.E. 1987. "Beyond Survival: Children's Growth for National Development." New York: UNICEF.

McGuire, Judith S. and Barry M. Popkin. 1989. "Beating the zero-sum game: Women and nutrition in the Third World. Part I." *Food and Nutrition Bulletin* 11:38-63.

Merchant, Kathleen M. and Reynaldo Martorell. 1988. "Frequent Reproductive Cycling: Does it Lead to Nutritional Depletion of Mothers?" *Progress in Food and Nutrition Science* 12:339-369.

Merchant, Kathleen M., Martorell, Reynaldo and Jere D. Haas. 1990a. "Maternal and Fetal Responses to the Stress of Lactation Concurrent with Pregnancy and of Recuperative Intervals." *American Journal of Clinical Nutrition* 52:280-288.

Merchant, Kathleen M., Martorell, Reynaldo and Jere D. Haas. 1990b. "Maternal and Fetal Responses to the stress of Lactation Concurrent with Pregnancy in Consecutive Pregnancies and of Recuperative Intervals." *American Journal of Clinical Nutrition* 52:616-20.

Merchant, Kathleen M. 1991. "Nutritional Antecedents to the Major Causes of Maternal Mortality." Paper presented at the 18th Annual NCIH International Health Conference. Arlington, VA.

Merchant, Kathleen M. and Jos* Villar. 1991. "Maternal stature relative to fetal size and risk of delivery." Presentation at the 39th Annual Clinical Meeting of the American College of Obstetrics and Gynecologists. New Orleans, LA.

Mock, Nancy B. and Mander K. Konde. 1991. "Correlates of Maternal Nutritional Status in the Republic of Guinea." Presentation at the 18th Annual NCIH International Health Conference. Arlington, VA.

Moerman, M.L. 1982. "Growth of the birth canal in adolescent girls." *American Journal of Obstetrics and Gynecology* 143(5):528-532.

Morrison, S.D. 1984. "Nutrition and Longevity," Ch.45 In: R.E. Olson, ed. *Nutrition Reviews*. Washington, D.C.: The Nutrition Foundation, Inc.

National Academy of Sciences. 1990. *Nutrition During Pregnancy*.

National Academy of Sciences. 1991. *Nutrition During Lactation*.

Payne, P.R. and M. Lipton. 1989. "How Third World Rural Households Adapt to Dietary Energy Stress: Statement of issues, outline of literature, research protocol." Washington, DC: International Food Policy Research Institute.

Rivera, Juan, Ruel, Marie T. and Reynaldo Martorell. 1991. "The Effects of Protein-Energy Supplementation in Early Infancy on the Anthropometry and Body Composition of Guatemalan Women at Adolescence." Presentation at the 18th Annual NCIH International Health Conference. Arlington, VA.

Royston, E. and S. Armstrong. 1989. *Preventing Maternal Deaths*. Geneva: World Health Organization.

Satyanarayana, K., Nadamuni Naidu, A., Swaminathan, M.C. and B.S. Narasinga Rao. 1981. "Effect of nutritional deprivation in early childhood on later growth - a community study without intervention." *American Journal of Clinical Nutrition* 34:1636-1637.

Schuette, S.A. and H.M. Linkswiler. 1984. "Calcium," Ch. 28. In: R.E. Olson, ed. *Nutrition Reviews*. Wasington, D.C.: The Nutrition Foundation, Inc.

Senapati, Shishir K. 1991. "Women's Work Pattern and Its Impact on their Health and Nutrition." Paper presented at the 18th Annual NCIH International Health Conference. Arlington, VA.

Shah, Kusum. 1991. "Methodological Issues in the Measurement of Maternal Nutritional Status." In Krasovec Katherine and Mary Ann Anderson, eds., *Maternal Nutrition and Pregnancy Outcome*. Washington, DC: Pan American Health Organization; Scientific Publication, No. 529. Pp. 132-137.

Soysa, P. 1987. "Women and Nutrition." *World Review of Nutrition and Diet* 52:1-70.

Taggert, N.R., Holliday, R.M., Billewicz, W.Z., Hytten, F.E., and A.A. Thomson. 1967. "Changes in skinfolds during pregnancy." *Journal of Nutrition* 21:439-451.

UN Population Division. 1986. "Contraceptive Practice: Selected findings from the World Fertility Survey Data." New York: United Nations.

UNICEF. 1990. "State of the World's Children."

UNFPA. 1989. "State of World Population 1989. Investing in women: The focus of the nineties." United Nations Population Fund.

WHO. 1989. "Global Nutritional Status: Anthropometric Indicators Update 1989." NUT/ANTREF/1/89 Geneva: World Health Organization.

WHO. 1986a. "Health Implications of Sex Discrimination in Childhood: A Review Paper and an Annotated Bibliography." WHO/UNICEF/FHE 86.2. Geneva: World Health Organization.

WHO Working Group. 1986b. "Use and interpretation of anthropometric indicators of nutritional status." *Bulletin of the World Health Organization* 64(6):929-941.

WHO/UNFPA/UNICEF. 1989. "The reproductive health of adolescents: A strategy for action." A joint WHO/UNFPA/UNICEF statement. Geneva: World Health Organization.

# 4

# Infection: Social and Medical Realities

*Jeanne McDermott, Maggie Bangser,*
*Elizabeth Ngugi, and Irene Sandvold*

The prevalence of infections in women is extensive, and current knowledge probably reflects only the tip of the iceberg. These infections include a broad range: sexually transmitted diseases (STDs), including human immunodeficiency virus (HIV) and acquired immunodeficiency syndrome (AIDS); overgrowth of endogenous organisms; infections acquired from unsafe abortions and deliveries, female circumcision, and unsafe practices during reproductive years; and endemic diseases, such as tuberculosis and malaria. Their consequences can be severe and lifelong, resulting in not only medically recognized mortality and morbidity, but also social ostracism due to either the physical symptoms and signs such as incontinence, painful sexual intercourse, foul-smelling vaginal discharge, and skin lesions or to their sequelae, including divorce due to infertility and the inability to work.

Reproductive-tract infections (RTIs) and HIV/AIDS dominated the sessions on infection at the 1991 NCIH conference, probably as a result of increased attention to the association of RTIs with HIV infection and to high maternal mortality and morbidity associated with sepsis of the reproductive tract. It is encouraging that international meetings have been convened recently by WHO, policy groups, and donor agencies to address priorities for research and intervention for RTIs.[1] These meetings indicate a growing awareness of the extent and consequences of these infections among the general population of women. The impact of malaria infection on pregnancy outcome and anemia in women (Jelliffe 1991) and the knowledge, attitudes, and practices of people in Nigeria related to guinea worm infection (Yacoob 1991) were the subject of two other papers presented at the meeting. Among discussions with the participants, many other infections were identified, including schistosomiasis, tuberculosis, and mastitis. However, little is known about the impact of many of these infections specifically on the health of women.

Because of the extent of infections in women, it is impossible to cover the whole subject in this chapter. We will focus on RTIs and HIV/AIDS because the majority of papers presented related to these infections and because these infections have important implications on the life and behavior of women.

This chapter summarizes content from the papers, which were country-specific in most cases. These presentations dealt with both the medical realities of the level and extent of these infections as they are defined by health professionals, and the social realities, such as the physical and social implications, of the infections as perceived by women. An attempt to merge these two realties has been identified as a key component in successful intervention programs described in the papers presented. The chapter concludes with policy, research, and program recommendations that arose from the presentations and from discussion among the participants at the meeting.

## Level and Trends of Infection

Reproductive-tract infections (RTIs) are defined as a "variety of bacterial, viral, and protozoal infections of the upper and lower reproductive tract of both sexes, and most of them are STDs" (Dixon-Mueller and Wasserheit 1991). Women are infected with RTIs through sexual intercourse, unsafe procedures related to family planning, childbirth, and abortion, as well as from unsafe personal hygiene, sexual, and cultural practices. Complications of lower and upper RTIs include emotional distress, social ostracism, chronic pelvic pain, infertility, HIV transmission, fetal and infant death, and death of the woman.

Estimates of the extent of RTIs are staggering, with much variation in the distribution of the causative organisms. WHO estimates that one out of five maternal deaths occurs around the time of delivery due to tetanus or sepsis (Gasse 1991). Chlamydia, a common cause of infertility in women, affects up to 23 percent of African women in certain populations (Dixon-Mueller and Wasserheit 1991). In a rural area in India, 92 percent of women in fifty-eight rural villages reported gynecological disorders; 50 percent of these were RTIs (Bang 1991). Of 702 women who were seen at a menstrual regulation clinic in Bali, Indonesia, 404 (58 percent) had clinically diagnosed RTIs, and 148 (37 percent) of these women had more than one infection. Candidiasis, an RTI resulting from an overgrowth of flora naturally occurring in the vagina, was the most common infection in these Balinese women, with a prevalence rate of 16 percent. Bacterial vaginosis and muco-purulent cervicitis were each found in 14 percent of the women. Gonorrhea and syphilis had prevalence rates of 1 percent, and no women had HIV infection (Susanti 1991).

In Africa, syphilis, gonorrhea, and HIV infection have very different prevalence rates. The prevalence of maternal syphilis in Africa ranges from 4 percent to 15 percent, with estimates of 20 percent–40 percent of women with untreated syphilis experiencing a fetal or neonatal loss (Schulz et al. 1987). Syphilis serology was reactive in 8.7 percent of 3,128 pregnant women tested in a rural district in Malawi in 1986–1990, and 15 percent–19 percent of fetal and neonatal loss among these women is estimated to be due to syphilis (McDermott 1991). Based on thirty-nine studies, the median estimate of the prevalence of gonorrhea in Africa is 10 percent (Dixon-Mueller and Wasserheit 1991).

The number of women infected with HIV is increasing dramatically. The HIV seroreactivity among prostitutes in Kenya has risen from zero in 1980 to 3.4 percent in 1981, 61 percent in 1985, and 88 percent in 1988 (Ngugi 1991). Similar dramatic increases in prevalence rates over a short period of time have also been reported among pregnant women, but such rates are lower (Miotti et al. 1990). In the major cities of the Americas, Western Europe, and sub-Saharan Africa, AIDS is now the leading cause of death for women 20–40 years old; up to 40 percent of women ages 30–34 years old in some central African cities were found to be infected with AIDS (Dixon-Mueller and Wasserheit 1991). These high prevalence rates contribute significantly to morbidity and mortality among women, particularly in developing countries.

Certain cancers also seem to be causally linked to RTIs. Cervical cancer is the leading cause of death from cancer among women in sub-Saharan Africa (Dixon-Mueller and Wasserheit 1991). The strong association between cervical cancer and human papilloma virus (Dixon-Mueller and Wasserheit 1991) and herpes (Adelusi 1984) increases the suspicion of a causal link between these RTIs and cervical cancer. This is further supported by the association with other risk factors such as multiple sexual partners and sexual activity begun at an early age common to both RTIs and cervical cancer. Hepatitis B is another sexually transmitted disease that has been causally linked to liver cancer, one of the more common cancers in developing countries. This infection, which is also transmitted from mother to fetus, is estimated to infect 95 percent of the adult population in sub-Saharan Africa and Southeast Asia. With the availability of a vaccine, programs to include hepatitis B vaccine in existing childhood immunization programs are currently being implemented in Cameroon, Indonesia, Kenya, the Philippines, and Thailand (Krieger 1991). The high cost of the vaccine in the United States compared with the much lower cost in European countries was discussed as a constraint to implementing a hepatitis B vaccine program in this country.

Women's perceptions of the severity and cause of many RTIs can differ drastically from those of the health-care provider. For example, in India women perceive "white discharge" as a serious chronic disease that drains off energy and blood from the body and leads to severe weakness (physical, mental, and sexual), anxiety, pain, loss of libido, painful sexual intercourse, and ultimately death. This condition is believed to be transmitted to a woman by a promiscuous or alcoholic husband; witchcraft and the use of some family planning methods are also cited as causes (Bang 1991). Despite these perceptions, RTIs, especially those associated with vaginal discharge, are not seen as important health problems by Western-trained health care providers because no direct mortality is associated with them. This lack of understanding of women's health conditions results in inappropriate treatment. Focus groups in Egypt demonstrated the wide gap between women's perceptions and pathophysiology taught in health services education (Khattab 1991). (See chapter "Health Women's Way.")

Access to and availability of culturally acceptable health care services determine the ability to measure the extent of RTIs in women. Women often do not seek diagnosis and treatment from the organized health care system. In the India study, although 92 percent of the women reported gynecological disorders, only 7.8 percent had sought and received any medical treatment (Bang 1991). The reasons for women not seeking care include nonavailability of doctors in rural areas, cultural inhibitions and communication barriers in consulting male doctors for gynecological care, lack of time and money, and feelings of shame regarding their physical condition. (See chapter "Access to Care.")

## Determinants of Infection

HIV and RTIs are associated with sexual practices, a subject that is often taboo to discuss between younger and older generations, men and women, health care providers and clients, and sexual partners. These discussions are, however, vital for prevention and treatment of these infections.

In most developing countries, women's vulnerability to RTIs and HIV is fostered by their low social status, severely limited means of protection against infection, and strong cultural prohibitions against denying sex to partners. Moreover, the lack of economic opportunities available to women can force women into risky behaviors, particularly sex for money (Ngugi 1991; Mataka 1991). ( See chapter "Women's Health.") Behavioral research is critically needed to understand sexual decision making and practices that leave women at risk of acquiring RTIs and HIV (Caravano 1991).

The risk of infection following a trans-cervical procedure such as IUD insertion, unsafe abortion (see chapter "Abortion"), or childbirth is increased when there is a concomitant RTI. Conversely, pelvic inflammatory disease (PID), which can result in infertility, potentially fatal ectopic pregnancy, chronic pelvic pain, and recurrent bouts of upper reproductive tract infection, is facilitated by these procedures (Dixon-Mueller and Wasserheit 1991).

The contribution of female circumcision, also referred to as female genital mutilation, to mortality and morbidity due to infection of girls at the time of the practice and to women at consummation of marriage and delivery, has been well documented. Sixty percent of the countries in Africa have populations that practice some form of female circumcision (Hosken 1991). The social, cultural, and medical implications of this practice, and examples of educational interventions to reduce female circumcision from Somalia (Mohamud 1991), Kenya (Naisho 1991), and Nigeria (Adebajo 1991) were discussed in a session devoted entirely to this issue.

## Challenges to Designing Interventions

The need for laboratory methods for the diagnosis of RTIs has frequently been cited as an obstacle to the development of effective treatment programs. The research studies reported at this meeting from India (Bang 1991), Indonesia (Susanti 1991), and Egypt (Khattab 1991) included methods for clinical and laboratory diagnosis of RTIs to establish their spectrum and prevalence. The studies have sought to close the gap between women's and health care providers' perceptions of RTIs, to improve services, and to develop practical mechanisms for community-based diagnosis and screening of RTIs with available resources. Many RTIs can be diagnosed with only a good history and simple physical exam, in combination with known epidemiological data. With the addition of only a microscope, the program in Indonesia was able to diagnosis 90 percent of the RTIs (Susanti 1991). Nonetheless, even when dealing with infections known to contribute significantly to mortality, providers frequently do not have the knowledge and communication skills necessary to obtain a good health history, and lack even simple equipment for diagnosis and supplies for treatment.

Challenges also exist in diagnosing syphilis. Syphilis serology tests have a false-negative rate of 0–25 percent and a false-positive rate of less than 5 percent, depending on the test used and the stage of the disease (Larsen et al. 1990). However, individuals who have received adequate treatment for syphilis may still react positively, and those with very early or late stages of the disease may not react with a particular test. In addition to the problems of diagnosis, an effective syphilis screening and treatment program during pregnancy requires an infrastructure that allows blood to be collected, sera to be serologically tested, and results to be reported in a timely manner so that women with reactive serology can be treated before the fetus dies. Such intervention also requires that women come for screening early in pregnancy. To overcome these obstacles, a screening program that can be implemented at the clinic level is needed so that, on her first antenatal clinic visit, a woman can be screened and treated if necessary. Although a low-technology test for screening pregnant women has been developed, it has not been widely implemented nor evaluated for use in a clinic-based screening program (McDermott 1991).

In addition to improving diagnostic accuracy, targeting problems that have the greatest impact on the health status of women is a challenge to program planners. To ensure that scarce resources are allocated to high prevalence/high risk health conditions, the causes of morbidity and mortality among women in a community need to be accurately identified and prioritized. The program for reproductive health in India was developed in response to a community survey that identified gynecological problems as a major cause of morbidity for women (Bang 1991). Although the purpose of the study in Malawi was to assess the efficacy of different regimens of malaria chemoprophylaxis to prevent poor pregnancy outcomes, syphilis-related perinatal mortality was investigated when perinatal mortality was identified as excessively high (McDermott 1991). To have the greatest impact, programs must assess the health problems of women in a community from both an epidemiological approach (medical reality) and an anthropological approach (social reality) and target those high prevalence/high risk problems that can be most effectively dealt with given the resources available.

## Examples of Existing Interventions

Several interventions presented at the NCIH Conference are described in this section; suggested strategies for additional interventions are presented in the "Recommendations" section of this chapter.

Interventions must fundamentally be based on the medical and social realities of women's lives. The cultural context of infection is crucial in the development of education programs for the community and for health care providers. STD- and HIV-prevention messages (use condoms, limit sex partners, practice safer sex) often conflict with traditional cultural norms prescribed for women (be submissive, do not deny sex to partners). This type of conflict needs to be recognized and discussed so that appropriate health education messages and media can be used (Convisser 1991). In many parts of the world, women are forced into behaviors—such as prostitution or sexual relations with a spouse who has multiple sexual partners—that significantly increase their vulnerability to infection. Interventions need to help both women and men to make safer decisions regarding sexual relations and to broaden women's economic opportunities so that they have options other than prostitution. (See chapters "Health Women's Way" and "Women's Health.")

Successful women's health programs in India, Indonesia and Egypt that have already been mentioned are important examples of simple, culturally appropriate interventions.

In Zaire, a four-part soap opera was developed for radio and television to motivate high-risk groups to adopt safer sex practices. The television viewing population in Zaire includes an estimated thirteen million urban residents. Frequently, several households share a television and all watch together. The soap opera focused on factors that increase the risk of becoming HIV-infected, and included messages to avoid multiple sexual partners, practice mutual fidelity, and use condoms in high-risk situations. The series was very popular. A post-test of a representative audience sample in Kinshasa revealed that more than two-thirds of the target audience watched each episode and retained the key messages. Seventy-five percent of the viewers stated that they intended to change their behavior, more than 50 percent discussed the soap opera with family and friends, and more than 90 percent wanted another episode. Other mass-media shows, including another soap opera, are planned (Convisser 1991).

In Zambia, a school program for teenagers was developed to promote communication and to provide accurate information concerning sexuality and, in particular, HIV. Cartoons and songs with health education messages were developed (Mataka 1991).

In Kenya, behavior-change messages that reflect and respect women's lives have been developed and marketed to reach people where they live and work. A program targeted for prostitutes in Kenya demonstrated that behavior change is possible in a high-risk group when it is implemented in a culturally appropriate, respectful, and caring manner. The messages encourage women to stop prostitution, reduce the number of partners, insist partners use condoms, avoid intercourse when any sexually transmitted disease is present, avoid intercourse when menstruating, and have regular medical examinations. These messages were marketed through radio, television, printed materials, and personal discussions with community leaders, various community groups, or one-on-one by leaders chosen by the prostitutes and provided with training. The program was evaluated after eleven months, and significant changes in all of the targeted behaviors were demonstrated. The incidence of STDs declined, as did the number of clients seen by each woman and the incidence of intercourse during menses. Notably, there was a remarkable increase in the number of women using condoms and a move out of prostitution altogether by some women (Ngugi 1991). Another project trained community motivators to distribute AIDS educational materials and to provide counseling to AIDS victims and their families in two urban slum communities, one peri-urban community, and one rural community in Kenya (Amayun 1991).

With the spread of HIV infection, family planning clinics have been identified as a key point of contact for health education messages. The International Planned Parenthood Federation/Western Hemisphere has developed a training program for family planning workers to integrate HIV/AIDS prevention education and counseling into their activities. Sessions are conducted in four areas: sexuality education and values clarification; education about sexually transmitted diseases, including HIV; counseling and interpersonal skills; and infection control. These sessions are conducted in a participatory manner, with open-ended questions and role play to promote discussion, and trainees are provided an opportunity to express their feelings and practice interpersonal skills. This program has not only incorporated HIV/AIDS health education messages into the care provided to patients but has also improved communication and interaction among staff and with patients to improve the overall quality of care (Smit 1991). A research grant program administered by AIDSCOM at the Academy for Educational Development has been established to support research to explore determinants of behavioral risk factors for HIV/AIDS among women. The findings can then be used to design, implement, and evaluate intervention programs (Caravano 1991).

Infection control guidelines for use in family planning/maternal child health clinics were discussed within the context of the prevention of HIV and hepatitis B infection. Descriptions of the four infection-prevention steps of waste disposal, decontamination, cleaning, and high-level disinfection or sterilization were given and included the substances to use in developing countries (Tietjen 1991; Angle 1991). Guidelines are available from the World Health Organization (WHO) and several other international family planning organizations

## Costs

One presentation at the NCIH Conference dealt specifically with the issue of estimating the cost of nursing care and medication for people with HIV/AIDS-related illnesses in Tanzania. This process includes eight steps:

1. Estimate the number of symptomatic adult and pediatric cases. Because most patients with HIV are not diagnosed and die of common conditions such as diarrhea, tuberculosis, pneumonia, and other infections, these estimates are based on seroprevalence data and on the expected number of HIV-related illnesses rather than on reported cases of HIV or AIDS.
2. Estimate the numbers of episodes of particular HIV-related illnesses per symptomatic patient. At present, these estimates are based on clinical impressions and a few small studies. Data from longitudinal cohort studies will provide better information.
3. Assess nursing care requirements per episode. The number of days and level of nursing care (hospital, health center, or home) is estimated for each treatment episode.
4. Estimate the cost per day of nursing care. Analysis includes average staffing by level of care and average salaries for different levels of staff.
5. Determine drug usage per episode using standard treatment regimens and guidelines.
6. Enter drug information as to unit size, pack size, and cost per unit.
7. Compute overall drug and nursing costs for each episode, each patient, and each illness.
8. Compare with available national data on expenditure. The costs in Tanzania based on these estimates were 31 percent of the annual health budget to care for approximately 56,000 adult and 38,000 pediatric cases of HIV-associated illnesses. Alternative models of care (e.g. decentralization of nursing care to more peripheral levels) or drug availability (e.g. improved availability of less expensive drugs) may need to be considered (Laing 1991).

This methodology can be used to estimate the basic costs of other diseases and infections. Obviously, it is a simplified methodology that does not include long range cost of facilities, equipment, logistics, and training and supervision of personnel.

The resources required for one screening program were discussed in the presentation on the Bali Indonesia program. They include a binocular microscope, slides, coverslips, colorpHast pH strips, Chemstripe, Gram stain for staining cervical smears, potassium hydroxide and saline for wet smears to diagnose candidiasis and trichomonas, and cotton swabs. More sophisticated supplies and training are needed for gonorrhea and chlamydia cultures and for syphilis and HIV testing (Susanti 1991). The discrepancy between lack of basic facilities at the peripheral levels and sophisticated technology at the tertiary levels was raised as an example of the need for political will to determine priorities for allocating limited resources.

## Recommendations

It is critical that policies and interventions respect women's descriptions and perceptions of their conditions, as well as the cultural context of women's experience with infection. In addition, they must recognize social and biological factors that make women vulnerable to infection. Women and women's healthcare providers should be actively involved in making policy decisions and designing programs to prevent, detect, and treat RTIs.

Building on this foundation, recommendations include:

## Policy:

1. Establish basic health facilities and services at primary levels rather than sophisticated technology at tertiary levels.
2. Establish safe, accessible services, including safe abortion, family planning, and childbirth services, to prevent maternal mortality and morbidity.
3. Integrate RTI screening and treatment into existing health programs such as maternal and child health, family planning, and primary care.
4. Draw on community-based advocacy efforts that articulate local demands for services, information, and allocation of resources.

## Program:

1. Educate health-care providers in simple diagnosis of RTIs (e.g. through history and speculum examination by field workers and clinicians), communication skills for prevention, diagnosis, and counseling efforts, and appropriate treatment of infections.
2. Establish minimum standards and guidelines for each level of the health-care delivery system to be used by health planners and program managers.
3. Adapt existing treatment guidelines such as those developed for urethral/vaginal discharge and genital ulcer disease (Meheus 1984).
4. Involve the community in the development of community education programs for prevention, early identification, and self-referral to appropriate resources for treatment of infection.

## Research:

1. Examine sexual behaviors and practices that make women vulnerable to infection.
2. Identify simple, low-cost diagnostic tools, methods of protection, including female controlled methods, and effective homeopathic and medical therapies for infection.

3. Develop virucides that do not act as spermicides.
4. Undertake random controlled clinical trials to assess outcome effectiveness of both homeopathic and medical treatments.
5. Promote and support national and international collaborative research related to the lay person's and health-care providers' knowledge, attitudes and practices related to infection.
6. Develop epidemiological surveillance systems.

## Note

1. Reports from meetings related to STD research needs include "Sexually Transmitted Diseases Research Needs," WHO Consultative Group convened in Copenhagen September 13–14, 1989; "Report of the Research Sub-Committee," WHO AIDS/STD Task Force convened in Geneva, May 23-31, 1990; WHO Sexually Transmitted Diseases Research Working Group convened in Geneva, April 22-24, 1991; International Conference on Reproductive-Tract Infections in the Third World: National and International Policy Implications, sponsored by International Women's Health Coalition and The Rockefeller Foundation, April 29–May 3, 1991 in Bellagio, Italy; and International STD Research Workshop: Priorities for the US Agency for International Development in the 1990's convened in Atlanta, Georgia, July 23–25, 1991. The Safe Motherhood Initiative was inaugurated at a conference sponsored by WHO, World Bank and UNFPA held February 10–13, 1987 in Nairobi, Kenya, and was a major topic at the International Congress of Midwives in 1987 at the Hague, Netherlands and in a 1990 meeting at Kobe, Japan.

## References

Adebajo, Christine. 1991. "A Grassroots Project by Nurses in Nigeria to Eradicate Female Circumcision." Paper presented at the 18th Annual NCIH International Health Conference, Arlington VA.

Adelusi, B. 1984. "Carcinoma of Cervix: Can a Viral Etiology Be Confirmed?" in *Virus-Associated Cancers in Africa, International Research on Cancer Scientific Publication #63*. pp.433-450.

Amayun, Milton. 1991 "HIV/AIDS Prevention in Four Communities of Kenya." Presentation at the 18th Annual NCIH International Health Conference, Arlington VA.

Angle, Marcia. 1991. "Infection Control: The Forgotten Factor in Providing Safe Family Planning and Maternal Health Services." Presentation at the 18th Annual NCIH International Health Conference, Arlington VA.

Bang, Rani. 1991. "The Context of Reproductive Tract Infections." Paper presentation at the 18th Annual NCIH International Health Conference, Arlington VA.

Carovano, Kathryn. 1991 "A Cross-Regional Assessment of Determinants of Women's Risk Behavior for HIV / AIDS." Presentation at the 18th Annual NCIH International Health Conference, Arlington VA.

Convisser, Julie. 1991. "Focusing on Women and AIDS: Using Television Drama in Zaire to Promote Safe Behaviors." Paper presented at the 18th Annual NCIH International Health Conference, Arlington VA.

Dixon-Mueller, Ruth and Judith Wasserheit. 1991 *The Culture of Silence: Reproductive Tract Infections Among Women in the Third World*. International Women's Health Coalition.

Gasse, Francoise. 1991. "Birth-linked Tetanus and Sepsis Must Stop." Paper presented at the 18th Annual NCIH International Health Conference, Arlington VA.

Hosken, Fran. 1991 "World Review of Traditional Practices Affecting the Health of Women and Actions for Change." Paper presented at the 18th Annual NCIH International Health Conference, Arlington VA.

Jeliffe, E.F. Patricia. 1991 "Malaria and Pregnancy." Presentation at the 18th Annual NCIH International Health Conference, Arlington VA.

Khattab, Hind. 1991. "Research Methods to Elicit Information from Women." Paper presented at the 18th Annual NCIH International Health Conference, Arlington VA.

Krieger, Laurie. 1991. "Immunizing Against Liver Cancer: Training and IEC for the Introduction of Hepatitis B Vaccine." Paper presented at the 18th Annual NCIH International Health Conference, Arlington VA.

Laing, Robert. 1991. "AIDS in Africa: The Cost of Drugs and Nursing Care." Paper presented at the 18th Annual NCIH International Health Conference, Arlington VA.

Larsen, Sandra, Stephen Kraus, and William Whittington 1990. "Diagnostic Tests." In *A Manual of Tests for Syphilis*, edited by Sandra Larsen, Elizabeth Hunter and Stephen Kraus. Washington D.C.:American Public Health Association.

Mataka, Elizabeth. 1991 "Listening to Zambian Adolescents Talk about AIDS." Paper presented at the 18th Annual NCIH International Health Conference, Arlington VA.

McDermott, Jeanne. 1991. "Syphilis-Associated Perinatal Mortality–A Quantifiable Problem with an Effective Intervention–Where is the Program?" Paper presented at the 18th Annual NCIH International Health Conference, Arlington VA.

Meheus, A.Z. 1984. "Practical Approaches in Developing Countries." In *Sexually Transmitted Diseases*, edited by King K. Holmes et al. New York:McGraw-Hill pp.997-10018.

Miotti, P., G. Dallabetta, E. Ndovi, G. Liomba, A. Saah, and John Chiphangwi. 1990. "HIV and Pregnant Women: Associated Factors, Prevalence and Estimate of Incidence, and Role in Fetal Wastage in Central Africa," in *AIDS* 4: 733-736.

Mohamud, Asha. 1991 "Medical and Cultural Aspects of Female Circumcision in Somalia and Recent Efforts for Eradication." Paper presented at the 18th Annual NCIH International Health Conference, Arlington VA.

Naisho, Joyce. 1991 "Discouraging Female Circumcision Among Selected Communities in Kenya." Paper presented at the 18th Annual NCIH International

Health Conference, Arlington VA.

Ngugi, Elizabeth. 1991. "Education and Counseling Interventions." Paper presented at the 18th Annual NCIH International Health Conference, Arlington VA.

Schulz, K.F., W. Cates, and P.R. O'Mara. 1987 "Pregnancy Loss, Infant Death, and Suffering: Legacy of Syphilis and Gonorrhoea in Africa." *Genitourinary Medicine* 63: 320-5.

Smit, Laura. 1991. "How AIDS Prevention Training is Improving the Quality of Care in Latin American and Caribbean Family Planning Programs." Paper presented at the 18th Annual NCIH International Health Conference, Arlington VA.

Steinglass, Robert. 1991. "Maternal Mortality Due to Tetanus: Magnitude of the Problem and Potential Control Measures." Paper presented at the 18th Annual NCIH International Health Conference, Arlington VA.

Susanti, Inne. 1991. "Research Methods to Screen, Diagnose, and Treat Reproductive Tract Infections." Paper presented at the 18th Annual NCIH International Health Conference, Arlington VA.

Tietjen, Linda. 1991. "Infection Prevention Guidelines: Effectiveness of Instrument and Equipment Processing Procedures." Paper presented at the 18th Annual NCIH International Health Conference, Arlington VA.

Yacoob, May. 1991 "Putting a Face on the Numbers: The Uses of Anthropology and epidemiology in Guinea Worm Control Among Women." Paper presented at the 18th Annual NCIH International Health Conference, Arlington VA.

# 5

## Family Planning:
## A Base to Build on for Women's
## Reproductive Health Services

*Andrea Eschen and Maxine Whittaker*

Family planning, though not always recognized as such, is one of the basic and most important preventative health care services for women. To maximize the health value of family planning, services must be available to women in a way that incorporates and satisfies their other primary or reproductive health care needs and is simultaneously responsive to the various stages of their reproductive lives. Enhancing and expanding family planning services may be one way to decrease the indefensible rate of pregnancy-related maternal morbidity and mortality women experience in developing countries.

Ninety-nine percent of maternal morbidity worldwide takes place in the developing world—nearly half a million women die each year as a result of pregnancy (Sai and Nassim 1989). In reality, the death toll may be quite a bit higher considering the number of women who die from the complications of unsafe induced abortion. It is estimated that 25–50 percent of the deaths due to pregnancy related causes are the result of poorly performed abortions (Winikoff and Sullivan 1987). At least one-third of the one billion people living in the developing world live in countries where abortion services are prohibited or severely restricted to cases of rape, incest, or saving a woman's life (Dixon-Mueller 1990), a situation that forces women to take extreme and dangerous measures to terminate pregnancy.

Preventing mortality is a strong argument for the importance of family planning services, but there are others that are equally valid and pressing. Although most women do not die from pregnancy-related causes, all women still require safe, effective, and accessible services to free them from the fear of unwanted pregnancy and the physical damage or infection that can result from unsafe induced abortion. Available and accessible family planning services enable women to time their pregnancies so that they choose to bear children when they are able to care and provide for them. They allow women to take responsibility for their reproductive life and their body.

However, many women in the developing world lack the opportunity and resources to manage their reproductive lives through family planning. The World Fertility Survey has shown that there is a large gap in the number of women who use contraception and their stated desired family size. In Africa, 23 percent of women not wanting additional children are practicing contraception; in Asia, this figure is 43 percent and in Latin America, it is 57 percent. In most developing countries less than one-third of couples are within reach of a family planning service. Women's ability to utilize family planning services refers not only to physical proximity, convenient hours of service, and suitable location, but also includes knowledge of services, acceptability of the contraceptive methods and services being provided, and lack of restrictions to receive services. In many countries access to family planning for some groups, such as the unmarried, adolescents, indigenous groups, and refugees, are restricted by social, legal, or geographical constraints. For others, the direct and indirect costs of the services inhibit access. (See chapter "Access to Care.")

## Contraceptive Use: What Choices Do Women Really Have?

Many women have to make difficult choices about contraceptive use not only because a limited number of methods may be available, but they may be unacceptable for reasons related to national policies concerning family planning, women's individual health and sexuality, or the financial and opportunity costs of obtaining a contraceptive. In choosing a method, women must weigh a variety of factors, including their health status, potential side-effects of a method, consequences of an unwanted pregnancy, desired family size, partner's cooperation, and cultural norms about childbearing. Every method has advantages and disadvantages, but even considering the total range of contraceptives available, there remain substantial difficulties in people's ability to control their fertility safely, effectively, and in personally and culturally acceptable ways during the different stages of their reproductive years. It is not surprising that many women find contraceptive use problematic and may be compelled to choose the potentially adverse consequences of an inappropriate method or no method at all.

### Government Policies Promoting or Hindering Contraceptive Use

Government policies, laws, and programs influence strongly the methods available to individuals and the way in which services are delivered. Programs making modern contraception available that are backed by government policies and endorsement, and education in combination with a favorable social setting, are the most effective in reducing fertility (Mauldin and Ross 1991). In the last decade, at least fifty countries have promulgated policies or laws supporting family planning to reduce population growth, reach national development objectives, support individuals' rights to determine family size, and/or ensure equity in the provision of services (Population Reports 1984). In some Asian countries, reduced fertility has been attributed to strong family planning programs and policies, relatively high levels of education, health, and income, and wide access to and demand for services. Along with this, however, there has been in some countries a heavy promotion of sterilization as the primary means of fertility control. Most Latin American and Caribbean countries have policies supporting family planning. These have been based on the premise that individuals have the right to use family planning for health measures, and to plan the number and spacing of their children. In sub-Saharan Africa, there have been some significant changes in governments' support of family planning in the past decade. At least thirteen countries have instituted policies advocating the adoption or expansion of family planning services, but about twelve countries, particularly in Francophone Africa, do not support family planning, and three sub-Saharan countries limit access to contraception. In North Africa and the Middle East, some countries offer services through the public and private sector, while other countries outlaw completely family planning.

Even in countries where a family planning policy is operational, there can be many limitations to obtaining services and methods (Population Reports 1984). Some countries prohibit advertising and distributing methods, prevent trained field workers from distributing contraceptives and basic medicines, or limit a capable cadre of health providers from giving particular services. For example, in some countries nurses and auxiliary nurses have been restricted from providing oral contraceptives, inserting IUDs, and performing mini-lap sterilizations despite the fact that throughout the world these health professionals have proved capable of performing these jobs. Services can be denied to women without spousal consent and to adolescents because service delivery to them is illegal. Still in other countries, the import duty on contraceptives is high and it can be cumbersome to clear them through customs.

The laws regulating voluntary surgical contraception, one of the most widely used methods in the world, are becoming better defined in Europe, Francophone Africa, and much of Latin America, and the limitations to its use are being reduced. The criminal codes of some countries in these regions prohibited "intentional bodily injury," (Population Reports 1984: E-127) which included surgical contraception. In countries where its legal status is not clear, individuals may not know the service is available and do not request it; and providers do not offer it because the circumstances in which it is legal are poorly defined (Isaacs and Fincancioglu 1987). Other countries such as Chile, Iran, Peru, Saudi Arabia, and Burma decree it illegal under statute.

## Women's Health Considerations in Contraceptive Decision Making

In deciding upon which contraceptive method to use and when, women consider how the method will affect their reproductive functioning, as well as their general well-being. One of the most commonly cited reasons for discontinuing contraceptive use is the perceived side-effects (Wasserheit et al. 1989). What some health professionals dismiss as normal "side-effects" may be of great personal or cultural importance to women. Women may blame any type of health problem, especially reproductive-tract problems, on their contraceptive method. This reaction results in part from poor counseling and education about the method and from information women receive about other women's experiences.

A study conducted by the World Health Organization of 5,322 parous women in fourteen cultural groups in developing countries has shown that many women discontinue using the IUD and oral and injectable contraceptives because they found some of the changes in their menstrual bleeding patterns unacceptable (World Health Organization 1981). They also have specific ideas about the normative length of their menstrual period and the amount of blood flow. The study results suggested that preferred contraceptive methods should (1) not cause amenorrhea; (2) not change the volume of blood loss; (3) ensure that bleeding is short and regular; (4) enable women to know when they will menstruate; and (5) not change the consistency or color of menstrual bleeding.

Findings of a study of NORPLANT® users in Brazil showed that 18 percent of the sample found menstrual irregularity problematic, and 79 percent said that bleeding interfered with sexual intercourse. Numerous fears were associated with this feeling, including fear of sexually transmitted disease, pain, and infection (Bruce 1987).

## Sexuality, Gender Roles, and Contraceptive Use

Women's feelings and beliefs about their bodies and sexuality cannot be overlooked in their decision to use contraception. Some women do not use barrier methods because of their reluctance to touch their genitals (Bruce 1987; Philliber 1989). Many do not want to alter their normal cycle fearing that extended bleeding may change patterns of sexual intercourse, and may encourage their husbands to have sexual relations with other women during this time (Bruce 1987). Extended cycles or intermittent bleeding may restrict participation in religious or cultural activities.

The sexual and power dynamics between men and women can also make contraceptive use awkward for women. Conflicts arise about when to have intercourse, which partner should make the decision about contraceptive use, which method to use, and how many children to have and when. A Sri Lankan woman expressed her frustration, stating: "What is the good of refusing (a husband's sexual demands); they will never let us alone. (If I refuse) he will go to some other woman and then what will become of me and my children?" (Dixon-Mueller 1989:146). Studies in Latin America found that women felt used and angry when their husbands refused to use contraception and that some of women's anger was due to "a sense of deep depersonalization, humiliation, and physical dissatisfaction" because their husbands treated them badly during sexual relations (Dixon-Mueller 1989:147).

Husbands' opinions on family planning can be strong enough to determine their wives' use of family planning. In Zimbabwe, a study of males' family planning knowledge, attitudes, and practice found that 80.6 percent of the sample had used contraception with their partners and 83.5 percent approved of family planning in general (Mbizvo and Adamchak 1991). Of the men who had ever used family planning, 58.8 percent said the male partner should have a "major say" in the decision to practice family planning; 48.3 percent said they were responsible for the decision to use a method; and 53.7 percent said that they decided on the number of children to have. Women had little involvement in the decision. A study of Sudanese men's attitudes, knowledge, and practice concerning family planning suggested that men made the decision about contraceptive use and were responsible for obtaining the method (Khalifa 1988). The choice of which method to use was left to the health professional. Contraceptive use was considered acceptable when it was related to the mother's health and the family's economic situation. In a study of five cities in Indonesia, husbands' approval was the most important factor in whether or not wives used contraception as husbands are seen as the protector and provider for the household and the decision makers (Joesoef et al. 1988). Nonetheless, some women practice contraception without the knowledge or approval of their husbands. These women tended to have two or more living children and a postelementary education. These findings suggest that although family planning programs are directed at women, it may be a strategic move to aim some program effort toward men.

In some cases, laws, regulations, and clinic guidelines require that women have their husbands' consent before they are able to obtain family planning services. Many cultures support the belief that men have rights to their wives' fertility (Cook and Maine 1987). The health and public perception of the law has a strong influence on how services are provided even if the law contradicts general practice. In Papua New Guinea, women cannot purchase contraceptives without their husbands' approval. In Turkey, the law requires a partner's consent when either wishes to undergo surgical contraception and husbands' consent when women want an abortion. In Niger, it is common practice that women cannot receive contraceptives without their husbands' authorization.

These conditions imply that husbands have a strong voice in wives' acceptance of contraception and the choice of methods creating a barrier to women's ability to contracept. Removal of spousal authorization laws and society's and providers' perceptions of these supposed or real laws has the potential to increase the number of women seeking services. In Ethiopia, the Family Guidance Association required husbands to sign a consent form to enable their wives to get contraceptives. Sixteen percent of women who requested supplies did not receive them. When the rule was repealed, clinic utilization increased by 26 percent within a few months, suggesting that many women never even came to the clinic for family planning.

Women may be given a sense of control when they are responsible for contraceptive use; but on the other hand, they may also feel resentful that they have to contend with their partners' sexual demands and bear the brunt of any real or perceived side-effects and health risks. Women may be afraid out of a sense of modesty or shame to talk to their partners about family planning and to contradict their partner's desire for intercourse or children (Bruce 1987). Some women choose to use contraception without the knowledge of their partners and run the risk of being thought of as promiscuous or being abandoned or divorced (Dixon-Mueller 1989: Bruce 1987).

## The Cost of Contraceptive Use to Women

Contraceptive users face a number of costs in obtaining and using contraception in addition to the cost of the method. The monetary price may not even be the most important cost factor to women (Lewis 1986). Nonmonetary costs they have to consider include the distance to the source of supply, the opportunity cost of time and the cost of transportation notwithstanding; the opportunity cost of waiting; the opportunity and travel costs of trips that, for one reason or another, do not result in getting a method or services; and the cost of resupply, including these same factors. Poor-quality services such as long waiting times, lack of privacy, or unsatisfactory interaction with the provider, add to the financial cost.

A review of studies on the effect of cost on the demand for family planning gave mixed results (Lewis 1986). Some studies indicate that consumers would rather pay for goods and services because they perceive they are getting higher-quality goods and are skeptical of free offerings. Some social marketing program strategies recommend that for these reasons a financial cost be attached to services. On the other hand, other studies indicate that when moderately priced or free products are provided through known, similar sources, the demand is not very different. It has been found, however, that low-income groups do have greater access to services when programs are subsidized. In a study in Brazil of discontinuation of contraceptive use, no one mentioned cost as a factor. Rather, reasons concerned pregnancy, fecundity, and side-effects. Overall, the study concluded that free services probably are not necessary and that reasonably priced methods and services may even be an incentive for family planning use because of its association with quality.

Few studies have been carried out on the costs to women in terms of opportunity and transportation or those related to their family. One example is a study of transportation among women living in the *pueblo jovenes*, (slum areas), in the outskirts of Lima, Peru (Anderson and Panzio 1986). Of the 190 women in two areas, 106 walked up to six blocks to receive health services. Those that were not able to walk to services had to use public transportation and make long trips, which could cause an extra financial burden. Seeking services often had to be coordinated with women's trips to work, children's travel to school, and purchases of other services and food. The routes used by the majority of buses in Lima were based on, in part, by large public-sector centers such as ministries, government offices, markets, and hospitals and posed time and financial inconveniences for women seeking services outside these sectors.

In deciding when to use contraception, women also consider their income earning opportunities. Effective contraceptive use relieves women of the uncertainty of when they will bear children, giving them the chance to devote their time and energy to their desired or necessary economic role in the household. It allows women the opportunity to continue their education and get a job (if these choices are available) and, therefore, potentially increase their economic productivity and social status (Birdsall and Chester 1987).

## What Family-Planning-Method Choices
## Can Women Anticipate?

Providing new methods of contraception—and, therefore, more choice—
may help overcome some of the current obstacles to its use. However, the
development of new contraceptives to add to the current array is sorely
lacking positive changes and innovation, and, in fact, the picture is almost
dismal. In the past twenty years, all but one of the U.S.-based pharmaceu-
tical companies conducting research on new contraceptives have discontinued this work (Mastroianni et al. 1990). This change has forced nonprofit
organizations and small companies to take on this effort, an initiative that
needs to be supported and encouraged. They, too, however, must face a
shortage of funds, lawsuits, jury awards, and a lack of liability insurance
(Wymelenberg 1990).

Any new contraceptive method requiring regulatory approval should
have reached the clinical investigation stage at this point in time if it is to be
used by the end of this century or in the early years of the next (Segal et al.
1989). Considering the increasing obstacles companies face in developing
and marketing new contraceptives, it is difficult to predict the methods that
will be available. Some of the methods that are currently being tested are
described below (Population Council 1991).

The *contraceptive ring*, inserted into the vagina, is shaped like a doughnut
and contains steroid—a progestin or a progestin plus estrogen—that is
released into the bloodstream. A contraceptive ring has a lower dose of
hormones than oral contraceptives, women can insert and remove the ring
themselves, and it does not need much attention once in place. One type of
ring, usable for breast-feeding mothers, is used for three months and is then
replaced. Another type of ring is left in the vagina for three weeks, removed
for one week during which time a woman experiences menstrual bleeding,
and then inserted again. It is expected to last for three to six months. Study
results on one type of ring indicated that there were low pregnancy rates
and that it was an acceptable method to women. Additional clinical trials of
these two types are now underway.

A reversible *antifertility vaccine* being developed for women causes anti-
bodies to interact with human chorionic gonadotropin (hCG), a hormone
that maintains pregnancy. Without hCG, the lining of the uterus sloughs off
carrying a fertilized egg, and menstruation takes place. Clinical trials are
testing the safety and efficacy of the vaccine. All women in the trial have
continued to ovulate and maintain regular menstrual cycles. Much remains
unknown about the hCG vaccine, but time and experience will provide
basic facts on effectiveness, schedule of boosters required, reversibility, and
side-effects (Segal et al. 1989).

*NORPLANT® II* shows advantages to the current form of NORPLANT® in that it requires only two subdermal implants, and is expected to be easier for health care professionals to insert and remove. Clinical trials are measuring efficacy and long-term effectiveness.

New forms of *injectable contraceptives* using microspheres or microcapsules are in the stage of human trials and may be available in the 1990s. These injectables are made of one or more hormones in a biodegradable capsule that releases hormones blocking ovulation. One injection can provide protection for one, three, or six months depending on its chemical makeup. A negative aspect of this method is that once it has been injected it cannot be reversed. This method shows a pregnancy rate similar to oral contraceptives and decreased incidence of side-effects.

*Transdermal patches* provide slow, steady release of contraceptive steroids to the bloodstream through the skin. Women can place the patches on their body and remove them at will. In one type of transdermal patch, a woman wears three patches, each effective for seven days, for three weeks. In the following week in which she wears either no patch or a placebo patch, menstruation takes place.

A new *T-shaped IUD* releases a low level of levonorgestrel for at least five years. A study of this IUD, completed in 1990, demonstrated high effectiveness against both unplanned pregnancy and menstrual bleeding (Toivonen et al. 1991). Disadvantages to the method include more hormonal side-effects and amenorrhea.

A *female condom* has the advantages of being female-controlled, preventing pregnancy, and reducing the risk of acquiring a sexually transmitted disease. Acceptability studies of the female condom showed there are some negative aspects to this method, but 56–58 percent of the study population would use it again (Contraceptive Technology Update 1991). Clinical tests demonstrated that slippage, leakage, breakage, and barrier effectiveness are better than those of the condom for men. One condom, *Femidon,* is on the market in Switzerland, and may be available to the public in the United Kingdom, France, and Italy by early 1993.

Studies on potential contraceptives for men are also being undertaken but new developments before the end of the century seem unattainable. Although much remains to be understood about the male reproductive system before new research ideas are tested (Segal et al. 1989), there are ongoing studies of potential methods. One of these is an *injectable vaccine coupled with an implant* containing androgen. The vaccine would inhibit hormones necessary for sperm and testosterone production, and the implant would strengthen the anti-fertility function of the vaccine while maintaining secondary sex characteristics and sexual behavior. The primary drawbacks with inhibiting testosterone production are that males' libido and potency are simultaneously reduced and that they affect secondary sex characteristics. The vaccine would be effective for one year.

Although it appears that there are new choices on the horizon, especially for women, it is highly unlikely that women in any country will have access to all possible methods available and that all individuals' needs and circumstances will be satisfied. Even though there is some progress in developing methods that are client-controlled (contraceptive ring, transdermal patch, female condom) many of the methods under investigation are hormonal and provider-dependent, a situation similar to the current one. To avoid some of the past problems associated with contraceptive introduction and acceptance, and to continue to increase accessibility and availability, it is important for providers to emphasize careful and thorough counselling and education with clients about contraceptive methods to allow them to make informed choices.

Before a method is made available and presumed to be an additional option, user-based research on values and beliefs concerning sexuality and contraceptive use, including the relationship between menstrual beliefs and behavior (WHO 1981) should be carried out. When new methods are introduced to any group of women (or men), it is necessary that complete and appropriate information be given to them about the correct use of the method, potential side-effects or bodily changes, and effectiveness. Providers have to be trained to counsel and inform clients, develop a positive provider–client relationship, administer and monitor the method, and manage side-effects.

## Strategies for Comprehensive Care

The international family planning community, including providers, program managers, policy makers, and donor agencies, recognizes that availability and acceptability of methods are only part of the condition that encourages contraceptive use. It is now paying closer attention to strategies to make services more accessible and acceptable to various subgroups of the population. One very strong thrust is improving the quality of care that each facility delivers. (See chapter "Quality of Care.") As an integral component of strengthening the quality of care, this community has recognized that service delivery strategies need to be more attentive to women's needs in accordance with different stages of women's reproductive lives. As aptly stated by Sai and Nassim (1989), comprehensive reproductive health care is preferable to programs focusing strictly on maternity or prevention of pregnancy because women's reproductive lives follow a continuum: it is difficult to make a distinction where one stage begins and another ends. Concerns about family planning and sexual health often begin in early adolescence, and the consequences of pregnancy and childbirth during this phase of life strongly affect current and future health and development in social, physical, and economic terms. A more comprehensive approach also begins to ensure that fertility and pregnancy are seen as part of a broader, integrated state of good health and well-being.

The notion is that services will be more acceptable and accessible to women if women can receive care for their family planning and reproductive health concerns as well as other types of primary care, including care for their children. Since many women have infrequent contact with health care services, it may be more feasible and effective to provide a variety of services in the same location at the same time. The following details some programs addressing women's reproductive health needs including and extending beyond family planning. These are selected examples of a variety of such programs, recognizing that no one approach is the most effective and that various political, social, cultural, and economic conditions determine the potential service delivery systems.

*Family planning services and primary health care.* The Bangladesh Women's Health Coalition is frequently singled out as a highly regarded example of a health facility providing integrated and high-quality services. The clinic offers a wide choice of contraceptive methods, including early termination of pregnancy, in an environment where women are made to feel comfortable and well- informed about the services they are receiving. At the Coalition, women are also able to get primary health services for themselves and their children, including treatment of gynecological problems, referrals to hospital for sterilization, prenatal care, treatment for early childhood diseases, and immunizations. These services were added to the Coalition's menstrual regulation program because so many clients requested these services—a need corroborated by the staff, who were well aware of clients' many health care demands. They also knew that many women seek care for their children before themselves (Kay and Kabir 1988).

The Coalition's operational philosophy is that each woman deserves respect, her needs are discussed with her, and she is given the information and counseling necessary for her to make her own choices concerning her reproductive health care. Informed choice is as integral to the Coalition as medical safety and access to contraceptives (Kay et al. 1991). The staff also try to help women, especially poor women, understand their rights to quality care (Kay and Kabir 1988). Clinics are convenient and attractive to women, are located in low-income areas of Dhaka as well as in semi-urban and rural areas, simply furnished and decorated, clean, and open five days a week. Women paramedics provide the services because Bangladeshi women prefer to be seen by women practitioners.

*Services for family planning and sexually transmitted diseases.* An increasing number of family planning institutions are taking the initiative to expand their programs to include other components of reproductive health services. With the rapid and worrisome rise in the transmission of the HIV virus, some family planning institutions have begun to incorporate information and education for both providers and clients about sexually transmitted diseases (STDs) and HIV/AIDS with family planning services. Although STDs traditionally have been treated in facilities distinct from family planning clinics, the programmatic association between services for each is inseparable. Family planning clinics seem to be a logical source for STD diagnosis, treatment, and services because of their experience in dealing with sensitive subjects, trained staff knowledgeable about family planning, IEC (information, education and communication) programs, and systems for contraceptive distribution, including condoms.

The traditional separation of services between family planning and diagnosis and treatment of STDs, the stigma attached to STDs, and limited financial and human resources to deal with either concern have been compounded to create large barriers to integrating these services. Services to diagnose and treat STDs are not usually available in primary health centers, including maternal–child health and family planning clinics, and are generally restricted to STD clinics which are frequented by men and prostitutes. This type of atmosphere is not the least bit inviting for women because the context emphasizes the sexual acquisition of the disease (Elias 1991) and services are geared to select groups which have very different needs than most women. Treatment for women may be more acceptable and effective if given in a place which can provide counseling, diagnosis, and treatment for STDs in the same context as attending to their family planning needs (Elias 1991). Indeed, many women only discover or discuss the presence of an STD or reproductive-tract infection (RTI) at the time of a family planning visit, or a method may be exacerbated or contraindicated by an existing RTI.

Realizing the dire need to take some action to address the rising concern about AIDS, the International Planned Parenthood Federation/Western Hemisphere Region (IPPF/WHR) instituted training for its family planning affiliates located in Latin America in the prevention of AIDS and STDs, and began to integrate AIDS prevention into its family planning programs (Smit, 1991). This was done not only to assist in the effort to slow the spread of AIDS but also as a part of its own mandate to provide high-quality family planning services. IPPF wanted to provide information, education, and counseling on STDs, relationship issues, and sexuality in the context of contraception and fertility. In launching this new program, however, it was clear that staff in the affiliates wanted to understand their own feelings and behavior and learn more about STDs and HIV/AIDS. IPPF began a training program for staff which they enthusiastically supported and went so far as to request additional work in counseling and interpersonal communication skills.

IPPF discovered that providers rarely talked about sexual behavior with their clients because they did not feel comfortable talking about sex and were unsure how to elicit conversation about sex from clients. Some of this hesitation was due to their own discomfort concerning sex and their lack of clarity concerning their own values, feelings, attitudes, and knowledge about sexual behavior. Staff were able to provide adequate information about contraception but were less able to counsel clients effectively concerning issues of reproductive health, sexuality, and relationships with family and husband. The program was designed around the needs of the trainees and as the program developed, the goals were expanded and tailored to the interests of the trainees. Some of the program objectives included 1) to provide simple, clear information on STDs, including AIDS, to family planning staff; 2) to promote the integration of STD prevention education and counseling into family planning clinics and community outreach programs (including teenagers and men); and 3) to strengthen the interpersonal communication and counseling skills of family planning staff.

Within two years, IPPF's training program resulted in a guide for trainers to integrate sexuality, counseling skills, prevention of STDs/AIDS, and infection control into a holistic approach to improve the quality of care provided in family planning programs. This guide is appropriate for nurses, doctors, paramedical staff, social workers, counselors, midwives, and other family planning workers.

PROFAMILIA, a private family planning organization in Colombia operating since 1965, decided in 1987 to incorporate an AIDS prevention program into its family planning work, although, at the time, other family planning agencies were shying away from this idea (Vernon 1990). PROFAMILIA felt this initiative was a large risk because it feared its public image would be tarnished and that the AIDS activities would overshadow or hinder the family planning work. On the other hand, PROFAMILIA felt this action was a positive one in that the organization was well established and had years of experience providing information, education, and communication services through its clinics and extensive network of field workers. It had systems for condom distribution within the community and provided family planning services to men and women. AIDS prevention activities could also help promote monogamy, abstinence, and condom and spermicide use in order to help prevent unwanted pregnancy. PROFAMILIA decided that it should use its institutional strengths and experience and focus on dissemination of information on AIDS prevention, distribution of condoms, and mass-media public education campaigns.

PROFAMILIA trained all of its instructors in the prevention of AIDS and STDs to equip them with the knowledge and counseling skills to talk about these issues with clients. PROFAMILIA found that women of reproductive age and adolescents demonstrated keen interest in receiving information on

AIDS from family planning field workers. The workers were able to provide this information to clients and still maintain their responsibilities for family planning work. Clinics showed videocassettes on AIDS and STDs in clinic waiting rooms and continued some aspects of the radio campaign to attract new clients. Despite PROFAMILIA's initial fears about providing AIDS prevention information along with family planning services, it resulted in an important and recognized step in service delivery and a potential model for other clinics in Latin America (Vernon 1990).

The Fundación Mexicana para la Planeación Familiar, A.C. (MEXFAM), a Mexican nonprofit family planning institution, undertook a similar type of initiative to determine the institution's effectiveness and capacity to incorporate AIDS prevention activities into two of its current programs, "Area de Promoción Intensiva" (API) and "Gente Joven" (GJ), and to determine the effect of this integration on its primary function, the promotion of family planning (Pacheco et al. 1990). API promotes family planning in peri-urban disadvantaged areas that lack medical and social services and GJ is a program for young people that provides information and services on reproductive health and sexuality. MEXFAM personnel and youth promoters devote time to this program in exchange for a small monetary remuneration. Each program carried out educational activities concerning STDs and AIDS for its particular clientele.

MEXFAM found that the incorporation of AIDS prevention activities in the two programs was successful from an operational viewpoint in that it did not interfere with the family activities, and clients found the new service acceptable. However, MEXFAM saw only a small increase in the clients' knowledge of AIDS, but a larger degree of positive change in their attitudes about people with AIDS and their ideas about mechanisms of HIV transmission. Overall, most MEXFAM clients supported the organization's involvement in AIDS prevention activities, and there were no adverse consequences of the new strategy on the organization.

*Contraceptive services for women after pregnancy termination.* Because most abortion services throughout the developing world are given on an emergency basis as a result of the consequences of unsafe induced abortion, the conditions for delivering family planning services to these clients are unique. These women require distinct family planning counseling and services because their circumstances are different compared to other family planning clients. However, there have been limited efforts and many barriers to linking postabortion care and family planning services (Leonard 1991).

One barrier is that ob/gyn units where abortion or postabortion services are performed are not connected to the family planning unit. Administrative practices, clinic hours, separate locations, and different responsibilities keep these two units apart. A second impediment is the lack of information on providers' attitudes and knowledge concerning the cause of induced abortion, feelings about women who have an unwanted pregnancy, and how these affect the way abortion and subsequent family planning services are delivered. If providers have negative attitudes toward clients presenting for induced abortion, this attitude can be reflected in clients' behavior in that many women do not believe they deserve good services because they have had a clandestine abortion.

A programmatic and managerial link between emergency abortion care and family planning services may help provide these women with contraceptive services at the time of abortion or at a follo- up visit and improve contraceptive acceptability. For some women this represents the first time that they have interaction with health providers and receive information on contraception, while others may know about and use a method and are in need of treatment because of contraceptive failure.

A study in Turkey was conducted among three groups of women to identify factors surrounding abortion clients' motivation for accepting contraception or switching from a relatively inadequate contraceptive method to a modern method (Bulut 1984). The first group was given routine family planning information following induced abortion; a second group of postabortion clients received routine family planning information and education on the health consequences of abortion; and members of the third group, who did not undergo abortion, received the routine and special education. Nurse-midwives made follow up visits to each group. During the visits to the second group, nurse-midwives provided special education immediately after the abortion. They encouraged the women to accept a modern method of contraception or switch from a relatively ineffective method to a better one if they wanted to prevent pregnancy. These women also had a physical exam and additional counseling from a doctor.

The findings show that women in the second group were the most highly motivated to adopt or switch methods. Thirty-six of forty-two women (86 percent) stopped using withdrawal and began to use the IUD, orals, or condoms. This compares to 45 percent in the first group and 18 percent in the third group. Three important points the researchers drew from the study are that 1) most of the women who had an induced abortion and used ineffective methods did not switch to an effective method if they were not encouraged to do so, 2) women who did not have an abortion were not as motivated to use contraception as women who did have an abortion, and 3) contraceptive information and services given within three months of an abortion or unplanned pregnancy were more effective.

Results from a study conducted in India also indicate that postabortion women are highly motivated to accept contraception (Chhabra et al. 1988). In India, the combination of pregnancy termination and family planning services is encouraged to increase contraceptive prevalence as well as to decrease the health risks of pregnancy and abortion. This study conducted at the Mahatma Ghandi Institute of Medical Sciences found that the contraceptive acceptance rate of married women immediately after an abortion was 88.2 percent. Among married women in the first trimester, 43.4 percent accepted an IUD after receiving counseling from staff. Among married women in the second trimester, 11.5 percent chose an IUD; 70.2 percent elected surgical contraception.

The investigators of this study concluded that it was acceptable to women following pregnancy termination to promote contraceptive use and discuss with clients the potential consequences of unsafe induced abortion or abortion by medical professionals in the second trimester. This type of integrated service can contribute to the reduction of the number of unwanted pregnancies, reduce the rate of abortion, and increase contraceptive prevalence.

The Bangladesh Women's Health Coalition learned from a study that it is cost-effective to provide clients undergoing menstrual regulation with contraceptives at the time of their visit (Kay and Kabir 1988). The cost in 1988 for both menstrual regulation and family planning services was about $3.83 per client in urban clinics and $2.82 in rural clinics compared to the cost of an MR client who returns for follow up at a cost of $5.68 for urban clinics and $5.58 for rural clinics. The Coalition has found that the utilization of clinics in rural areas has increased by 15 percent each year and has attributed this rise to the popularity of integrated health services.

*Family planning services and postpartum care.* Postpartum women's special contraceptive needs often have been met immediately after delivery through IUD insertion or sterilization; but, in fact, much is in doubt as to the best time to offer contraceptive services during the postpartum period. It has been thought that the most effective time to provide postpartum women with contraception is after delivery, when they will be highly motivated to prevent another pregnancy and when the woman is still within the reach of the health care system. Current thought argues this approach stating that there is little scientific evidence supporting this trend, and what there is, is based on research on program effectiveness and coverage, not on women's perceptions and needs concerning contraception during the postpartum period (Winikoff and Mensch 1990; Thapa et al. 1991).

An analysis of data from twenty-five countries included in the "first phase" of the Demographic and Health Surveys provides some thought to challenge these notions about the optimal time for postpartum services (Thapa et al. 1991). The results show that women's desires for additional children vary during the two-year postpartum period (DHS's definition of the length of the postpartum period). It was found that women in the immediate postpartum period (0–3 months) are not more likely to want to prevent additional pregnancies than women in the later stages (7–9 and 13–18 months). The number of women in the later stages of the postpartum period who want to space or limit their pregnancies is higher than or equal to the number of women in the immediate postpartum period in nine of thirteen countries. Data also indicate that most women do have interaction at least once with health service personnel in the ante- and postnatal periods, which suggests that there are other opportunities to discuss and provide contraception rather than around the time of delivery.

The findings of a study conducted by the Association for Voluntary Surgical Contraception (Verme and Landry 1991) on contraception during the postpartum period also support the notion that women would be receptive to, and even prefer, information on contraception at a time other than delivery. In a three-country study (Colombia, N=108; Kenya, N=109; and Turkey, N=100), women interviewed felt that receiving family planning information during delivery was the least appropriate time in relation to when they are not pregnant, during the antenatal period, before they leave the hospital, or during the postpartum period. When asked if it was appropriate to receive family planning information during delivery, 4.6 percent of the Kenyan women and 1.0 percent of the Turkish women agreed to this. (The answers from Colombia were found unreliable for this question.) In the three countries, 99.1, 94.5, and 97.0 percent of the women, respectively, believed that receiving this information during postpartum visits was appropriate. Percentages in this range were obtained when women were asked about receiving family planning information when a woman is not pregnant and after the birth of the baby before leaving the hospital.

An innovative program integrating postpartum care and contraception with primary health care comes from the Tunisian Office National de la Famille et de la Population (ONFP), the national family planning program (Coeytaux 1989). The ONFP in discussion with a small group of physicians recognized the philosophical and programmatic importance of recognizing a postpartum mother and her infant as a "synergistic pair," the "couple *mère-enfant*," and the opportunity to care for both the mother and her child during the same postpartum visit. They realized that the fortieth day postpartum, which has great cultural significance for new mothers and infants in Tunisia, could be used as a signal for women to come back to the health facility for a checkup. The fortieth day is when the mother is able to attend to her household responsibilities again and be seen in public after forty days of confinement and care for her and her infant within the household. The fortieth day is a lso important to the community's understanding of the child's health and development, for this marks the time when a baby sleeps through the night and remains awake during the day. Capitalizing on this symbolic day, ONFP and the group of physicians established the "fortieth-day consultation visit."

At the fortieth-day visit, the mother returns to the service delivery site for care for her infant and for herself. Pediatric care is provided at the same time that gynecological and family planning services are offered. Between 1983 and 1987, the number of women returning for the fortieth-day consultation at the Maternal and Neonatal Hospital of Sfax had risen from 60 to 83 percent. Of the 7,686 women who returned for a postpartum visit, 55.6 percent accepted a contraceptive method during that visit.

Because of the positive outcome of this program at Sfax, the ONFP is considering using this model for postpartum services. From this experience, ONFP gleaned some useful lessons for replicating the program elsewhere: (1) contraceptive care can be given with postpartum services if done at an appropriate time; (2) the importance of the fortieth day was a key part in drawing women back to the clinic and helping them appreciate their health needs and those of their infants; (3) the concept of the *mère-enfant* influences many aspects of the program; (4) expanding the choice of available contraceptive methods to postpartum women could help meet their needs on an individual basis; and (5) staff providing care need time to understand and adapt to a new program.

*Family planning programs for adolescents.* Although adolescents make up a significant portion of the population in developing countries–a large number of them are sexually active–they often have no or little access to family planning information and services. In Guatemala, Jamaica, and Mexico the average age for beginning sexual activity is between twelve to fifteen for males and thirteen to seventeen for females (Morris et al. 1987). In the Latin America and Caribbean region, 20-30 percent of females under twenty years old become pregnant in any given year (Ross et al. 1988). Despite this obviously high level of sexual activity, adolescents' reproductive health concerns often go completely unrecognized because of societies' misconceived beliefs and attitudes about adolescent sexual behavior and needs for contraception, and because of the subsequent political regulations preventing adolescents from receiving services. In Latin America, only three governments—Brazil, Colombia, and Mexico—have policies supporting adolescent health programs (Paxman et al. 1991). It is important to look at areas where these attitudes and restrictions are beginning to change and find practicable models for instituting services to this large and important sector of the population.

In an industrial working-class suburb of Sao Paulo, Brazil, a group of assistant professors associated with the ABC Medical School began a program in 1984 based in an out-patient clinic that offers gynecological services, prenatal care, contraceptive methods, individual and group counseling, psycho-social support, referral to other services at the Medical School, and social services to adolescents (Shepherd et al. 1989). The average age of the client is 16.5 years and most clients live in the neighboring slums.

An evaluation of this clinic found that the community looks upon the clinic's work favorably, in part because of the committed director and staff.

The counseling group sessions encouraged participation and were well organized and attended. Program staff also recognized the value of convenient public transportation to the clinic and its location near the target population (Shepherd et al. 1989).

MEXFAM designed and implemented a program to provide family planning and reproductive health services for adolescents called "Gente Joven" (GJ) (Bouzidi and Korte 1990). The program was initiated in thetwenty-eight provinces where MEXFAM is located, and was subsequently extended to forty-two Mexican cities and 50,000 users in these provinces. GJ targets males and females between ten and twenty years of age who live in marginal areas. MEXFAM's general approaches to the GJ program are that the focus should be on health education, particularly reproductive and sex education; that it should be structured around the needs of adolescents based on their input and participation; and that parents, teachers, and community members should be involved.

The education component consists of information on sexual development, reproduction, sexuality, prevention of STDs, and contraception and prevention of unwanted pregnancy. The education sessions of two hours each take place in schools, recreation and sports centers, youth clubs, and factories with adolescent employees. The advantages of this type of operation is that MEXFAM does not have to pay for the facilities, there is wide coverage and a low number of project staff, and the project can be easily integrated into the institutions. The service delivery component includes services and provision of condoms and spermicides to males and females over the age of sixteen.

Some key ingredients for a utilized and community-supported youth program have emerged as these various institutions have initiated programs for adolescents (Monroy 1989). One is the participation of adolescents in identifying problem areas in services, helping design programs, promoting the programs, teaching, organizing activities, distributing information and over-the-counter contraceptives, and making their stories and information available to policy makers. Teenagers working for the program work on-site in schools, factories, community groups, and other places where teenagers congregate. Some of their most useful tools are acting, singing, art, and games, as well as short stories, photography, and discussion groups. These youths tend to have strong leadership abilities, acceptance in the school or community, interest in helping others, and ease with figures of authority.

*Expanding family planning services to include men.* In the past decade family planning programs have made an attempt to broaden their outreach and expand their services to different clientele, including males. This effort has not been taken up with much force because of the limited knowledge and understanding of men's reproductive health and sexual lives and the fact there is little data on how these services should be structured. Should they be directed at males alone or somehow be combined with family planning services for women? How should the clinic and services be organized? What services should be included? What makes men want to come to family planning clinics and what services do they need and require once there? Are men willing to talk about their sexual lives and health care concerns with male and/or female providers? Little is known about answers to these questions but there is clear evidence that men's needs are different than women's and that given the opportunity to utilize special services designed for males, men can be interested and committed clients.

The PROPATER Men's Reproductive Health Clinic in São Paulo, Brazil, is exemplary of a facility that has been successful in promoting male involvement in family planning and offering a broad range of services (Rogow 1990). It was designed as "a space for men to participate more fully in family planning." In 1981, at a time when vasectomy was practically unheard of and rarely done in Latin America, PROPATER opened a vasectomy clinic to complement its sexuality counseling, screening and treatment for sexual dysfunction, and infertility counseling. It aims to provide the most "professional" care possible with attention to the quality of services. This means informed choice, thorough counseling, built-in waiting periods, competent clinical care, and follow-up. The clinic waiting room is attractive and comfortable, interviews are conducted privately, and the lab is strikingly clean. To encourage men to visit the clinic, PROPATER carries out educational and promotional programs in factories for groups from twenty-five to sixty workers.

PROPATER attributes its success to its excellent counseling and technical services and to the increasing interest in and prevalence of vasectomy in Brazil. PROPATER has low complication and failure rates and high client satisfaction. It sees itself as a family planning organization aiming to increase the number of contraceptive methods available, to include vasectomy, in order to promote client and couple satisfaction, rather than control the size of the population. Its sexual-dysfunction and infertility counseling services aid the organization to respond to the multiple concerns of men and act as a link to reproductive health and family planning.

Another example of a successful service delivery program for men comes from PROFAMILIA's Clinica para el Hombre in Colombia (Rogow 1990). After years of abandonment of the vasectomy program due to an increase in tubal ligations performed and, therefore, less demand for male surgical contraception, PROFAMILIA reinstituted vasectomy services in 1985, but this time it was integrated with other reproductive health services for men. The new services were designed to respond to a growing interest and expressed need for various services, but also to maintain financial solvency.

The clinic provides testing and treatment for urological problems, sexual problems, infertility, and sexually transmitted diseases. It also offers family planning education, condoms, and general physical exams. Both male and female nurses are trained to interview each client and determine the appropriate service for him. It was over the course of these interviews in the early stages of the program that PROFAMILIA gained reassurance that men are willing to talk about their reproductive care needs as long as they feel comfortable in the clinic environment and that their privacy is respected.

Both PROFAMILIA and PROPATER provide useful paradigms for instituting and delivering services for men (Rogow 1990). The clinics offer services in a separate clinic or section of the clinic from women, an important logistical move to maintain and ensure men's privacy. The counseling covers a wide range of sexual health issues and is not limited to vasectomy. The variety of services provided addresses a wide range of reproductive health matters and are treated as part of a whole. These additional services outside the vasectomy program also generate income, some of which is used to sustain the vasectomy program. Both institutions have made vasectomy, condom use, and participation in family planning more acceptable and approachable for men by providing high-quality services in an environment tailored to males, and, by putting family planning in a context of comprehensive reproductive health.

The Ghana National Family Planning Program began its services for men based on the male population's participation in a program designed primarily for women (Bouzidi and Korte 1990). When GNFPP began in 1970, it initiated a program to serve rural populations using mobile family planning teams complemented by the services provided by the Maternal and Child Health Centers and village-based primary health care workers. In one rural area, Danfa, almost half of the clients were men even though the program was intended for women. Men seemed to be more consistent users of contraception and better advocates for family planning. They recommended using contraception as well as particular methods to other men. As a result of the services directed toward men in the Danfa program, the fertility rate has dropped and there are fewer unwanted pregnancies. Men said they wanted to use contraception to ensure the health of their children and wives, and that it was easier to educate their surviving children when there were fewer of them.

## Conclusion

This chapter points to some of the current constraints to contraceptive use, the importance of improved and extended family planning services, and alternative strategies to deliver these services. Family planning can be included with other primary and reproductive health services to be responsive to the entire sphere of women's reproductive health needs. Behind an integrated program, there have to be acceptable, safe, and effective methods of contraception that are appropriate and utilizable for women in the different stages of their reproductive lifetime. In order for any program to satisfy clients and care for their reproductive health needs, a chosen contraceptive method must suit a woman whether she is young or old, breast-feeding, spacing pregnancies, engaging in intercourse only occasionally, or planning to end childbearing. They must also be socially and sexually acceptable without having an adverse impact on overall health and well-being. Users' perspectives on health, contraceptive use, and sexuality in each cultural setting must be taken into consideration in planning new program strategies.

When contraceptives fail or women have no access to them, resulting in an unwanted pregnancy, safe and legal abortion services must be available. There are currently effective methods of pregnancy termination, such as menstrual regulation, used in only a limited number of institutions so far; and new technologies, including medical abortifacients such as RU 486, that have great potential as acceptable choices for women.

Financial resources are increasingly limited, forcing programs to operate cost-effectively while providing adequate services. It behooves program managers to experiment with strategies that combine services to achieve more effective programs in terms of client satisfaction, accessibility, and cost for different sectors of the population which have a continuum of reproductive and primary health care needs.

Only when a wider choice of contraceptive methods is available and services more responsive to the totality of women's reproductive health care needs and desires will family planning goals begin to be achieved. Women can play a larger role in this effort, and, as Toro states (1989:120), "be invited to expand their consciousness of their sexual and reproductive rights as a necessary step towards total health."

## Recommendations

### Policy

1. Governments need to enact population policies providing accessible methods and services and demonstrate their commitment to them. They also should continue to reduce barriers to services.

2. Population policies should be reoriented to integrate family planning services with other primary health and/or reproductive services to maximize resources, enable clients to take care of different health needs simultaneously, and be responsive to the range of women's reproductive health needs throughout their lifetime.
3. Recognizing that methods fail and unwanted pregnancy will continue to occur, governments should provide legal, safe, and accessible abortion services.
4. Trained health professionals such as nurses and auxiliary nurses should be enabled to expand their duties, giving them greater flexibility to provide services.
5. Adolescents, unmarried women, minority ethnic groups, and other underserved sectors of the population have a right to family planning as a part of health care, and services should be made legal and accessible to these groups.

## Programs

1. There is a need for better in-service training for management and administration, counseling and education activities, especially as institutions integrate additional services into their ongoing program. For example, counseling on STDs and AIDS prevention, working with adolescents and understanding their different approach to family planning, and attending to the unique needs of postpartum and postabortion women, are training measures to increase the staff's understanding and knowledge of the new or expanded services.
2. Program managers and policy makers should heed the expressed needs and perceptions of women and include them in redesigning services to make them more acceptable and utilizable.
3. Contraceptive services for postabortion women should be linked to the ob/gyn unit on administrative and service delivery levels.
4. Postpartum women should be able to choose when they wish to resume contraception and be provided with information on all the appropriate methods available to them.
5. Family planning institutions can set up special hours and services either in an existing or new facility to provide family planning and reproductive health services for men and adolescents.
6. Adolescents can be very effective in helping to plan, organize, and work in family planning programs and with other youths.
7. Service delivery sites have to be convenient to the target population in terms of location, availability of public transportation, and hours of

service and should be provided in a neighborhood and facility comfortable for clients.

8. Institutions must have mechanisms to follow up their clients over the long term in terms of contraceptive use and general reproductive health.

## *Research*

1. Research efforts to improve family planning methods and service delivery should address women's perception of and needs for family planning, and should include their beliefs, attitudes, and practices concerning their health and sexuality within their cultural norms.

2. Studies should be undertaken to find cost-effective and practical ways to integrate family planning and reproductive health care.

3. Research will give better indications of the right time, place, and combination of family planning services to provide to postpartum or postabortion women.

4. Research on methods to link post abortion clients with family planning services can be carried out to allow better information and access to contraceptive methods.

5. New contraceptives for men and women must be developed and tested for safety, efficacy, and acceptability.

6. Development of medical abortifacients and testing their acceptability and feasibility should continue full force.

7. Research needs to be carried out to identify strategies to increase men's utilization of family planning and reproductive health services.

8. Studies can be conducted on male's perceptions of reproductive health and sexuality so that services can be developed according to these findings.

## References

Anderson, Jeanine and Nelson Panzio. 1986. "Transportation and Public Safety: Services that Make Service Use Possible," in Schmink, Marianne, Bruce, Judith, and Marilyn Kohn eds., *Learning about Women and Urban Services in Latin America and the Caribbean.* New York: The Population Council.

Birdsall, Nancy and Lauren A. Chester. 1987. "Contraception and the Status of Women: What is the Link?" *Family Planning Perspectives* 1:14-18.

Bouzidi, Mohammed and Rolf Korte. 1990. *Family Planning for Life: Challenges for the 1990s.* London: International Planned Parenthood Federation and Deutsche Gesellschaft fHr Technische Zusammenarbeit.

Bruce, Judith. 1987. "Users' Perspectives on Contraceptive Technology and Delivery Systems." *Technology and Society*. 9: 359-383.

Bulut, Aysen. 1984. "Acceptance of Effective Contraceptive Methods after Induced Abortion." *Studies in Family Planning* 15: 281-284.

Chhabra, S., Gupte, N., Mehta, Anita, and Arti Shende. 1988. "Medical Termination of Pregnancy and Concurrent Contraceptive Adoption in Rural India." *Studies in Family Planning* 19: 244-247.

Coeytaux, Francine. 1989. *Celebrating Mother and Child on the Fortieth Day: The Sfax, Tunisia Postpartum Program.* Quality/Calidad/Qualit*, no. 1. New York: The Population Council.

Contraceptive Technology Update. "Female condoms scheduled to reach the U.S. market this year." 1991. *Contraceptive Technology Update*. 12:117-132.

Cook, Rebecca J. and Deborah Maine. 1987. "Spousal Veto over Family Planning Services." *American Journal of Public Health* 77:339-344.

Dixon-Mueller, Ruth. 1990. "Abortion Policy and Women's Health in Developing Countries." *International Journal of Health Services* 20: 297-314.

Dixon-Mueller, Ruth. 1989. "Psychosocial Consequences to Women of Contraceptive Use and Controlled Fertility." In Allan M. Parnell, ed., *Contraceptive Use and Controlled Fertility*. Pp. 140-159. Washington, D.C.: National Academy Press.

Elias, Christopher J. 1991. "Sexually Transmitted Diseases and the Reproductive Health of Women in Developing Countries." New York: The Population Council.

Isaacs, Stephen, Cook, Rebecca J., Pile, John M., Smit, Larua, Levitt, Larua, Cairns, Gail, and Nancy Heckel. 1984. "Laws and Policies Affecting Fertility: A Decade of Change." Population Reports, Series E, Number 7. Baltimore: Population Information Program, Johns Hopkins University

Isaacs, Steven and Nuray Fincancioglu. 1987. "The Policy and Programme Implications of Promoting Family Planning for Better Health." Background paper for Better Health for Women and Children through Family Planning Conference, Nairobi, Kenya, 1987. New York: The Population Council.

Joesoef, Mohamad R, Baughman, Andrew L. and Budi Utomo. 1988. "Husband's Approval of Contraceptive Use in Metropolitan Indonesia: Program Implications." *Studies in Family Planning* 19:162-168.

Kay, Bonnie J., Germain, Adrienne, and Maggie Bangser. 1991. *The Bangladesh Women's Health Coalition*. Quality/Calidad/Qualit*, no. 3. New York: The Population Council.

Kay, Bonnie J. and Sandra M. Kabir. 1988. "A Study of Costs and Behavioral Outcomes of Menstrual Regulation Services in Bangladesh." *Social Science Medicine* 26: 597-604.

Khalifa, Mona A. 1988. "Attitudes of Urban Sudanese Men Toward Family Planning." *Studies in Family Planning* 19:236-243.

Leonard, Ann. 1991. "Post-Abortion Family Planning." Paper presented at the 18th Annual NCIH International Health Conference, Arlington, VA.

Lewis, Maureen. 1986. "Do Contraceptive Prices Affect Demand?" *Studies in Family Planning* 17:126-135.

Mastroianni, Luigi, Donaldson, Peter J., and Thomas T. Kane, eds. 1990. *Developing New Contraceptives: Obstacles and Opportunities.* Washington, D.C.: National Academy Press.

Mauldin, Parker and John Ross. 1991. "Family Planning Programs: Efforts and Results." *Studies in Family Planning* 22: forthcoming.

Mbizvo, Michael T. and Donald J. Adamchack. 1991. "Family Planning Knowledge, Attitudes, and Practices of Men in Zimbabwe." *Studies in Family Planning,* 22:31-38.

Monroy, Anameli. 1989. "Adolescent Participation in Health Programs." Paper presented at the International Conference on Adolescent Fertility in Latin America and the Caribbean. Oaxaca, Mexico.

Morris, Leo, Nunez, Leopoldo, Bailey, Patricia, Monroy, Anemeli, Whatley, Anne, and Carmine Cardendas. 1987. "Young Adult Reproductive Health Survey - Mexico." Final English-Language Report. Atlanta, GA: Centers for Disease Control.

Pacheco, Maria Edith, Rodriguez, Gabriela, Lopez, Alfonso Juarez, Varela, Luis, and Nancy Murray. 1990. "The Impact of Incorporating Educational Strategies for AIDS Prevention and Control into Family Planning Programs." Final Technical Report. Mexico City: Fundacion Mexicana para la Planeacion Familiar, A.C. and the Population Council.

Paxman, John M., Rizo, Alberto, Shepard, B.L., Stern, Claudio, and Kathryn Tolbert. 1991. *Overview: International Conference on Adolescent Fertility in Latin America and the Caribbean.* Oaxaca, Mexico: The Pathfinder Fund/The Population Council.

Philliber, Susan. 1989. "Psychosocial Factors in Contraceptive Efficacy." In Segal, Sheldon, Tsui, Amy O., and Susan M. Roger, editors, *Demographic and Programmatic Consequences of Contraceptive Innovations.* New York: Plenum Press.

Population Council. "Contraceptives Under Development by the Population Council". 1991. News Release. New York: The Population Council.

Rogow, Debbie. 1990. *Man/Hombre/Homme: Meeting Male Reproductive Health Care Needs in Latin America.* Quality/Calidad/Qualit*, no. 2. New York: The Population Council.

Ross, John A., Rich, Marjorie, Molzan, Janet P., and Michael Pensak. 1988. "Family Planning and Child Survival: 100 Developing Countries." New York: Centre for Population and Family Health, Columbia University.

Sai, F.T. and J. Nassim. 1989. "The Need for a Reproductive Health Approach." *International Journal of Gynecology and Obstetrics Supplement 3, Women's Health in the Third World: The Impact of Unwanted Pregnancy*: 103-113.

Shepherd, B.L., Garcia-Nunez, Jose, Miller, J.T., Levitt, Peggy, and Alberto Rizo. 1989. "Adolescent Program Approaches in Latin America and the Caribbean: An Overview of Implementation and Evaluation Issues." Paper presented at the International Conference on Adolescent Fertility in Latin America and the Caribbean. Oaxaca, Mexico.

Smit, Laura. 1991. "How AIDS Prevention Training is Improving the Quality of Care in Latin American and Caribbean Family Planning Programs." Paper presented at the 18th Annual NCIH International Health Conference, Arlington, VA.

Thapa, Shyam, Kumar, Sushil, Cushing, Jeanne, and Kathy Kennedy. 1991. "Contraceptive Use and Needs Among Postpartum Women in 25 Developing Countries: Recent Patterns and Programmatic Implications." Research Triangle Park, NC: Family Health International.

Toro, Olga. 1989. "Commentary on Women-Centered Reproductive Health Services." *International Journal of Gynecology and Obstetrics Supplement 3, Women's Health in the Third World: The Impact of Unwanted Pregnancy*: 119-123.

Toivonen, Juhani, Luukkainen, Tapani, and Hannu Allonen. 1991. "Protective Effect of Intrauterine Release of Levonorgestrel on Pelvic Infection: Three Years' Comparative Experience of Levonorgestrel- and Copper-Releasing Intrauterine Devices." *Obstetrics and Gynecology*. 77:261-264.

Verme, Cynthia Steele and Evelyn Landry. 1991. "Contraception During the Postpartum Period: Perspectives From Clients and Providers in Three Regions." Paper presented at the 18th Annual NCIH International Health Conference, Arlington, VA.

Vernon, Ricardo. 1990. "Incorporating AIDS Prevention Activities into a Family Planning Organization in Colombia." *Studies in Family Planning* 2: 335-343.

Wasserheit, Judith N., Harris, Jeffrey R., Chakraborty, J., Kay, Bradford A., and Karen J. Mason. 1989. "Reproductive 'Tract Infections in a Family Planning Population in Rural Bangladesh." *Studies in Family Planning* 2: 69-80.

Winikoff, Beverly and Maureen Sullivan. 1987. "Assessing the Role of Family Planning in Reducing Maternal Mortality." *Studies in Family Planning* 18: 128-143.

Winikoff, Beverly and Barbara Mensch. 1991. "Rethinking Postpartum Family Planning." *Studies in Family Planning*. 22:294-307.

Wymelenberg, Suzanne. 1990. *Science and Babies: Private Decisions, Public Dilemmas.* Washington, D.C.: National Academy Press.

# 6

# Abortion

*Francine M. Coeytaux, Ann H. Leonard,*
*and Carolyn M. Bloomer*

## Scope and Magnitude of the Problem

Three inescapable facts about abortion make it a public health problem that must be addressed:

1. unsafely performed abortions are a major cause of mortality and morbidity among women;
2. the need for induced abortion is a prevalent and persistent reality; and
3. women need not die or suffer from the consequences of unsafe abortion because—when hygienically and correctly induced—abortion is extremely safe.

In short: mortality and morbidity due to abortion is almost totally preventable.

### A Major Cause of Maternal Mortality and Morbidity

Complications from unsafe abortions account for approximately 40 percent of maternal deaths worldwide (Coeytaux et al. 1989; Royston and Armstrong 1989). This means that at least 200,000 of the estimated 500,000 women who die every year from causes related to pregnancy and childbirth die as a result of poorly performed abortions (Germain 1989; Gay and Underwood 1991; McLaurin et al. 1991; Baker 1991; Coeytaux 1988). Moreover, many experts agree that the incidence suggested by these figures is almost certainly underestimated because considerable underregistration in maternal death counts is a pervasive problem (ranging from about one-third underregistration in the U.S. to multiples of three or four in Egypt and other countries), and because the subject of clandestine abortion is a

133

sensitive issue (WHO 1987; Royston 1989; Coeytaux et al. 1989). In all events, abortion-related deaths account for a very large proportion of maternal mortality; and these deaths are, by their very nature, largely preventable.

Death is not the only human cost of unsafe abortion. In addition to the women who die, hundreds of thousands more women survive, only to suffer serious complications. These include sepsis, hemorrhage, uterine perforation, and cervical trauma, which often lead to permanent physical impairment, chronic morbidity, infertility, and psychological damage (Coeytaux 1990; McLaurin et al. 1991).

The morbidity associated with unsafe abortion remains a severely neglected public health problem. Until very recently, abortion has been the primary method of fertility control in Eastern Europe, where the data paint a very grim picture. In Romania, the Ministry of Health estimates that one out of five women of reproductive age now suffers from infertility caused primarily by unsafe abortions (Marinescu 1990). The same proportion (21 percent) has been reported from Armenia (Donnay 1990). Even though data about the precise magnitude of the problem are inadequate, there is no question that unhygienically performed abortions are a major cause of reproductive-tract infections leading to infertility.

In addition to health problems, numerous other human costs accrue as well. For women these include: stigma, loss of time, psychological stress, financial costs, and a myriad of other personal burdens. From families and communities, unsafe abortions exact still more tolls. Of these, motherless children are perhaps the most poignant and devastating. More than half of the married women suffering from septic abortion already have two or more children (Coeytaux 1988). Every year, 1.5 million children become motherless as a result of maternal mortality (WHO 1987)—and few of these children survive the loss of their mother.

In addition to these unacceptably high human costs, treating abortion complications places heavy financial burdens on health systems in developing countries, where 99 percent of the world's maternal deaths occur. In these countries, treating abortion complications may consume as much as 50 percent of hospital budgets (WHO 1990, 1987), thus draining resources that are already very meager. As a result, entire health care systems in these countries are strained; the risks for mortality and morbidity are thereby increased among women who do not have abortions as well as among those who do. A final irony is that the cost of emergency services to clean up botched abortions is substantially greater than the cost of performing hundreds more medically safe abortions. For example, when abortion was briefly legalized in Chile in the early 1970s, approximately U.S. $200,000 were saved when a high proportion of clandestine abortions were replaced with medical termination procedures (Potts et al. 1977).

## The Persistence and Prevalence of Abortion

No society has been able to eliminate induced abortion as an element of fertility control. Induced abortion is the oldest and, according to some experts, perhaps the most widely used method of fertility control (Royston and Armstrong 1989). Worldwide, about fifty-five million unwanted pregnancies (between one-fifth and one-third of all pregnancies) are terminated each year by induced abortions (Jacobson 1990; Henshaw 1986; David 1989). Of these abortions, about half are illegal and occur primarily in the Third World. The rest are legal abortions performed mainly in the developed world, China, and India (Population Crisis Committee 1989; McLaurin et al. 1991).

The fact that women have abortions is a reality that is not going to go away. If anything, the incidence of induced abortion is increasing worldwide (Toubia 1989), despite legal codes, religious sanctions, and personal dangers. Women of all backgrounds resort to abortions. The factors contributing to this increase include desires for smaller families, increases in the absolute number of women of childbearing age, shifts from rural to urban communities, and increased incidence of nonmarital sexual activity (Coeytaux 1990). Women and couples "make their reproductive decisions according to their personal moral values and [they] use the methods to which they have access, be they legal or illegal, safe or unsafe" (Barzelatto 1989).

While strengthening contraceptive services is essential to reducing the number of unwanted pregnancies, contraception will not altogether remove the need for abortion (Toubia 1989). Moreover, the contraceptive methods that exist to date are far from perfect; correct usage is not easy and virtually all methods have some failure rate, even when used correctly. Until we develop the "perfect contraceptive" and are able to prevent *all* unwanted pregnancies, some women will choose to terminate those pregnancies, despite potential complications and adverse consequences.

Preventing unwanted pregnancies depends on three factors: the availability of contraceptive methods, the effective use of those methods, and the inherent effectiveness of the methods. It is important to note, however, that even when a 95 percent contraceptive usage and effectiveness rate is assumed, demographers estimate that reducing fertility to an average of two births per woman would still require that seven out of ten women have one abortion at some point in their reproductive years (Tietze and Bongaarts 1975). Thus, while family planning programs can reduce the number of unwanted pregnancies, they cannot completely eliminate the necessity for abortion.

## Mortality and Morbidity Due to Abortion Is Preventable

While unsafely induced abortion is the greatest single cause of mortality for women, it is also the most preventable. Of all the major causes of maternal death, those that lead to abortion deaths are the best understood (Maine 1991). Women need not die or suffer medical consequences from abortions because abortions do not kill women; it is, rather, *unsafely performed* abortions which kill. Deaths per 100,000 legal abortion procedures range from 0.1 in industrialized countries to six in developing countries (Centers for Disease Control 1990; Hogberg 1985; Sai and Nassim 1989). In the U.S. legal abortion is eleven times safer than tonsillectomy or childbirth. When hygienically performed, abortion is extremely safe.

Lack of access to safe abortion—rather than any risk inherent in abortion itself—explains the unacceptably high levels of abortion mortality and morbidity. Legal restrictions on induced abortion, together with barriers arising from logistics and policies, force many women to rely on clandestine providers who are often poorly trained and work in unhygienic conditions. Alternatively, women may attempt to terminate the pregnancy themselves using dangerous methods such as the ingestion of poisonous substances or the insertion of sharp objects. Mortality from clandestine (and generally unsafely performed) abortion is estimated to run from fifty to 100 deaths per 100,000 procedures (Liskin 1980); some investigators place the risk of death from unsafe abortion at 100 to 500 times greater than that of abortions performed in safe circumstances (Royston and Armstrong 1989).

Although maternal mortality rates in the developed countries have declined significantly in recent years, little progress has been evidenced elsewhere (WHO 1987). Great disparities remain between women who can afford and have access to adequate medical care and those who are forced to resort to unsafe practices. Unfortunately, this differential access to safe abortion services results in a disproportionate distribution of health risks among poor women (Jacobson 1990; WHO 1987). In fact, maternal mortality rates are often the best public health indicators of inequalities between rich and poor (Fathalla 1988b; Barroso 1991). Ensuring broader access to safe abortion services, then, is one of the most effective ways to prevent hundreds of thousands of women's deaths.

## Tackling the Problem:
## The Need for a Comprehensive Approach

The World Health Organization recognizes abortion as a crisis issue, and in 1991 recommended action to "encourage governments to do everything possible to prevent and eliminate the severe health consequences of unsafe abortion" (WHO 1991). WHO has also made induced abortion a priority topic in the research and development of fertility regulation methods (WHO 1991) and is preparing a book on the technical and managerial aspects of emergency abortion care (WHO forthcoming). In 1987, The Safe Motherhood Conference concluded that the unsafe abortion of unwanted pregnancies causes 25 to 50 percent of maternal deaths because women lack access to family planning services, to safe procedures, and to humane treatment. The Safe Motherhood action program includes interventions to reduce the incidence of unsafe abortion and to improve the management of abortion complications (Family Care International n.d.; Mahler 1987).

Effective action on any of these fronts requires a better understanding of how women make reproductive decisions—including whether or not to terminate a particular pregnancy —and how such decisions are influenced by cultural values placed on fertility, by conditions affecting access to contraception, and by ways in which social change and economic development affect women's status, roles, and opportunities (Coeytaux 1988). But the need for greater insights into women's experiences and needs does not excuse inaction. Two ways to reduce and eventually to eliminate mortality and morbidity from unsafe abortion are already clear: 1) ensuring women's access to timely, safe, effective, and humane abortion care, using existing technologies; and 2) linking abortion care to high-quality family planning services.

## Safe and Effective Abortion Technologies

Safe and effective abortion technologies that could greatly reduce abortion-related deaths and injuries already exist, yet they are not being utilized to the fullest possible extent. Without dispute, vacuum aspiration (VA) has been shown to be the safest surgical technique for uterine evacuation in the first trimester (Grimes et al. 1977), whether employed for induced abortion or for treating incomplete abortion. It is the technique used for most induced abortions in the developed world. The World Health Organization recommends vacuum aspiration (also called "suction curettage") as the procedure of choice for first-trimester uterine evacuation, and lists it as an essential obstetric service to be made available at all first-referral-level hospitals (WHO 1986).

In spite of the safety advantages of VA, however, dilation and curettage (D&C) remains the most common method employed in the developing world for inducing abortions and for treating abortion complications. In tertiary-level hospitals, physicians typically perform D&Cs in operating theatres using general anesthesia or sedation; women usually remain at

least overnight in the hospital. These logistical necessities limit the availability of abortion services; in addition they unnecessarily appropriate
higher-level and more costly resources for abortion care. Hence, persistent
use of this outdated medical technique exacerbates the problem of unsafe
abortion.

Abortion care providers in the developing world continue to rely on
D&Cs for a number of reasons, chief among them being lack of access to
electric vacuum aspiration technology. But other alternative procedures, if
widely adopted, could make safe abortion care accessible to women in
remote areas throughout the world. One such technology is manual vacuum
aspiration (MVA).

MVA is a variation of vacuum aspiration which uses a hand-held syringe
as a vacuum source, and is not dependent on electricity. MVA usually
requires only verbal reassurance, paracervical block, or mild analgesia; it
thus reduces the risks associated with anesthesia, the need for overnight
hospitalization, and the costs to both patients and institutions (Benson
1991). This simple procedure for early uterine evacuation can be employed
by trained paramedical personnel, and consequently allows care delivery to
be decentralized to a variety of settings. Replacing D&C with MVA would
expand the number of sites at which care can be delivered and allow
outpatient delivery of abortion care; it would thus increase women's access
to services and greatly reduce consumption of health care resources (IPAS
1991a; McLaurin et al. 1991).[1]

Other existing technologies could also greatly increase access to safe
abortion services and reduce the morbidity and mortality associated with
unsafe methods. The most promising of these is RU486, a procedure for
early first-trimester abortion now used extensively in France and approved
for introduction in England. RU486 is an abortifacient that acts by preventing
uterine implantation of the blastocyst, or, if implantation is complete, by
preventing gestation. RU486 is 87 percent effective when used alone, and 96
percent effective in combination with prostaglandin (Maria et al. 1988;
Silvestre et al. 1990).

Unfortunately, RU486 is not yet available to most women. Antichoice
groups have exerted political pressure on the manufacturer of the drug, and
as a result, the company has limited its distribution to only two developed
countries. While the body of scientific knowledge about RU486 continues to
expand, little is known about users' perspectives on this technology or
about the service delivery requirements for introducing this method in
developing countries (Brady 1989). Urgently needed are studies on the
acceptability and feasibility of providing RU486 in a variety of countries
and cultural settings.

## Abortion and Family Planning

The conceptual link between abortion and family planning is obvious and fundamental: effective contraception is the most efficacious means of preventing unwanted pregnancies and so preempting the need for abortions. All methods of contraception are subject to failure, however; even couples practicing contraception with an effective method may find themselves faced with an unwanted pregnancy. In the absence of safe contraceptive backups, women will continue to be forced to employ unsafe means for terminating unwanted pregnancies.

Many developed countries provide abortion care as an integral component of family planning. In most developing countries, however, international and local pressures have forced programs to stop providing *any* abortion-related services—even education and referrals (Coeytaux 1990). This artificial separation, or "disintegration," of abortion and family planning has led millions of women to continue their postabortion lives in the absence of contraceptive protection and has thus contributed to the epidemic of unwanted pregnancies and unnecessary abortion deaths (Leonard 1991).

Research in many countries shows that women are most receptive to contraceptive counseling immediately following abortion. In countries where abortion is illegal or difficult to access, women are doubly disadvantaged: they are unlikely to get contraceptive guidance from clandestine abortionists, and consequently they remain vulnerable both to repeated unwanted pregnancies and to dangerous, illegal abortions (Royston and Armstrong 1989). Tragically, even if these women enter formal medical systems for treatment of complications from clandestine abortions, they will still not be offered family planning services because the systems fail to link family planning and emergency abortion care services.

This failure to combine such fundamental services is symptomatic of the broader failure to view abortion and family planning as integral components in comprehensive reproductive health services. Approaching reproductive health needs as single, self-contained services contributes to fragmentation in care and to the failure to meet women's needs.

Ameliorating the problem of unsafe abortion requires (1) integrating abortion care into existing reproductive health care services; and (2) increasing access to safe abortion services. We cannot ignore the fact that ensuring access to safe abortion services remains the most effective way to prevent hundreds of thousands of women's deaths and untold suffering. Examples abound of how quickly and how dramatically mortality can be reduced; in the U.S. and Romania, abortion deaths dropped 85 percent and 67 percent, respectively, after the legalization of abortion (Population Crisis Committee 1989; Tietze 1981; Romanian Ministry of Health 1991); and comparable reductions have been reported from other countries. Even in countries with legal restrictions, abortion risks can be drastically reduced by timely access to humane treatment. The safety of emergency treatment for abortion complications can be improved; and programs can be implemented to train health personnel in the use of safe techniques such as manual vacuum aspiration (McLaurin et al. 1991).

## Ensuring Access to Care

Access to safe, effective early abortion, as well as to timely treatment of abortion complications, represents for women the realization of the right established a quarter of a century ago by United Nations General Assembly Resolution 2200 (1966): "to enjoy the benefits of scientific progress and its applications" (cited in Cook 1989). "Benefits of scientific progress" are here recognized not as a privilege of wealth and social class, but as a *human* right that cuts across the inequalities of socioeconomic disparities. For poor women, Resolution 2200 establishes the right to an exit off "the road to *preventable* death" through access to new, safe, and affordable technologies that will preserve their reproductive health.

Making this right a reality involves, in many instances, liberalizing laws related to contraception and abortion. But while this is an important step toward facilitating women's access to safe and effective reproductive care, it does not, unfortunately, guarantee a supportive infrastructure (Fathalla 1988a; McLaurin et al. 1991; Population Crisis Committee 1989). The actual availability of abortion services depends on:

- the organization and policies of health care systems (e.g. distribution of money, facilities, equipment, personnel, and supplies; administrative bureaucracy; protocols for screening, referral, transportation, and treatment; etc.);
- health care providers (e.g. their training, caseloads, social and ideological attitudes and pressures); and
- women themselves (e.g. their awareness of services, physical distance from service sites, perceived quality of care and caregivers, community and familial pressures) (McLaurin et al. 1991; IPAS 1991b; Thaddeus and Maine 1990; WHO forthcoming).

The time between the onset of complications and receiving adequate treatment is critical in preventing the vast majority of pregnancy-related deaths. Thaddeus and Maine (1990) have identified three phases of delay which influence this time period. They are:

- delay in deciding to seek care,
- delay in reaching an adequate facility, and
- delay in receiving adequate care.

Barriers such as age limits, spousal notification, and narrow criteria for induced abortion limit women's access to services that would allow them safe fertility control. In some countries with liberal laws, such as India and Zambia, administrative or logistical hurdles are so burdensome that abortion procedures legally allowable under the law are effectively unavailable to most women, and unsafe, illegal practices persist (IPAS 1990). Unless health care systems respond to liberal laws with administrative and structural support, women may be denied care, even when it is legally allowable.

WHO has identified the decentralization of care as an essential element in expanding access to safe health services (WHO forthcoming). Linking community, primary, and other care levels in an interactive network enables safe, appropriate care to be delivered at the lowest, most accessible levels possible (McLaurin et al. 1991). In smaller, local centers, health services can be implemented by paramedical personnel, and care can be delivered to rural women who are unable or unwilling to journey to centralized sites, and who would otherwise be deprived of potentially life-saving and timely treatment (IPAS 1991a, b).

Integral to the problem of decentralization is the current absence of providers trained in safe abortion care and related services. Existing clinical programs in much of the world neglect to train the skills required for safe abortion care. Because well-trained providers are essential to high-quality abortion services, health systems must adopt a proactive approach to training providers, especially those who will serve populations in remote or underserved areas, and to equipping them to provide the safest and most appropriate care (McLaurin et al. 1991).

A final obstacle to implementing abortion services has been the United States government's restrictions on funding abortion services. Since 1974, U.S. foreign aid for most activities related to abortion has been prohibited. In 1984, at the Second International Conference on Population, held in Mexico City, the United States government announced additional abortion restrictions (the "Mexico City policy"), further prohibiting the funding of nongovernmental organizations that provide any form of abortion-related service. These restrictions—by one of the biggest international donors of population and family planning assistance—have severely damaged the ability of health systems in the developing world to deliver safe services to women in need (Leonard 1991). Until such restrictive policies are reversed, barriers to access will continue to exist, and women will continue to be forced to rely on unsafe abortions which threaten their health and their lives.

## Unsafe Abortion: A Call for Action

All over the world, women have begun to voice outrage over the millions of women who die each year from preventable causes (Barroso 1991). The toll from unsafe abortion is particularly unacceptable because these deaths and suffering *could have been prevented.*

Explicit in the call for action for women's health in the 1990s is the call for universal access to safe abortion and the elimination of all restrictions and barriers which hinder such access. The recommendations of the 18th Annual NCIH International Health Conference on Women's Health[2] regarding abortion include:

1. an open acknowledgment by health authorities worldwide of the severity and magnitude of the problem of unsafe abortion;
2. universal access to comprehensive reproductive health services that include safe abortion services;
3. the elimination of all legal and other restrictions and barriers that hinder the provision of safe voluntary abortion services; and
4. the development of new, safer methods of fertility control including both contraceptives and abortifacients (Institute of Medicine and National Research Council 1990).

During the coming decade, we could eliminate, once and for all, the millions of unnecessary deaths and untold suffering that are generated by denying women access to safe abortion services. While daunting, the task is achievable. Women deserve no less.

## Notes

1. At Ahmadu Bello University Teaching Hospital (ABUTH) in Zaria, Nigeria, for example, 98 percent of cases that previously would have been treated with D&C are now managed with MVA in outpatient facilities. A total hospital stay for treatment of abortion complications now rarely exceeds two hours; previously women waited up to seventy-two hours just to be treated. In Zambia, the introduction of MVA at University Teaching Hospital in Lusaka (UTH) and district/provincial hospitals throughout the country has increased women's access to legal procedures. Before the introduction of MVA, only one in twenty-five abortion cases was legally

induced; all the others were admitted for treatment of complications of unsafe abortion. Today, that ratio is one-to-five.

2. Resolution entitled "Support for Safe Abortion Services as a Component of Comprehensive Reproductive Health Care" submitted to the NCIH Governing Board, September 1991.

The authors wish to thank Vicki Henderson for her assistance in bibliographic research and in the production of the paper.

## References

Baker, Jean. 1991. "Impact of Induced Abortion on Women's Health in Kenya." Paper presented at the 18th Annual NCIH International Health Conference. Arlington, VA.

Barroso, Carmen. 1991. "Women's Health: Towards an Agenda for the Nineties." Keynote Address presented at the 18th Annual NCIH International Health Conference. Arlington, VA.

Barzelatto, José. 1989. "Reflections About Ethics and Human Reproduction and the Sense of the Conference." In Z. Bankowski, J. Barzelatto and A.M. Capron, eds., *Ethics and Human Values in Family Planning*. Geneva: Council for International Organizations of Medical Sciences (CIOMS). [cited in Ford Foundation 1991]

Benson, Janie. 1991. "Women Don't Have to Die: An Underutilized Technology Can Make a Difference." Paper presented at the 18th Annual NCIH International Health Conference. Arlington, VA.

Brady, Martha. 1989. "Medical Abortifacient: A New Technology Requiring New Research." In Francine Coeytaux, Ann Leonard and Erica Royston, eds., *Methodological Issues in Abortion Research*. Pp. 107-109. New York: The Population Council.

Centers for Disease Control, U.S. Department of Health and Human Services, Public Health Service. 1990. *Morbidity and Mortality Weekly Report (MMWR)*. Abortion Surveillance, 1986-1987. CDC Surveillance Summaries, 39:SS-2.

Coeytaux, Francine. 1988. "Induced Abortion in Sub-Saharan Africa: What We Do and Do Not Know." *Studies in Family Planning* 19(3):186-190.

_____. 1990. "Abortion, Sexually Transmitted Diseases, and Infertility: Reproductive Health Problems Family Planning Programs Can No Longer Ignore." Paper presented at the 17th Annual NCIH International Health Conference. Arlington, VA.

Coeytaux, Francine, Leonard, Ann and Erica Royston. 1989. *Methodological Issues in Abortion Research*. Proceedings of a seminar presented under the Population Council's Roger H. Ebert Program on Critical Issues in Reproductive Health. New York: The Population Council.

Cook, Rebecca J. 1989. "Antiprogestin Drugs: Medical and Legal Issues." *Family Planning Perspectives* 21(6):267-272.

David, Henry P. 1989. "Methodological Realities in Service-oriented Abortion Research." In Francine Coeytaux, Ann Leonard and Erica Royston, eds., *Methodological Issues in Abortion Research.* Pp. 9-11. New York: The Population Council.

Donnay, France. 1990. Personal Communication, Paris.

Family Care International. n.d. *Safe Motherhood Initiative.* New York: Family Care International.

Fathalla, Mahmoud F. 1988a. "Health Care Systems: The Seven Sins." In P. Belfort, J. A. Pinotti, and T.K.A.B. Eskes, eds., *Advances in Gynecology and Obstetrics.* Proceedings of the 12th World Congress of Gynecology and Obstetrics, Rio de Janeiro. Vol. 4. Pp. 3-13.

_____. 1988b. "Safe Motherhood." *International Journal of Gynecology and Obstetrics* 26:347-48.

Ford Foundation. 1991. *Reproductive Health: A Strategy for the 1990s.* New York: Ford Foundation.

Gay, Jill and Tamara Underwood. 1991. "Women in Danger: A Call for Action." In *Women's Health: The Action Agenda for the 90s.* 18th Annual NCIH International Health Conference. Arlington, VA. Pp. 63-74.

Germain, Adrienne. 1989. "The Christopher Tietze International Symposium: An Overview." In A. Rosenfield, ed., Women's Health in the Third World: The Impact of Unwanted Pregnancy. *International Journal of Gynecology and Obstetrics* Supplement 3:1-8.

Grimes, David A., Schulz, K.F., Cates, W., Tyler, C.W. Jr. 1977. "The Joint Program for the Study of Abortion/CDC: A Preliminary Report," in W. Hern and B. Andrikopoulos, eds., *Abortion in the Seventies.* Pp. 41-54. New York: National Abortion Federation.

Henshaw, Stanley K. 1986. "Induced Abortion: A Worldwide Perspective." *Family Planning Perspectives* 18(6):250-254. [cited in Royston and Armstrong 1989]

Hogberg, U. 1985. "Maternal Mortality: A Worldwide Problem." *International Journal of Gynecology and Obstetrics* 23:463-470.

Institute of Medicine and National Research Council. 1990. *Developing New Contraceptives: Obstacles and Opportunities.* Washington, D.C.: National Academy Press.

International Projects Assistance Services (IPAS). 1991a. "IPAS' Initiative for Influencing Change in Reproductive Health Care Policy in Mexico." Carrboro NC: IPAS

_____. 1991b. *Strategy for the Next Decade.* Carrboro NC: IPAS.

_____. 1990. "Zambia Project Assessment Report." Carrboro NC: IPAS

Jacobson, Jodi L. 1990. "Abortion in a New Light." *World Watch* March/April:31-38.

Leonard, Ann. 1991. "Falling Through the Cracks: Post-Abortion Family Planning." Paper presented at the 18th Annual NCIH International Health International Health Conference. Arlington VA.

Liskin, Laurie S. 1980. "Complications of Abortion in Developing Countries." *Population Reports.* Series F(7):106-155.

Mahler, Halfdan. 1987. "The Safe Motherhood Initiative: A Call to Action." *Lancet* March:668-670.

Maine, Deborah. 1991. *Safe Motherhood Programs: Options and Issues*. New York: Columbia University Center for Population and Family Health.

Maria, Bernard, Stampf, F., Goepp, A., Ulmann, A. 1988. "Termination of Early Pregnancy by a Single Dose of Mifepristone (RU 486), a Progesterone Antagonist." *European Journal of Obstetrics and Gynecology and Reproductive Biology* 28:249-255.

Marinescu, Bogdan (Minister of Health, Romania). 1990. Personal Communication, Paris.

McLaurin, Katie E., Hord, Charlotte E. and Merrill Wolf. 1991. *Health Systems' Role in Abortion Care: the Need for a Pro-Active Approach*. Carrboro, NC: IPAS.

Population Crisis Committee. 1989. *Fact Sheet*. Washington, DC: Population Crisis Committee.

Potts, Malcolm, Diggory, P., Peel, J. 1977. *Abortion*. Cambridge: Cambridge University Press.

Romanian Ministry of Health, Directorate for Maternal and Child Health. 1991. *Mortalitatea Materna*. Bucharest (unpublished).

Rosenfield, A., Fathalla, M.F., Germain, A., Indriso, C.L. 1989. Women's Health in the Third World: The Impact of Unwanted Pregnancy. *International Journal of Gynecology and Obstetrics* Supplement 3.

Royston, Erica. 1989. "Estimating the Number of Abortion Deaths." In Francine Coeytaux, Ann Leonard and Erica Royston, eds., *Methodological Issues in Abortion Research*. Pp. 23-28. New York: The Population Council.

Royston, Erica and Sue Armstrong. 1989. *Preventing Maternal Deaths*. Geneva: World Health Organization.

Sai, F. T. and Janit Nassim. 1989. "The Need for a Reproductive Health Approach." In A. Rosenfield, ed., *International Journal of Gynecology and Obstetrics* Supplement 3:103-113.

Silvestre, L., Dubois, C., Renault, M., Rezvani, Y., Baulieu, E., Ulmann, A. 1990. "Voluntary Interruption of Pregnancy with Mifepristone and a Prostaglandin Analogue: A Large-scale French Experience." *New England Journal of Medicine*, 322(10):645-648.

Thaddeus, Sereen and Deborah Maine. 1990. *Too Far to Walk: Maternal Mortality in Context* (Findings from a Multidisciplinary Literature Review). New York: Columbia University Center for Population and Family Health.

Tietze, Christopher. 1981. *Induced Abortion: A World Review, 1981*, 4th ed. New York: The Population Council.

Tietze, Christopher and John Bongaarts. 1975. "Fertility Rates and Abortion Rates, Simulations of Family Limitations." *Studies in Family Planning* 6:114.

Toubia, Nahid. 1989. "Measuring the Rising Costs of Unwanted Pregnancy in Khartoum, Sudan." In Francine Coeytaux, Ann Leonard and Erica Royston, eds., *Methodological Issues in Abortion Research*. Pp. 70-76. New York: The Population Council.

World Health Organization (WHO). 1986. *Essential Obstetric Functions at First Referral Level*, FHE/86.4. Geneva: WHO.

_____. 1987. "Maternal Mortality: The Dimensions of the Problem." Draft chapter of WHO Monograph. Nairobi: Safe Motherhood Conference.

_____. 1990. *Maternal Health and Safe Motherhood Programme Progress Report 1987-90*. Geneva: WHO.

———. 1991. "Summary Report and Recommendations of the Meeting on "Women's Perspectives on the Introduction of Fertility Regulation Technologies," Special Programme of Research, Development and Research Training in Human Reproduction and the International Women's Health Coalition. Geneva: WHO.
———. In press. *Technical and Managerial Guidelines on Abortion Care.* Geneva: WHO.

Woman preparing tortillas in Guanacaste, Costa Rica (courtesy of the Agency for International Development)

Woman shepherd in Ecuador (courtesy of the World Bank)

Women sewing in a factory in Brazil (courtesy of the World Bank)

Woman painting a new house in Chile (courtesy of the Agency for International Development)

Girl on street, U.S.A. (photo taken by Carissa Etheridge, age 15, courtesy of Shooting Back)

Urban slum in El Salvador (courtesy of the World Bank)

Woman farming in Ecuador (courtesy of the World Bank)

Mother and child in Liberia (courtesy of the United Nations, UN photo 33096/
Davis)

Women carrying newly harvested sorghum in Mali (courtesy of the Agency for International Development)

Women pounding grain in Burkina Faso (courtesy of the World Bank)

Women and children at a family planning clinic in Indonesia (courtesy of the World Bank)

Woman and child in doorway in Indonesia (courtesy of the World Bank)

Girl and women carrying fuel wood in Nepal (courtesy of the Agency for International Development)

Women waiting for services at a family planning clinic in Bangladesh (courtesy of the World Bank)

Woman with child on her back in the Philippines (courtesy of the Agency for International Development)

# 7

# Women's Mortality:
# A Legacy of Neglect

*Lynn P. Freedman and Deborah Maine*

Virtually everywhere in the world, women live longer than men (UN 1991). Yet this simple fact is deceptive, for not only does it mask a very different profile of morbidity (as documented throughout this book), it also obscures the millions of premature deaths that women experience because they are women. In some cases—such as the domestic battering that kills at least 1,500 women in the United States every year (FBI 1989), or the dowry deaths and bride burnings that take the lives of thousands more in India (Heise 1990)—women die purely and simply because of their gender. But in a far greater number of cases, women die because of biological events that occur in a social context in which their needs, their contributions—indeed, their very lives—are undervalued.

Women's inferior social status influences their mortality not just in the poorest communities of the developing world, but in the most sophisticated urban centers of the industrialized world as well. Thus, as we explain in some detail below, girls die in rural Bangladesh because the meager resources available in the poorest households are distributed to boys first. At the same time, women die in the high-tech, high-cost world of American health care because the massive resources available to American medicine also are disbursed through a system plagued by gender bias.

The interplay between biological and social forces is often difficult to identify and even harder to quantify. Yet the recognition that this phenomenon exists is crucial, since without an explicit acknowledgment that the circumstances of women's lives—and of their deaths—are influenced by pervasive gender bias, truly effective policy solutions will remain beyond reach.

The task of isolating those deaths that have a gender component is fraught with methodological and conceptual difficulties, aggravated by the lack of reliable sex-specific data. Nevertheless, even a general examination of how and why females die at each stage in the life cycle leads to two central conclusions:

1.  A shamefully large number of girls and women die each year because of the unique risks inherent in being female in a world where females are second-class citizens.

2.  The great majority of these deaths will not be eliminated as an incidental benefit of socioeconomic development or even through the conscientious, but gender-neutral, application of the principles of primary health care that dominate thinking in international health today. Rather, a dramatic decline in gender-influenced deaths will come about only when the health establishment, program planners and managers, and public-policy makers give specific attention to the plight of women as women, valued for their own sake and in their own right.

In the sections that follow, we examine some salient issues concerning women's mortality at three separate stages of the life cycle: infancy and childhood, the reproductive years, and midlife and older years. We do not attempt to catalogue every major cause of death for women around the globe. Many of the most important health problems, such as AIDS and other infectious diseases, violence, and malnutrition, are treated extensively elsewhere in the book; our omission of them here is not meant to downgrade their importance as factors in women's mortality. But our aim is a different one. By looking at mortality from a different angle for each stage in the life cycle, we hope to give a sense of the complex range of ways in which gender influences health in order to demonstrate that gender must be an explicit element in the design of policies and programs intended to improve women's survival.

## Infancy and Childhood

Discrimination against girls happens in many parts of the world; but in some places, under some circumstances, gender discrimination kills. Thus the study of sex differentials in infant and child mortality throughout the world raises provocative questions about the role of gender in the allocation of household resources and in the delivery and use of primary health care under various socioeconomic circumstances and cultural conditions.

### Sex Differentials in Infant and Child Mortality

In every country in the industrialized world and in the majority of countries in the developing world, male infants and children have a higher mortality rate than females. In the neonatal period, excess male mortality is due primarily to higher rates of respiratory distress syndrome among males (indicative of the greater immaturity of the lungs of male babies at birth) and to higher death rates for congenital anomalies and intestinal infections as well (Waldron 1987). In the later childhood years, excess male mortality is due primarily to accidents and violence, which are generally thought to reflect a difference in the socialization of the two genders (this time to the detriment of males), although there is some suggestion that biological factors may play a role here as well (Waldron 1986).

This is the picture that prevails in countries with higher life expectancies (over sixty-five years) and thus lower infant and child mortality rates. The key point here is this: where male infants and children have higher mortality than females, it is *not* because males are denied equal access to resources; it is because of inherent biological differences that influence mortality in the neonatal period, and socialization differences that, in later childhood, lead males to engage in more dangerous behaviors.

A very different picture emerges in the countries where girls have a higher mortality rate than boys. Although excess female mortality has been studied most thoroughly in South Asia, evidence compiled by Elsa Gómez and presented at the NCIH Conference indicates that this occurs in the Americas as well (Gómez 1991). In both regions, during the perinatal period, where death is due almost entirely to biological conditions present at birth, male mortality is consistently higher than female mortality (Waldron 1987). It is only after the neonatal period that female mortality suddenly surges ahead. Some explanation can be found by examining sex differentials for different causes of death. Accidents and violence still kill more boys than girls (Waldron 1987). But these deaths are outweighed by the fact that, in countries with excess female mortality, girls die in far higher numbers than boys from a wide range of other causes including intestinal diseases, respiratory diseases, and nutritional deficiencies (Waldron 1987). These are the causes of death that predominate whenever infant and child mortality is high. They are associated with poverty, with poor sanitation and hygiene, with malnutrition and infection and with the absence of basic health care.

Are girls biologically more susceptible to death when exposed to such poor conditions? Or can excess female mortality be attributed to gender discrimination (i.e. to differential access to the basic resources needed to survive)? Available evidence indicates that gender discrimination is the culprit. First, many societies suffer from dire poverty and the inadequate resources associated with it, but only some of those societies have higher death rates for girls. Second, studies of communities with excess female mortality show that the high female death rates are associated with discrimination against girls in feeding and access to health care. These studies found that girls were often given less and lower-quality food; they were brought for treatment in health centers less often than boys, and at a later stage in their illness (when recovery was less likely) (Koenig and D'Souza 1986). Further evidence that the excess in female mortality stems from discriminatory treatment of girls exists at the population level as well. For instance, Waldron has shown that the ratio of female-to-male mortality in different states in India correlates strongly with an index of son preference expressed by adults in those states (Waldron 1987).

Identifying the connection between excess mortality among female children and gender discrimination is only half the job; it is essential to probe why parents treat sons and daughters differently. While pockets of excess female mortality in particular stages of childhood are found in many parts of the developing world, the problem has been studied most intensively in countries of South Asia—India and Bangladesh—where it is especially severe. Evidence from these countries indicates that the disparate treatment of sons and daughters has both economic and cultural components.

The economic rationale that often underlies gender discrimination in the allocation of household resources can be simply put. Boys represent a net asset to parents: They can work in the fields or for wages, and they will provide for parents in their old age. By contrast, girls are a net drain on family resources: They have limited prospects for earning substantial income; they are likely to marry early and at high cost (because of the dowry that must be paid), and the benefit of their labor will then accrue solely to their husbands' families.

When household resources are severely limited, some parents make what they perceive to be an economically rational decision: they invest in the child most likely to yield the highest return. Evidence from Matlab, Bangladesh supports this view (Koenig and D'Souza 1986). There, gender discrimination in feeding began only when infants reached an age where breastmilk had to be supplemented with scarce and costly weaning foods. At that point boys received more and better-quality foods; girls began to show higher levels of malnutrition. Although the incidence of various infections was the same for boys and girls, girls' illnesses were longer and more severe, probably due to their poor nutritional status. Despite this fact, parents were willing to incur the time and opportunity costs of going to the clinic far more often if the sick child was a son than if it was a daughter. Under the poor environmental conditions in rural Bangladesh, such differential treatment ultimately manifested itself in mortality statistics: Data for two different birth cohorts at Matlab indicate that, between the ages of one and four years, female mortality exceeded male mortality by 59 to 77 percent.

Population-based statistics from India further substantiate the view that gender discrimination in nutrition and health care has a strong economic component. In a review of evidence from different parts of India, Chatterjee concludes that as the perceived economic value of women relative to men increases, the ratio of female-to-male mortality in children declines. For example, an analysis of data from rural households throughout India showed that where female employment went up, thereby improving the potential economic value of girls, their relative share of household re- sources went up and their survival rate relative to boys went up as well. Interestingly, there is also a relationship between female labor force partici- pation and dowry costs: As women join the labor force (thus increasing their economic value), the amount that their families must pay in dowries for them drops. And where dowry and marriage costs (and thus the financial burden of daughters) are lower, female to male mortality ratios are lower as well (Chatterjee 1990).

However, a strictly economic explanation of excess female mortality is dangerously simplistic. The perception that women have low economic value is legitimated and reinforced by culture. Socially constructed gender roles relegate women to a set of duties and obligations that are typically given little value. Consequently, "women's work," such as housework, child-rearing or certain agricultural tasks, is routinely dismissed from official calculations of productivity regardless of how critical that work is to family and community welfare. And critical it is indeed. For example, as of 1985, it was estimated that if women's unpaid household labor alone were given economic value, it would contribute an additional one-third—$4 trillion—to the world economic production (Sivard 1985). Women's agri- cultural labor is especially critical to many communities' very survival: In Africa women produce 60 to 80 percent of all food; in Latin America they produce 40 percent (Joekes et al. 1988).

Thus, women's work is devalued not because it is unimportant, but be- cause it is women who are doing it. This becomes even more apparent when men's and women's earnings in the wage-labor market are compared. Almost everywhere in the world, jobs dominated by women are paid less than jobs dominated by men; where men and women do the same job, women often earn a lower wage (UN 1990; Commonwealth Secretariat 1989). This tendency to denigrate women's work complicates efforts to improve their real and perceived economic contributions. Among other things, it means that at the heart of the economic calculus that parents do, whether consciously or unconsciously, lurks a deeply embedded, culturally validated belief that women are inherently less capable of being contribut- ing, productive members of a household and community, and so less deserving of an equal share of scarce resources.

To summarize then, excess female mortality in infancy and childhood is largely attributable to gender discrimination in the allocation of basic resources such as food and health care. Such gender discrimination results from parents' preference for sons, which in turn is based on a perception, legitimated by culture, that boys have a higher economic value than girls.

## Policy Implications

What implications do these findings have for public policy? The immediate problem is that girls are denied access to sufficient resources to survive. However, simply increasing the total resources at the family's disposal by relatively small amounts—such as by the additional amount that girls need to survive—will not solve the problem, because the added resources will not necessarily be allocated according to need and so will not automatically reach the girls who lack them. Indeed, some evidence indicates that, within communities suffering excess female mortality, the ratio of girls' deaths to boys' deaths is actually higher among children in better-off families than in poorer families. When income or available resources increase, the families simply invest even more in boys, thus bringing down male mortality while female mortality stays at the same high level (Chatterjee 1990). Of course, in the very long run, greatly improved living conditions in these societies would probably eliminate the sex differential in mortality, even if it did nothing to eliminate discrimination per se. In the current economic climate, however, that level of increased resources is but a wish and a prayer.

For the foreseeable future, excess female mortality in children will not be eliminated by an across-the-board increase in resources; it will only be eliminated by attacking the discrimination first. In the long term, that means attacking the causes and symptoms of gender discrimination throughout the society; in particular, it means recognizing and valuing women's work and their contributions to households, communities, and the broader economy. In the short run, it means paying specific attention to girls by devising "affirmative action"-style programs to make sure they get equal access to the basic resources that all children need to survive and thrive.

## The Reproductive Years

Once a girl has survived childhood and entered her reproductive years, the relationship between female mortality and the allocation of community and household resources takes a very different turn. Especially in the developing world, among the biggest threats to women's lives during these years are the risks inherent in pregnancy and childbirth. These are risks that men do not run. Thus the problem should not be framed as one of getting women better access to the same resources that sustain men.

Instead, the challenge of reducing women's mortality in the reproductive years can be understood as a two-step process. First, there must be a clear recognition of the uniqueness of women's health risks and a broad consensus about the interventions necessary to lower their mortality. Second, there must be a political commitment to the notion that women's health is important because women themselves are important; that suffering and death come no more "naturally" to women than they do to men; and that a society's investment in alleviating sickness and death among women can yield at least as high a return as a comparable investment in men. To meet that challenge, health planners will have to break out of conventional modes of thinking about public health and look with new vision at the lives of women.

## Maternal Mortality

Nowhere is the need for innovative analysis more acute than in the area of maternal mortality.[1] The World Health Organization estimates that every year some 500,000 women die in pregnancy and childbirth (WHO 1986). That is nearly one every minute. Ninety-nine percent of those deaths take place in the developing world; 89 percent in Africa and South Asia alone.

The profound difference in maternal mortality between developing and developed countries is expressed even more starkly by a comparison of lifetime risk: One in every twenty-one women in Africa will die of complications of pregnancy or delivery, compared to only one in every 9,850 in Northern Europe (Rochat 1987). Although women who live in countries with high maternal mortality also die more often of other causes than do women in industrialized countries, maternal deaths in developing countries still account for a dramatically higher proportion of all deaths of women in their reproductive years. In Bangladesh, Egypt, India and Indonesia, for instance, more than one out of every five deaths among women in their childbearing years are related to pregnancy. By contrast, in the United States, only one out of every 200 deaths among women of reproductive age is a maternal death (Maine 1991).

While maternal mortality thus appears to be another of the scourges of poverty, historical evidence demonstrates that its relationship to socioeconomic development and to household and community resources is strikingly different from that of almost every other major cause of death that afflicts the developing world. For example, infant and child mortality in the United States and Europe declined dramatically between 1900 and 1930 because of very significant improvements in nutrition and sanitation that accompanied broad-based socioeconomic development. However, during this same period, maternal mortality did not decline (Loudon 1991). The key difference was that, while the causes of infant death are extremely sensitive to environmental factors, the majority of obstetric complications that cause maternal deaths cannot be averted simply by improving women's overall health status, nutrition or hygiene (Loudon 1991).

Consequently, the aspects of socioeconomic development that drastically reduced infant and child mortality by improving basic health status actually had very little effect on maternal mortality. It was not until the mid-1930s, with the introduction of medical technologies to treat obstetric complications, that maternal mortality began to decline. Indeed, once antibiotics, blood transfusions, and improved surgical techniques used in cesarean sections and safe abortions became routinely available in the industrialized world, its maternal mortality all but disappeared (Loudon 1991).

However, for developing countries mired in economic crisis and facing a wholly different set of cultural and political constraints, the routes to lower infant and maternal mortality taken by industrialized countries in the first half of this century now hold little promise. Those routes will have to be short-circuited. For infant and child survival, a clear course has already been charted. Primary Health Care (PHC) is the strategy that has been designed and promoted in a concerted effort to bypass the long process of general economic development by concentrating immediately and directly on the factors of nutrition and infection so influential in child survival.

But history and a growing body of data about women's reproductive health teach us that PHC alone is not the solution for preventing maternal mortality in the developing world. Without widespread access to emergency medical care to treat the most common life-threatening obstetric complications, no amount of PHC will substantially improve a woman's chance of safely giving birth.

The challenge then is to zero in on a set of realistic, cost-effective actions that can substantially reduce maternal mortality in developing countries without awaiting the huge transformation in health care systems and physical infrastructure that, in industrialized countries, made possible the widespread availability of emergency medical care and with it, the virtual elimination of maternal mortality. To do this, we first need to evaluate the most important causes of maternal deaths in developing countries and then make a realistic assessment of what we know about how those deaths can be prevented.

### The Causes and Cures of Maternal Mortality

By definition, a maternal death can only occur when three events happen in sequence: (1) a woman becomes pregnant, (2) she develops obstetric complications, and (3) the complications result in death.[2] This implies three points of intervention: preventing pregnancy, preventing the development of complications and preventing complications from resulting in death. As we show in the two sections that follow, preventing pregnancy will reduce maternal mortality mainly by reducing the sheer number of times that women run the risk of obstetric complications. However, the primary aim of the Safe Motherhood Initiative is not to stop women from having children; rather, it is to ensure that when women choose to have children they can do so safely. Contrary to the intuition of many in the public health field, it is in third point of intervention, the treatment of obstetric complications, and not in their prevention, that the best hope for the rapid elimination of maternal mortality lies.

*Treatment and Prevention of Obstetric Complications.* Maternal deaths can be classified according to their immediate medical causes as "direct" or "indirect" obstetric deaths. Indirect obstetric deaths are those due to pre-existing medical conditions such as malaria, hepatitis or anemia, which are made worse by the pregnancy. In developing countries, these account for 25 percent of all maternal deaths. Direct obstetric deaths are those due to complications of pregnancy, delivery or the postpartum period, of which the most important are hemorrhage, induced abortion, hypertension, infection, and obstructed labor. The vast majority of maternal deaths—75 percent—are direct obstetric deaths. Using data from eleven population-based studies, the relative importance of the different complications can be estimated as shown in Figure 7.1.

FIGURE 7.1 Medical Causes of Direct Obstetric Deaths in Developing Countries

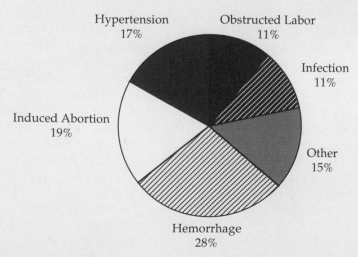

Source: Deborah Maine, *Safe Motherhood Programs: Options and Issues.*, New York, NY: CPFH, Columbia University, 1991.

For over half a century, we have had the technology to deal effectively with these medical conditions. That technology is relatively simple. It includes blood transfusions for hemorrhage, antibiotics for infection, and cesareans for obstructed labor. Although there are some techniques that lay people can use to slow the progress of these complications, only emergency medical treatment can actually save most lives once complications have developed (Winikoff et al. 1991).

In countries suffering high maternal mortality rates, such emergency obstetric care is scarce (or nonexistent) and costly. Conventional wisdom in the public health field would suggest that, under such circumstances, the most efficient way to provide emergency services would be to screen out those women most likely to develop complications and take steps to ensure that emergency care is available when they deliver.

Sadly, in the case of obstetric complications, screening turns out to be both inefficient and ineffective. The problem is that we do not know why obstetric complications develop in the great majority of cases, and there are often no early warning signals that an emergency complication is likely to occur. Thus, most complications occur in low-risk women who would not be identified through screening (Maine 1991).

Certainly there are women who are at higher risk for developing complications because of such factors as physical stature (related to cephalopelvic disproportion and, therefore, to the risk of obstructed labor), age and parity, or preexisting conditions such as diabetes and hypertension. Even though such women are more likely to develop complications than are women without any risk factors, the vast majority of high-risk women will still have normal deliveries.

Hence, screening programs have poor predictive power: Any attempt to screen out women likely to develop obstetric complications will result in a high number of both false positives (high-risk women who deliver normally) and false negatives (low-risk women who develop life-threatening complications). This is demonstrated by a study undertaken in 1971–75 at the Kasongo health center in Zaire (Kasongo Project Team 1984). All pregnant women who came to the clinic were evaluated for their risk of developing obstetric complications. Women with a poor obstetric history were found to be ten times as likely as women without such a history to have obstructed labor. Nevertheless, of 156 women determined to be high-risk based on screening, only fifteen (9.6 percent) actually had obstructed labor. Moreover, those fifteen high-risk women ultimately accounted for only 29 percent of the total cases of obstructed labor at Kasongo. Thus over two-thirds of the cases of obstructed labor were among low-risk women who were not and could not have been identified through screening.

Data from Guatemala presented at the NCIH Conference by Alfred Bartlett tell a similarly pessimistic story about screening. In his project, maternal risk factors associated with over 80 percent of all interpartum and day-one neonatal deaths were identified through retrospective studies. However, a screening program using these risk factors would end up identifying 70 percent of all pregnant women as being at high risk and referring three women for every hospital bed, thereby overwhelming the referral and emergency care systems (Bartlett 1991).

Not only do we lack feasible tests for predicting in advance which women in any given population will require emergency treatment, it appears that even a woman's overall health status has surprisingly little to do with the chance of developing a complication. Thus PHC programs aimed at improving the general health status of all women in a community have not been shown to lead to any substantial reduction in the incidence of complications in that community. This is even true when the PHC program includes prenatal care specifically designed to prevent and/or predict serious complications at delivery. For example, a prospective study of pregnancy outcome was conducted in a rural area of Gambia that had no facility for treatment of serious complications anywhere nearby. The women in the study received high-quality prenatal care: They were visited once a month, they had all illnesses treated, and their urine was checked for signs of toxemia. Nevertheless, they experienced an astronomically high level of maternal mortality (twenty-two maternal deaths per 1,000 live births)— deaths which the researchers felt could only have been prevented if there had been access to emergency treatment facilities (Greenwood et al. 1987).

In fact, once a serious complication has developed, even a woman in superb physical condition will have little chance of survival without access to emergency medical care. One striking piece of research that tends to prove this point is a study done on maternal mortality among a religious sect in the United States called the Faith Assembly of God (Kaunitz 1984). Its members are well-educated, well-fed and relatively wealthy. However, they do not use modern medical services even in the case of emergency. Among the Faith Assembly in 1983, there were 872 maternal deaths per 100,000 live births, compared to only eight deaths per 100,000 live births for the United States as a whole. In fact, the level of maternal mortality for this sect was higher than in contemporary urban India, and comparable to rural India.

This is not to say that prenatal care, improved nutrition, and proper hygiene are useless and irrelevant. Certainly these can be important in averting some number of "indirect" obstetric deaths by preventing and treating underlying diseases. It would also be absurd to suggest, for example, that a severely anemic woman is just as likely to survive a hemorrhage as a woman with an adequate blood count. On the other hand, if untreated, a major hemorrhage will kill anyone, anemic or not. In fact, given what we know about the most common life-threatening obstetric

TABLE 7.1 Estimated Average Interval from Onset to Death for
Major Obstetric Complications

| Complication | Hours | Days |
|---|---|---|
| Hemorrhage | | |
|   Postpartum | 2 | |
|   Antepartum | 12 | |
| Ruptured uterus | | 1 |
| Eclampsia | | 2 |
| Obstructed labor | | 3 |
| Infection | | 6 |

*Source:* Deborah Maine, et al., "Prevention of Maternal Deaths in Developing
Countries: Program Options and Practical Considerations," Paper presented at
the International Safe Motherhood Conferece, Nairobi, February 10-13, 1987

complications, it is clear that no amount of prevention or screening will
significantly reduce maternal mortality in the absence of emergency medical treatment.

Emergency medical care must therefore be the centerpiece of any plan
to ensure that women can give birth safely. The historical evidence from the
United States and Europe cited earlier indicates that the widespread availability of such care was the single most important factor in eliminating
maternal mortality in industrialized countries. The challenge facing the
international health community is to develop a plan to make the same basic
services available *now* under the radically different and immensely varied
conditions that prevail in the parts of the world that still suffer shockingly
high levels of maternal death.

*Program Priorities.* This brief review of the medical causes of maternal
mortality suggests certain broad priorities for Safe Motherhood programs
(Maine 1991).

### • Priority One: Ensure Access to Medical Treatment for Obstetric Emergencies

The chance of surviving an obstetric complication is excellent if a woman
receives medical care in time. For most complications, "in time" is a matter
of hours or days, not minutes. While a serious hemorrhage can kill a woman
in less than an hour, in many cases women arrive at hospitals alive after
bleeding for much longer. And for the other common complications—
infection, obstructed labor, eclampsia—there are usually several days be-

tween the time the condition becomes obvious and death, as shown in Table 7.1 (Maine et al. 1987).

While these are only general estimates of average time intervals, they illustrate an extremely important point: To save the lives of the vast majority of women who develop obstetric complications we do *not* need to build a hospital in every village and hamlet and insist that all women deliver there. We do, however, need to assist communities in developing plans to ensure that, when a complication does develop, quick action can and will be taken to reach emergency medical treatment.

In that connection, it is useful to analyze separately each of three steps that must be taken in order for a woman to get life-saving treatment: (1) there must be a decision to seek medical care for a woman who has developed a complication, (2) she must reach an appropriate medical facility, and (3) once at the facility she must receive adequate care (Thaddeus and Maine 1990). Delay at any one of these three stages can spell death. Consequently, any effective Safe Motherhood program must have elements addressing all three.

Obviously, every community has its own unique geographic and environmental obstacles, cultural conditions, administrative barriers, and economic constraints. However, certain general suggestions for improving access to emergency obstetric care are applicable almost everywhere that maternal mortality is high.

*Improve emergency treatment for obstetric complications in existing referral facilities.* At present, women with complications often manage to reach a hospital only to die there for lack of adequate care. In many developing countries hospitals are unable to treat common obstetric complications due to a lack of supplies, of properly trained personnel, and of good management. Thus the first requirement is to improve the quality of existing facilities so that they can provide at least the following "essential obstetric functions" identified by WHO (1986):

- perform cesarean sections
- administer anesthesia
- give blood transfusions
- perform vacuum extractions
- perform manual removal of placentas
- carry out suction curettage for incomplete abortion
- insert intrauterine devices
- perform contraceptive sterilizations

This program priority is listed first because, without the availability of adequate emergency care, many other program options, such as the implementation of referral and transport systems or training in early recognition of complications, are truly useless.

*Upgrade peripheral facilities and services to provide obstetric first aid.* There is much that can be done in peripheral facilities to improve the chance that a woman will survive once she does reach the hospital. These measures include starting antibiotics for women with obstructed labor or premature rupture of the membranes, starting a drip of plasma-expander and oxytocic drugs for women with hemorrhage, and administering sedatives for women with eclampsia.

Indeed, preliminary data from an experiment conducted in the Matlab area of Bangladesh and presented at the NCIH Conference, indicate that, given adequate support systems, community services provided by trained nurse-midwives could be associated with a substantial decline in maternal deaths (Fauveau et al. 1991). It should be emphasized that in this experiment the nurse-midwives were not working on their own. They had drugs and supplies; they were affiliated with long-established MCH/FP clinics; a maternity clinic with twenty-four-hour coverage by paramedics and female physicians was installed; and the referral chain was strengthened—beginning with round-the-clock availability of a boatman and helper to transport women, and ending with an ambulance to transport women from the clinic to the hospital. Under these circumstances, maternal deaths in the investigation area declined by more than half, while in the control area there was no decline.

*Inform the community about danger signs during pregnancy and delivery.* In many cases women reach the hospital when it is too late to save them. Often this happens because too much time has elapsed before a decision to seek treatment is made. Sometimes the delay is attributable to cultural reasons (as when a woman is forbidden to leave home without her husband's permission) or to logistical problems, or to a simple lack of recognition that a medical crisis is impending. Thus a critical element of Safe Motherhood strategies is information programs directed to the people in the community who make or approve the decision to seek medical care, including religious leaders, traditional birth attendants (TBAs), men and mothers-in-law.

*Work with the community to improve access to emergency care.* While a lack of vehicles and poor roads are problems in many areas, there are often ways in which the community can improve access to medical care in an emergency. For example, women's groups can put aside small amounts of money every month to be used in emergencies. Or community revolving funds can be set up to reimburse local vehicle owners for fuel if they will transport women to the hospital.

• *Priority Two: Reduce Exposure to the Risks of Unwanted Pregnancies*

*Provide accessible and acceptable family planning services.* Every time a woman becomes pregnant she runs the risk of developing fatal complications. By reducing the total number of pregnancies, family planning can reduce the number of maternal deaths. Thus, family planning will have a significant impact on maternal mortality rates if women want to have fewer children and can use contraception to reduce the total number of pregnancies they have.[3]

World Fertility Survey data collected in the period 1974–82 showed that, of currently married, fecund women of reproductive age, approximately 50 percent in Asia and Latin America and another 16 percent in Africa want no more children. But well over half of these women were not using an effective method of contraception, and so were still exposed to the risk of pregnancy. It has been estimated that if all women who said they want no more children were able to avoid future pregnancies, the drop in maternal deaths would be substantial: seventeen percent of all maternal deaths in Africa would be averted, 33 percent in Latin America, and 35 percent in Asia (Maine et al. 1987).

Family planning as an essential component of women's health services is treated separately in chapter "Familly Planning."

*Provide safe abortion services.* Once a woman is pregnant, there is little that can be done to prevent or predict the onset of most obstetric complications. There is one major exception: the complications resulting from illicit induced abortion. As discussed in detail in Chapter 6, a properly performed abortion is a safe procedure that rarely leads to any kind of medical complications. The horrifyingly high levels of maternal mortality attributable to induced abortion are the result of unsafe abortion techniques used under clandestine circumstances. Even with vigorous family planning programs, there will always be a demand for abortions. We know from painful experience in both developed and developing countries that criminalizing abortion does not stop abortion; rather, it endangers women's lives by forcing those who want abortions into the hands of unskilled practitioners operating under unsafe conditions (Dixon-Mueller 1990). We also know very well how to prevent deaths from abortion complications: make them legal, make them readily available, and make them safe.

• *Priority Three: Establish and Impove Other Maternal Health Services*

Prenatal care for mothers has been demonstrated to have a positive impact on the survival of their infants (Levano et al. 1985). But as the study from Gambia cited earlier graphically demonstrates, prenatal care will do little to lower maternal death rates unless women also have access to emergency medical treatment (Greenwood et al. 1987). Once emergency care is accessible, however, prenatal care and maternal health services can contribute significantly to reductions in maternal mortality. Thus, the third program priority includes the following:

*Establish and equip community maternities.* Community maternities, where local women can come once labor begins, can be run by a trained TBA or midwife. The use of such maternities would facilitate early recognition of complications and would make it easier to organize transportation to a medical facility in the event of an emergency. Moreover, in some places, scarce hospital beds are currently occupied by low-risk women who come to the hospital on their own accord (Bartlett 1991). If such women were screened out by hospital staff and referred to local maternities or birthing centers, hospital resources could be freed up for those in need of emergency obstetric treatment.

*Train TBAs to refer and treat women with complications.* Once a functioning treatment and referral system is in place, then it will make sense to train TBAs to refer women for treatment of complications. TBAs can also be trained, supplied and supervised to treat or provide simple first aid for some complications (e.g. hemorrhage and prolonged rupture of the membranes).

*Improve prenatal care services.* Although many women in developing countries receive some form of prenatal care, it is often of poor quality. For example, the supply of iron tablets and antimalarial drugs is insufficient, women are not asked about crucial symptoms, links to treatment centers are nonexistent, and staff members are not supervised. Once emergency medical care is available, improvement of prenatal care services may increase a woman's chance of surviving a complication both by improving her physical stamina and by facilitating early recognition of complications.

*Establish maternity waiting homes.* In some countries, women who live in remote rural areas can be several day's walk from the nearest road. Even when they reach the road, vehicles for transport to the hospital may be scarce. In these situations, gathering women together near the hospital during their last few weeks of pregnancy could be a great help in case of emergency. An alternative would be to establish community maternities beside the nearest main road. These could be built and maintained by the community, and women with normal deliveries could give birth there and then return home. In the event of an obstetric emergency, transportation to a hospital would be much more readily accessible.

## The Status of Women and Maternal Mortality

Maternal mortality is intimately related to the status of women in a society—but in a way that is different from almost every other health problem discussed in this book. Many aspects of women's poor health—for example, nutritional deficiencies, sexually transmitted diseases, and occupational injuries—are directly traceable to their low status in the home and society, so that improvements in these social factors can be expected to have a direct effect on women's health. By contrast, the usual indices of women's status (e.g., literacy, nutrition, employment) appear to have little association with the incidence of obstetric complications. For that reason, the program priorities discussed above address the immediate medical causes of maternal deaths rather than more general elements of women's status.

It is critical to recognize, however, that the *implementation* of a strategy centered around access to emergency obstetric care still depends fundamentally on the status of women in a society because it requires governments and communities to make a conscious and explicit political commitment to devote resources to ensuring the safety of women—and not just of children—during pregnancy and childbirth. That, in turn, requires a society and its members to value women and their health for their own sake.

Of course there are some non-medical steps related to women's status that can influence maternal mortality levels and these should surely be part of a comprehensive Safe Motherhood Initiative. For example, raising the legal minimum age for marriage (and enforcing that law) can eliminate some high-risk deliveries by decreasing the incidence of pregnancy among girls whose pelvises are not yet mature. Similarly, some laws or customs prevent women from obtaining contraception if they are unmarried or if they do not have their husbands' permission; others prevent women from leaving home to seek emergency treatment without their husbands' permission or without appropriate male escorts. Changing these laws and practices can contribute to a reduction in maternal mortality. Still, the vast majority of maternal deaths will be prevented only when emergency obstetric care is made widely available.

Put bluntly, the improvement of women's status along parameters such as equality in education, employment, or legal rights is virtually important for many reasons, not least of which is women's overall health. But we can not delude ourselves into assuming that such advances will automatically cause maternal mortality to disappear. A dramatic reduction in maternal deaths will happen only when there has been the explicit decision to make emergency obstetric care accessible to all women. Yet whether or not a society makes that decision is itself a measure of women's status. Consequently, every comprehensive evaluation of the status of women in a society should properly include an assessment of their access to emergency obstetric care.

There is a another, analytically distinct way in which maternal mortality relates to the status of women. A key indicator of women's status is reproductive freedom—the right to choose freely the number and spacing of one's children. Typically, reproductive freedom is considered to be safeguarded by the right to contraception and safe abortion. But for many women, this is a hollow freedom if it does not also include the right to bear children safely. Based on our analysis, then, access to emergency obstetric care must be recognized as a crucial element of reproductive freedom and as an important index of the status of women in any society. Conceptualizing safe pregnancy and childbirth in this way helps keep the focus on maternal mortality as a political issue, since it is from the political arena that the support for an effective program to prevent maternal deaths must ultimately emerge.

## Midlife and Older Age

Infant mortality and maternal mortality are problems that plague primarily the developing world, embedded as they are in the tragic dynamics of poverty. But gender does not cease being an important influence on mortality when poverty ceases to be an all-consuming problem. In affluent countries, the most important causes of death for women are diseases that strike most often in midlife and older age: cardiovascular disease and cancer. While gender is obviously relevant to the life-style and environmental factors that can increase the risk for these diseases, gender is now also acknowledged to be a critical determinant of actions taken by the medical community in two key areas: research and clinical treatment.

### Research

Gender bias taints medical research in multiple ways. This has been documented in the United States, and we will use that country as our example since there is little reason to believe that it is unusual in this regard. First, the proportion of resources spent on women's health problems is shockingly low. Every year the U.S. federal government alone spends more than $8 billion on medical research. Yet the National Institutes of Health (NIH) determined that in 1987 only 13.5 percent of this funding ($778 million) was devoted to health issues of particular importance to women (Kirschstein 1991).[4]

Among the diseases allocated a disproportionately low share of resources is breast cancer, which will strike one in ten American women sometime in their lives but receives only $77 million, less than 1 percent of all research dollars—and of that, only $17 million is spent on basic research on the disease (Lloyd 1990; Women's Health Research 1991).

Even in research on diseases that affect both men and women, gender bias regularly skews the outcome. One serious problem is that women are routinely excluded from clinical studies of the very diseases that most often claim their lives. Physicians treating women are thus forced to extrapolate from findings of studies conducted solely on men, even when there is no basis for believing that such extrapolation is clinically appropriate.

Cardiovascular disease is the most glaring example. It kills half a million women in the United States every year (more than twice the number who succumb to all forms of cancer combined). According to the National Center for Health Statistics, one in nine women aged 45–64 has some form of cardiovascular disease, and that ratio reaches one in three at age 65 and over. More than 90,000 women die of strokes each year compared to 59,061 men. And of the 520,000 heart attack deaths each year, approximately 257,000 are women. In fact, half of all women age 55–74 have high cholesterol, putting them at risk for heart attack and stroke (Dingell 1990). In addition, there is evidence that in significant ways, cardiovascular disease in women differs from the same disease in men (AMA 1991).

Despite this overwhelming evidence of the importance of cardiovascular disease in women's mortality, almost all of the significant studies on its causes and treatment have been done solely on men. For example, the Physician Health Study, which demonstrated the effectiveness of daily low doses of aspirin in preventing cardiovascular disease, involved 22,071 men and no women. The Multiple Risk Factor Intervention Trials (the "Mr. FIT" study), which evaluated life-style factors related to cholesterol and the development of heart disease, involved 15,000 men and no women (Women's Health Research 1991).

## Clinical Treatment

Recent studies have documented that gender is often a significant factor in clinical decision making involving heart disease, with men receiving more diagnostic procedures and more aggressive treatment (Ayanian and Epstein 1991; Steingart et al. 1991). Summarizing this and other evidence, the American Medical Association's Council on Ethical and Judicial Affairs recently issued a report in which it concluded that gender bias inappropriately affects access to and use of medical care in this country (AMA 1991).

For example:

- A study on data from 1981–1985 showed that women undergoing renal dialysis were approximately 30 percent less likely than men to receive a cadaver kidney transplant. The discrepancy remained even after controlling for age; indeed, for the age group 46–60 years, women had only one-half the chance of receiving a transplant.
- Although men and women with similar cigarette-smoking practices have essentially the same risk of lung cancer, certain diagnostic tests for the disease were ordered twice as often for men as for women.
- A 1987 study showed that cardiac catheterizations (a procedure necessary for coronary bypass surgery) were ordered far more often for men than for women. Interestingly, of patients whose exercise radionuclide scans were abnormal, men were 6.5 times more likely than women to be referred for catheterization; while women were twice as likely as men to have their symptoms attributed to somatic, psychiatric or other non cardiac causes.

The AMA Council concluded that part of the problem in treating women heart patients was that the lack of research done specifically on women has led to a failure to develop appropriate diagnostic criteria and treatment for them. However, with respect to all three diseases cited in their report— kidney disease, lung cancer, and cardiovascular disease—the AMA ultimately concluded that gender does indeed play an *inappropriate* role in physicians' decision making. They speculated that the gender disparities that result in preferential treatment for men may be fueled by a "general perception that men's social-role obligations . . . [and] their contribution to society are greater than women's" (AMA 1991; 561).

The undervaluation of women is therefore a prime factor in women's health at every stage of the life cycle and in every part of the world. Although precious little has been written about the health of elderly women in the developing world, where a much smaller percentage of the population is over age 60 (UN 1991), demographic trends indicate that as the populations in these countries age, women's mortality profile will come to look increasingly like that of the United States (AARP 1991). Thus the resolution of the controversies that surround the health of older women in the U.S. today may have significant ramifications for the health of women in the developing world tomorrow.

In the United States, gender bias in medicine has now become a decidedly political issue. The Women's Health Equity Act of 1991 (H.R. 1161, S. 514) is a comprehensive piece of legislation, now being considered in the U.S. Congress, that is designed to address these and other aspects of inequality and neglect in women's health care. Its significance lies not only in its substantive provisions, but in the recognition by some of America's most powerful policy makers that women's health and lives will be given appropriate attention only when gender becomes an explicit element in the elaborate process by which the enormous financial and human resources available to American medicine are distributed.

## Conclusion

Whether we speak of children, mothers or elderly women, whether we focus on the most desperately poor parts of the globe or its most affluent populations, one thread binds all women together: gender. Gender quietly, insidiously, skews the way that households, health systems and governments allocate the resources that profoundly influence women's health. The bias against women is rarely overt or even fully intentional; thus its effects creep into health and social policies without discussion or plan. In this sense women's mortality is less often the legacy of deliberate or malicious actions than of a long history of neglect. To reverse that tragic legacy, the health community must take the lead by making gender an explicit part of its own efforts to address mortality in every part of the world.

## Notes

1. WHO defines a maternal death as "the death of a woman while pregnant or within 42 days of termination of pregnancy, irrespective of the duration or site of the pregnancy, from any cause related to or aggravated by the pregnancy or its management, but not from accidental causes" (WHO 1977, 763-764).

2. These three "outcomes"—pregnancy, complications, death—can be understood as the final elements in a complex chain of events including biological, social and cultural factors. An analytical model for conceptualizing the intermediate and more remote causes of maternal mortality and their relationship to each other is developed in McCarthy and Maine (Forthcoming).

3. Family planning could help an individual woman avoid a high-risk pregnancy. But, at the population level, there is little evidence that family planning programs reduce the total number of pregnancies that are high-risk. Indeed, data from Matlab, Bangladesh suggest that family planning reduced maternal mortality by reducing the sheer number of pregnancies and not by selectively eliminating high-risk pregnancies. While the treatment area in Matlab with special family planning programs had a lower maternal mortality *rate* (maternal deaths per 100,000 women aged 15-44) than the control area, the two areas had very similar maternal mortality *ratios* (maternal deaths per 100,000 live births). (Koenig et al. 1988).

4. In arriving at the $778 million figure, NIH defined women's health issues to include: diseases or conditions *unique* to women or some subgroup of women; diseases or conditions *more prevalent* in women; diseases or conditions *more serious*

among women or some subgroup of women; diseases or conditions for which the *risk factors* are different for women or some subgroup of women; or diseases or conditions for which the *interventions* are different for women or some subgroup of women (Kirschstein 1991).

# References

American Association of Retired Persons. 1989. *Midlife and Older Women in Latin America and the Caribbean.* Washington, D.C.: Pan American Health Organization.

American Medical Association, Council on Ethical and Judicial Affairs. 1991. "Gender Disparities in Clinical Decision Making." *Journal of American Medical Association* 226:559-562.

Ayanian, John A. and Arnold M. Epstein. 1991. "Differences in the Use of Procedures Between Women and Men Hospitalized for Coronary Heart Disease." *New England Journal of Medicine* 325:221-225.

Bartlett, Alfred V. 1991. "More Risk than Resources: Evaluating Alternatives for Obstetric Risk Management in a Developing Population." Paper presented at the 18th Annual NCIH International Health Conference, Arlington, VA.

Chatterjee, Meera. 1990. *Indian Women: Their Health and Economic Productivity.* World Bank Discussion Papers No. 109. Washington, DC: The World Bank.

Commonwealth Secretariat. 1989. *Engendering Adjustment for the 1990s.* Report of a Commonwealth Expert Group on Women and Structural Adjustment. London: Commonwealth Secretariat.

Dingell, Deborah I. 1990. Testimony before the Subcommittee on Housing and Consumer Interests of the Select Committee on Aging of the United States House of Representatives. July 24, 1990.

Dixon-Mueller, Ruth. 1990. "Abortion Policy and Women's Health in Developing Countries." *International Journal of Health Services.* 20:297-314.

Fauveau, Vincent, Wojtyniak, Bogdan, Koenig, Michael, Chakroborty, J., and A.I. Chowdhury. 1989. "Epidemiology and Cause of Deaths Among Women in Rural Bangladesh," *International Journal of Epidemiology* 18:139-145.

Fauveau, Vincent, Stewart, K., Khan, S.A., and J. Chakroborty. 1991. "Mortality Impact of a Community-Based Maternity Care Programme in Rural Bangladesh." Paper presented at the 18th Annual NCIH International Health Conference, Arlington, VA.

Federal Bureau of Investigation, United States Department of Justice. 1989. *Uniform Crime Report for 1988.* Washington, D.C.: U.S. Government Printing Office.

Gómez, Elsa. 1991. "Sex Discrimination and Excess Female Mortality Among Children in the Americas." Paper presented at the 18th Annual NCIH International Health Conference, Arlington, VA.

Greenwood, A.M., Greenwood, B.M, Bradley, A.K., Williams, K., Shenton, F.C., Tulloch, S., Byass, P., and F.S.J. Oldfield. 1987. "A Prospective Survey of the Outcome of Pregnancy in Rural Areas of the Gambia." *Bulletin of the World Health Organization* 65: 635-643.

Heise, Lori. 1990. "Crimes of Gender." *Women's Health Journal*. ISIS. Latin American and Caribbean Women's Health Network. 17:3-11.

International Center for Research on Women. 1989. *Strengthening Women: Health Research Priorities for Women in Developing Countries*. Washington, DC: International Center for Research on Women.

Joekes, Susan, Lycette, Margaret, McGowan, Lisa, and Karen Searle. 1988. *Women and Structural Adjustment. Part II: Technical Document*. Washington, D.C.: International Center for Research on Women.

Kasongo Project Team. 1984. "Antenatal Screening for Fetopelvic Dystocias. A Cost-Effectiveness Approach to the Choice of Simple Indicators for Use by Auxiliary Personnel." *Journal of Tropical Medicine and Hygiene* 87:173-183.

Kaunitz, A.M., Spence, C., Danielson, T.S., Rochat, R.W., and D. Grimes. 1984. "Perinatal and Maternal Mortality in a Religious Group Avoiding Obstetric Care." *American Journal of Obstetrics and Gynecology*. 150: 826-831.

Kirschstein, Ruth L. 1991. "Research on Women's Health." *American Journal of Public Health* 81:291-293.

Koenig, Michael A. and S. D'Souza. 1986. "Sex Differences in Childhood Mortality in Rural Bangladesh." *Social Science and Medicine* 22(1):15-22.

Koenig, Michael A., Fauveau, Vincent, Chowdhury, A.I., Chakroborty, J., and M.A. Khan. 1988. "Maternal Mortality in Matlab, Bangladesh: 1976-85." *Studies in Family Planning*, March/April 1988, 19(2):69-80.

Law, Maureen, Maine, Deborah and Marie-Thérèse Feuerstein. 1991. *Safe Motherhood: Priorities and Next Steps*. United Nations Development Program.

Levano, K., Cunningham, F.G., Roark, M.C., Nelson, C.D., and M.L. Williams. 1985. "Prenatal Care and the Low Birth Weight Infant." *Obstetrics and Gynecology*. 66:1439-1444.

Lloyd, Marilyn. 1990. Statement of Honorable Marilyn Lloyd, Chairman of the Subcommittee on Aging and Consumer Interests of the Select Committee on Aging of the United States House of Representatives. July 24, 1990.

Loudon, Irvine. 1991. "On Maternal and Infant Mortality 1900-1960." *Social History of Medicine* 4:29-73.

Maine, Deborah. 1991. *Safe Motherhood Programs: Options and Issues*. New York: Center for Population and Family Health, Columbia University.

Maine, Deborah, Rosenfield, A., Kimball, A.M., Kwast, B., and S. White. 1987. "Prevention of Maternal Deaths in Developing Countries: Program Options and Practical Considerations." Paper presented at the International Safe Motherhood Conference, Nairobi, February 10-13, 1987.

McCarthy, James and Deborah Maine. "A Framework for Analyzing the Determinants of Maternal Mortality: Implications for Research and Programs." Forthcoming in *Studies in Family Planning*.

Ravindran, Sundari. 1986. *Health Implications of Sex Discrimination in Childhood: A Review Paper and an Annotated Bibliography*. Geneva: World Health Organization and UNICEF. WHO/UNICEF/FHE86.2.

Rochat, R.W. 1987. "Table 2: Estimated Lifetime Chance of Dying from Pregnancy-Related Causes, by Region, 1975-84." In A. Starrs (ed.), *Preventing the Tragedy of Maternal Deaths: A Report on the International Safe Motherhood Conference, Nairobi, February, 1987*. Washington, D.C.: World Bank.

Sivard, Ruth L. 1985. *Women... A World Survey.* Washington, D.C.: World Priorities.

Society for the Advancement of Women's Health Research. 1991. *Women's Health Research: Prescription for Change.* Annual Report January 1991.

Stein, Zena and Deborah Maine. 1986. "The Health of Women." *International Journal of Epidemiology* 15:303-305.

Steingart, Richard M., Packer, Milton, Hamm, Peggy, et al. 1991. "Sex Differences with the Management of Coronary Artery Disease." *New England Journal of Medicine* 325:226-230.

Thaddeus, Sereen and Deborah Maine. 1990. *Too Far to Walk: Maternal Mortality in Context.* New York: Columbia University Center for Population and Family Health.

Verbruggi, Lois M. and Deborah L. Wingard. 1987. "Sex Differentials in Health and Mortality." *Women and Health* 12:103-145.

Waldron, Ingrid. 1986. "What Do We Know About Causes of Sex Differences in Mortality: A Review of the Literature." *Population Bulletin of the United Nations* 18-1985:58-76.

Waldron, Ingrid. 1987. "Patterns and Causes of Excess Female Mortality Among Children in Developing Countries." *World Health Statistics Quarterly* 40:194-210.

Winikoff, Beverly, Carignan, Charles, Bernardik, Elizabeth, and P. Semeraro. 1991. *Medical Services to Save Mothers' Lives: Feasible Approaches to Reducing Maternal Mortality.* Population Council, Working Papers No. 4.

World Health Organization. 1986. *Essential Obstetric Functions at First Referral Level to Reduce Maternal Mortality: Report of a Technical Working Group, June 23-27, 1986.* Geneva: World Health Organization. (FHE/86.4).

World Health Organization. 1986. *Prevention of Maternal Mortality: Report of a World Health Organization Interregional Meeting, November 11-15, 1985.* Geneva. (FHE/86.1).

World Health Organization. 1977. "Definitions and Recommendations." In *Manual of the International Statistical Classification of Diseases, Injuries, and Causes of Death.* Vol. 1. Geneva.

United Nations. 1991. *The World's Women: Trends and Statistics: 1970-1990.* New York: United Nations.

United Nations Economic and Social Council, Commission on the Status of Women. 1990. *Development: Negative Effects of the International Economic Situation on the Improvement of the Status of Women.* Reprint of the Secretary General. E/CN.6/1990/3.

UNICEF. 1990. *The Girl Child: An Investment in the Future.* New York, NY: UNICEF.

# 8

## Violence Against Women: The Missing Agenda

*Lori Heise*

Violence against women is perhaps the most pervasive yet least recognized human rights abuse in the world. It is also a profound health problem sapping women's physical and emotional vitality and undermining their confidence—both vital to achieving widely held goals for human progress, especially in the developing world.

As yet there is no universal agreement on a definition of violence against women. At its most basic, gender violence includes any act of force or coercion that gravely jeopardizes the life, body, psychological integrity or freedom of women, in service of perpetuating male power and control.[1] Included here would be rape, battery, homicide, incest, psychological abuse, forced prostitution, trafficking in women, sexual harassment, genital mutilation, and dowry-related murder. Also relevant would be various forms of medical violence such as gratuitous cesarean sections and forced sterilization.

A more expansive definition would move beyond individual acts of violence to include forms of institutionalized sexism that severely compromise the health and well-being of women. This wider framework includes discrimination against girl children in food and medical care, female feticide, lack of access to safe contraception and abortion, and laws and social policy that perpetuate female subordination.

This chapter explores a subset of these abuses to help frame violence against women as an issue worthy of international action and concern. It details what we know about the prevalence and impact of different forms of violence and relates violence to issues already high on the international health agenda. Most importantly, it documents a vast amount of energy Third World women are investing to mobilize against abuse. In multiple ways, women are saying that safety is a priority for them, and they are acting on that conviction—setting up crisis centers, seeking legal reform, and challenging the sexist attitudes and practices that undergird male violence.

## Domestic Violence

The most endemic form of violence against women is wife abuse, or more accurately, abuse of women by intimate male partners. Study after study has documented severe and ongoing woman abuse in almost every culture of the world save a handful of small-scale societies where wife beating occurs only rarely[2] (Levinson 1989; Counts et al. 1991). While surveys document that women also hit men on occasion, it is usually in self-defense. The vast majority of injuries resulting from domestic violence are borne by women (Gelles and Cornell, 1990).

It is hard to make accurate cross-cultural estimates of wife assault because only a few countries have attempted a nationwide accounting. But the data that do exist give cause for concern (See Table 8.1). In the United States, for example, former Surgeon General C. Everett Koop (1989) estimated that three to four million American women are battered each year; roughly half of them are single, separated or divorced. Population-based surveys suggest that between 21 and 30 percent of U.S. women will be beaten by a partner at least once in their lives (National Committee 1989). Battering also tends to escalate and become more severe over time. Almost half of all batterers beat their partners at least three times a year (Straus et al. 1980).

A similar country-wide estimate is available for Colombia, which recently completed a national study of family violence as part of its Demographic and Health Survey (DHS Colombia 1991). The study shows that one out of every five Colombian women have been beaten by a partner; one out of every three have been emotionally or verbally abused. In Papua New Guinea (PNG) comparable figures are even higher: 67 percent of rural women and 56 percent of urban women have been physically abused, according to a survey conducted by the PNG Law Reform Commission (Bradley 1988a). And in Norway, 25 percent of female gynecology patients have been physically or sexually abused by their mates (Schei and Bakketeig 1989).

The health consequences of such violence are immense. In the United States, battery is the greatest single cause of injury to women, accounting for more injury than auto accidents, muggings and rape combined (Stark and Flitcraft 1991). It also provides the primary context for many other health problems. Battered women are four to five times more likely to require psychiatric treatment and five times more likely to attempt suicide than

TABLE 8.1 Prevalence of Domestic Violence, Selected Studies*

---

- In Papua New Guinea, 67 percent of rural women and 56 percent of urban women have been victims of wife abuse, according to a national survey conducted by the PNG Law Reform Commission (Bradley 1988a).
- In a detailed family planning survey of 733 women in the Kissi district of Kenya, 42 percent said they were beaten regularly by their husbands (Raikes 1990).
- In one study of 109 households in an Indian village, 22 percent of higher caste husbands and 75 percent of Scheduled Castes (lower) husbands admitted to beating their wives. The Scheduled Caste wives reported that they were "regularly beaten" (Mahajan 1990).
- A survey done in Santiago, Chile indicates that 80 percent of women have suffered physical, emotional or sexual abuse by a male partner or relative; 63 percent report that they are currently being abused (Moltedo 1989).
- A statistical survey conducted in Nezahualcoyotl, a city adjacent to Mexico City, found that one in three women had been victims of family violence; 20 percent report blows to the stomach during pregnancy (Valdez Santiago and Shrader Cox 1991).
- A study using children as informants reported that 57 percent of wives in San Salvador were beaten by their husbands (Cañas 1990)

---

* The studies cited are the most reliable surveys currently available.

nonbattered women (Stark and Flitcraft 1991). About a third of battered women suffer major depressions, and some go on to abuse alcohol or drugs.[3] Studies show, however, that most battered women begin to drink only after the onset of abuse, suggesting that women are using alcohol to escape an intolerable situation (Amaro et al. 1990; Stark et al. 1981)

Data from developing countries also highlight a link between violence and health. A study from Lima, Peru documents that one out of every three women in the city's emergency rooms are victims of domestic violence (Byerly 1984). A United Nations case study on wife abuse in China reports that domestic violence is the cause of 6 percent of serious injuries and death in Shanghai (Wu Han 1986). And 18 percent of *all* wives surveyed in urban areas of Papua New Guinea had received hospital treatment for injuries inflicted by their husbands. As Christine Bradley (1988b) of the country's law-reform committee observes, "In PNG, where many women have enlarged spleens due to malaria, a single blow can kill them." Health professionals have not begun to contemplate what other conditions may act synergistically to exacerbate the impact of violence in Third World countries.

Indeed, one should not underestimate the lethality of violence against women. Through both forced suicide and murder, gender violence kills. After reviewing evidence from the United States, for example, Stark and Flitcraft (1989) conclude that "abuse may be the single most important precipitant for female suicide attempts yet identified."[4] One out of every four suicide attempts by women are preceded by abuse, as are half of all attempts by African American women (Stark 1984). A cross-cultural survey of suicide by Counts (1987) draws the same conclusion, positing that in some Oceanic societies, female suicide operates as a culturally recognized behavior that enables the "politically powerless...to revenge themselves on those who have made their lives intolerable." Counts finds support for her argument in cultures from Africa, Peru, Papua New Guinea and other Melanesian islands. Among Fijian Indian families, for example, 41 percent cite marital violence as the cause of their loved one's suicide (Haynes 1984). Nor is suicide an inconsequential form of death. In Sri Lanka—a country with reasonably accurate mortality statistics—the rate of suicide death in young women aged fifteen to twenty-four is five times that from infectious diseases and fifty-five times the rate of obstetric related deaths (WHO 1985).

The relationship between domestic violence and homicide, however, may be even more profound. In Bangladesh, for example, assassination of wives by husbands accounts for 50 percent of *all* murders (Stewart 1989). In Canada, 62 percent of women murdered in 1987 died as a result of domestic violence (Canadian Centre 1988). And in Papua New Guinea, almost three-fourths of women murdered were killed by their husbands (Bradley 1988). Studies from a variety of cultures confirm that when women kill men, it is often in self-defense, usually after years of persistent and escalating abuse (Browne 1987; Walker 1989). Ironically, in the United States and elsewhere, a woman is more likely to be assaulted, raped or killed by a male partner than by any other assailant (Browne and Williams 1989).

### Dowry Deaths

On the Indian subcontinent, tradition has combined with greed to forge a particularly deadly form of wife abuse known locally as "bride burning" or "dowry deaths." Decades ago, dowry referred to the gifts that a woman received from her parents upon marriage. Now dowry has become an important part of premarital negotiations and refers to the wealth that the bride's parents must pay to the groom and his family as part of the marriage settlement.

Once a gesture of love, ever-escalating dowry now represents a real financial burden to parents of unwed daughters. Increasingly, dowry is being seen as a "get rich quick" scheme by prospective husbands, with young brides suffering severe abuse if ongoing demands for money or goods are not met. In its most severe form, dowry harassment ends in the woman's suicide or her murder, freeing the husband to pursue a more lucrative arrangement.

Dowry deaths are notoriously undercounted, largely because the husband and his relatives frequently try to disguise the murder as a suicide or an accident, and the police are loathe to get involved. A frequent scam is to set the woman alight with kerosene and then claim she died in a kitchen accident—hence the term bride-burning. In 1990, the police officially recorded 4,835 dowry deaths in all of India, but the Ahmedabad Women's Action Group estimates that 1,000 women may be burned alive annually in Gujurat State alone (Kelkar 1991; Crossette 1989).

A quick look at mortality data from India reveals the reasonableness of this claim. In both urban Maharashtra and greater Bombay, one out of every five deaths among women fifteen to forty-four are due to "accidental burns." For the younger age group fifteen to twenty-four, the proportion is one out of four (Karkal 1985). Also, female deaths due to burns have been increasing since 1979, corresponding to the recent commercialization of dowry demands (Pawar 1990). Clearly, homicides and suicides are being recorded as "accidents" instead of intentional injuries. Women advocates from India are quick to point out, however, that "bride-burning" is but the most visible and sensational symbol of a continuum of violence. More hidden and less newsworthy is the everyday battering that plagues women everywhere.

### Rape and Sexual Assault

On July 10, 1991, seventy-one teenage girls were raped by their male classmates, and nineteen others died in a night of dormitory mayhem at St. Kizito's coed boarding school in Meru, Kenya. Apparently the boys attacked the girls after the girls refused to join them in a protest strike against the school's headmaster. In a report splashed across the front page of the *Kenya Times*, the newspaper called the rape of St. Kitzito coeds a "common occurrence" sanctioned by the principal and his staff. The paper quoted the deputy principal as saying, "The boys never meant any harm against the girls. They just wanted to rape" (Perlez 1991).

These are the attitudes that women around the world must face when seeking justice and compassion after being sexually violated. Rape is either seen as a man's prerogative or a crime against the honor of a woman's family or husband, not a violation against the woman. In fact, the Latin root of rape means "theft," and most cultural responses to such violence emphasize reclaiming the woman's lost value, not prosecuting the offender. In many countries—including Fiji, the Philippines, Thailand, Mexico, and Peru—the cultural "solution" to rape is to have the young woman marry her rapist, thus legitimizing the union and preserving the family honor.[5]

Due to the stigma and shame associated with rape, sexual assault may be one of the most underreported crimes. But even the official, undercounted figures are chilling. In the United States, the Department of Justice reports that every hour, sixteen women confront rapists, and every six minutes a woman is raped. Studies indicate that one in five American women has been the victim of a completed rape (Sorenson et al. 1988). Researchers estimate that only 34 percent of stranger rapes and 13 percent of acquaintance rapes are reported (Koss et al. 1990).

TABLE 8.2 Statistics on Sexual Crimes, Selected Countries[a]

|                  | Percent of perpetrators known to victim | Percent of survivors 15 years and under | Percent of survivors 9 years and under |
| --- | --- | --- | --- |
| Lima, Peru       | 60      | —       | 18      |
| Malaysia         | 68      | 58      | 18[b]   |
| Mexico City      | 67[c]   | 36      | 23      |
| Panama City      | 63      | 40      | —       |
| Papua New Guinea | —       | 47      | 13[e]   |
| United States    | 80      | 33[f]   | 11[g]   |

[a] Studies include rape and sexual assults such as attempted rape and molestation.
[b] Percentage of survivors age six and younger
[c] Data from *Carpeta Basica*. 1991. Mexico City: Procurador de Justicia del Distrito Federal de Mexico
[d] Percentage of survivors age 10 and younger.
[e] Percentage of survivors age 7 and younger.
[f] Percentage of survivors age 17 and younger.
[g] Percentage of survivors age 12 and younger.

*Source:* Malaysia data from (Consumer's Association 1988); Panama City data from (Perez 1990); Peru data from (Portugal 1988); Papua New Guinea data from (Brandley 1990); Mexico City data from (COVAC 1990); United States data from (Koss et al. 1990; Illinois Coalition 1991).

Estimates of rape incidence are even more speculative in the developing world, but many countries—including Bangladesh, India, Korea, Malaysia, and South Africa—have noted dramatic increases in reported rape in recent years.[6] Rates of rape in South Africa appear to outstrip even those in the United States. Police reports document 19,308 rapes in 1988, but the National Institute of Crime Prevention and the Rehabilitation of Offenders estimates that only one in twenty rapes are reported, bringing the true total closer to 386,160 (Russel 1991; Vogelman 1990). That figure averages one rape every minute and a half, or thirty-four rapes per 1,000 adult women compared to the U.S. rate of eighteen per 1,000 women.[7]

Studies around the world also demonstrate a remarkable consistency in the demographics of sexual assault. Contrary to popular perception, the majority of rape survivors know their assailants, a reality confirmed by studies in Malaysia, Mexico, Panama, Peru and the United States (see Table 8.2). Also, a large percentage of rapes (40 to 47 percent) are perpetrated against girls fifteen years or younger, with a shocking percentage against girls younger than nine (see Table 8.2). It may be that rapes of young girls are simply reported more often, but in the United States this is not the case: Girls under eighteen are less likely to report their assault than older women (Ten Facts 1990).

Sexual assaults can cause physical injury and profound emotional trauma. A study of rape in urban and rural areas of Bangladesh, for example, reports that 84 percent of victims suffered severe injuries and/or unconsciousness, mental illness or death following the rape incident (Shamim 1985). Survivors also run the risk of becoming pregnant or contracting STDs, including AIDS. In Third World settings, the risk of unwanted pregnancy is high: Mexican rape crisis centers report 15 to 18 percent of their clients become pregnant because of the rape (COVAC 1990; CAMVAC 1985). Women raped in Mexico have more options than most—a new law requires judges to rule on a rape survivor's request for an abortion within five working days of her appeal. Thousands of others who live in countries where abortion is illegal must suffer the double humiliation of being raped and then having to bear the rapist's child.

Rape survivors also exhibit a variety of trauma-induced symptoms including sleep and eating disturbances, depression, feelings of humiliation, anger and self-blame, nightmares, fear of sex, and inability to concentrate. One study from the United States found that rape victims were nine times more likely than nonvictims to have attempted suicide, and twice as likely to experience a major depression (Kilpatrick 1990).

Perhaps most devastating, however, are the cultural consequences of rape in societies that highly value a woman's virginity. Many Asian, Middle Eastern, and African cultures equate a young woman's worth with her virginity. As Vincent Faveau (1989) describes in his ground-breaking study of injury in rural Bangladesh, "Even when women are victims, a premarital sexual relation is said to spoil something intrinsic in their physical and moral person.... Their ruined reputation cannot be amended." Faveau cites numerous case studies of women who were beaten, murdered or driven to suicide because of the dishonor that rape or illegitimate pregnancy brought upon their family. In Faveau's study, deaths from injury (suicide, homicide, assault, and complications from induced abortion) were 130 percent greater among unmarried versus married teenage girls, reinforcing his qualitative data on deliberate violence toward girls who are raped or become pregnant outside of marriage (Acasadi 1990).

## Violence Against Refugee Women

Such cultural attitudes combine with the perils of flight, to make sexual violence a particularly devastating experience for female refugees. It is estimated that 75 percent of the world's eighteen million refugees are women and girls (Overhagen 1990). Unfortunately, repeated and often brutal rapes are an all-too-common aspect of the female refugee experience. Refugee women are subject to sexual violence and abduction at every step of their escape, from flight to border crossings to life in the camps. United Nations High Commission on Refugees (UNHCR) data on violence against Vietnamese boat people, for example, indicate that 39 percent of women are abducted and/or raped by pirates while at sea. These statistics likely underestimate the problem given women's reluctance to admit violation and the difficulty of documenting abductions (Mollica and Son 1989).

Even when the immediate threat of rape is gone, the stigma of violation lingers on. Many refugee women who have been raped are shunned by their families and isolated from other members of their community. As Richard Mollica (1989), director of Harvard's Program in Refugee Trauma, observes, "In Southeast Asian cultures, a husband will often reject his wife if she has been sexually violated because she is perceived as having been "used," "violated," or "left over" by the rapist(s)." A Vietnamese proverb regarding rape summarizes this sentiment: "Someone ate out of my bowl and left it dirty."

Refugee workers also note a link between rape and subsequent domestic violence, especially by men whose wives or daughters have been raped in their presence. As Amy Friedman (1991), of the Washington-based Refugee Women in Development (Ref-WID), observes, "Refugee men often feel victimized by their experience and feel that they have failed in their obligation to protect their families. This vulnerability, compounded by the frustration of resettlement, often leads refugee men to resort to domestic violence to recover power and control." Ref-WID has developed and tested a training program to help U.S. service providers identify and respond to domestic violence within the refugee community.

## Female Circumcision

In parts of Africa and the Middle East, young girls suffer another form of violation, known euphemistically as female circumcision. More accurately, this operation—which removes all or part of the clitoris and other external genitalia—is a life-threatening form of mutilation. In its most severe form, known as infibulation, the clitoris and both labia are removed, and the two sides of the vulva are sewn together except for a small opening to allow urine and menstrual blood to pass. According to the World Health Organization, more than eighty-four million women alive today have undergone sexual surgery in Africa alone (Rushwan 1990).

While female circumcision has its origin in the male desire to control female sexuality, today a host of other beliefs sustains the practice. Many Moslems mistakenly believe that it is demanded by the Islamic faith, although it has no basis in the Koran. Others believe the operation will increase fertility, affirm femininity or prevent stillbirths. Ultimately, what drives the tradition is that men will not marry uncircumcised women, believing them to be promiscuous, unclean and sexually untrustworthy (Mohamud 1991).

The medical complications of circumcision can be severe. A study from Sierra Leone, for example, found that 83 percent of all women circumcised required medical attention sometime in their life for problems related to the procedure (Hosken 1988). Immediate risks include hemorrhage; tetanus and blood poisoning from unsterile and often primitive cutting implements (knife, razor blade or broken glass); and shock from the pain of the operation, which is carried out without anesthesia. In Sudan, where infibulation—the most extreme form of circumcision—is practiced, doctors estimate that 10 to 30 percent of young girls die from the operation, especially in areas where antibiotics are not available (Lightfoot-Klein 1989).

The long-term effects, in addition to loss of sexual feeling, include chronic urinary-tract infections, pelvic infections that can lead to sterility, painful intercourse, and severe scarring that can cause tearing of tissue and hemorrhage during childbirth. In fact, women who are infibulated must be cut open on their wedding night to make intercourse possible, and more cuts are necessary for the birth of a child. Among thirty-three infibulated mothers in Somalia's Benadir Hospital, all had to have extensive episiotomies during childbirth, their second-stage labor was five times longer than normal, and five of their babies died and twenty-one suffered oxygen deprivation due to the long and obstructed labor (Hosken 1988).

In recent years African women have begun to organize to combat circumcision and other traditional practices harmful to women and girls. In 1984, at a conference sponsored by the World Health Organization in Dakar, Senegal, groups joined together to form the Inter-African Committee on Traditional Practices Affecting the Health of Women and Children, an umbrella organization of twenty-two national committees working to eradicate genital mutilation. In the words of Berhane Ras Work, the consortium's president: "Female circumcision is a clear example of social violence which women have to bear in silence as a price for marriage and social identity."


## Discrimination Against Girl Children

While less overt, the preference for male offspring in many cultures can be as damaging and potentially fatal to females as rape or assault. The same sentiment that once motivated infanticide is now expressed in the systematic neglect of daughters—a neglect so severe that in India's Punjab state, girls aged two to four die at nearly twice the rate of boys (Das Gupta 1987).

"Eighteen goddess-like daughters are not equal to one son with a hump," goes a proverb in China, a country that shares its strong preference for male children with the rest of Asia and the Indian subcontinent. In these cultures and others, sons are highly valued because only they can perpetuate the family line and perform certain religious rituals. Even more important, sons represent an economic asset to the family and a source of security for parents in their old age.

Studies confirm that where preference for sons is strong, girls receive less food and inferior medical care and education. In rural Bangladesh, for example, malnutrition was found to be almost three times more common among girls than among boys (Bhatia 1985; Chen et al. 1981). Not surprisingly this discriminatory treatment shows up in mortality statistics for girls and women. Among forty-five developing countries for which recent data are available, there are only two where mortality rates for girls ages one to four are not higher than that of boys (UNICEF 1986).

In fact, the pressure to bear sons is so great in India, China and Korea that women have begun using amniocentesis and ultrasound as sex-selection devices to selectively abort female fetuses. Until protests forced them to stop, Indian sex-detection clinics boldly advertised that it was better to spend $38 now on terminating a girl than $3,800 later on her dowry. One study of amniocentesis in a large Bombay hospital found that 95.5 percent of fetuses identified as female were aborted (Ramanamma 1990).

## Women Fight Back

Women have not sat idle in the face of such abuse. Around the world they are organizing crisis centers, lobbying for legal reform, and fighting the sexism that underlines male violence.

Today, the vast majority of countries in Latin America, the Caribbean, Asia and the Pacific have at least a handful of nongovernmental organizations dedicated to changing public attitudes toward violence, and to providing services for victims of abuse. Some with more mature movements, such as Mexico, India, and Ecuador, have organized nationally to push for legal reform and to orchestrate major educational campaigns. A handful, including Brazil, Papua New Guinea, and Malaysia have initiated widespread reform and have marshalled considerable government support for services and public education. Feminists in Brazil, for example, have successfully lobbied for the creation of all-female police stations to assist victims of violence. Brazil now has roughly eighty-four such stations, and the country's new constitution requires the state to "create mechanisms so as to impede violence in the sphere of family relationships" (Pitanguy 1991).

Women's resistance to violence has taken many forms. In India, activists are using street theater to raise women's consciousness around dowry, wife beating and women's low status in society (Patel 1989). In Kingston, Jamaica, women have formed a "Women's Media Watch" that monitors the media, and agitates against imagery that contributes to sexual violence (Tribune Center 1991). And in San Juan de Miraflores, a shantytown of Lima, Peru, women carry whistles to summon other women in case of attack (Heise 1989). At least thirty developing countries also have shelters and/or crisis centers for survivors of violence, but most exist only in major urban centers.[8]

In Africa, organizing has focused more on genital mutilation than on other forms of abuse, although groups in Zimbabwe, Uganda, Nigeria, and Kenya have developed materials to raise awareness around wife beating and rape.[9] Some of the most innovative programs working to abolish female circumcision rely on mobilizing action at the grassroots. The National Association of Nigeria Nurses and Nurse-Midwives, for example, has orchestrated a series of regional workshops to train its own 60,000 members and other community leaders about the hazards of circumcision. Workshop members then develop a state plan of action, including health messages communicated through songs, comic books, and local theater groups (Adebajo 1991).

In recent years, individual country efforts have begun coalescing into a true international movement against gender violence. Through a series of regional and international conferences and networks, women have begun to share strategies and compare notes. Especially significant has been the contribution of Isis International, a women's resource center based in Santiago, Chile. With funding from the United Nations Fund for Women (UNIFEM), Isis has developed a computerized data base of information and organizations working against violence. The project's program directory lists 379 separate groups fighting violence in Latin America alone (Isis 1990a).

## A Call to Action

Despite the wealth of grassroots activity around violence there has been little recognition of the problem within mainstream development organizations, especially among those dedicated to health. The World Health Organization and a handful of nongovernmental organizations (NGOs), including the International Planned Parenthood Federation and the Population Crisis Committee, have supported efforts to eliminate female circumcision, but abuses such as battery, rape and incest have largely been ignored (The Canadian NGO, MATCH International is a notable exception). There are five compelling reasons, though, why the international health community should embrace the issue of gender violence and begin supporting research, services, and prevention activities designed to combat it.

### 1. Gender violence is a significant cause of morbidity and mortality among women.

A simple but powerful illustration of the cumulative impact of discrimination and violence on women's health comes from Amartya Sen, an Indian economist now teaching at Harvard University. Dr. Sen compared the sex ratios between women and men in countries where both sexes receive similar care, such as North America and Europe, to countries where females are highly discriminated against, as in China and India. In more egalitarian countries the female/male ratio is about 1.05 or 1.06, reflecting women's biological advantage. But in South Asia, West Asia, North Africa and China the ratio is typically .94 or lower. If countries in these regions had the 1.05 ratio typical in other parts of the world (including some of sub-Saharan Africa), the world would have 100 million more women alive today. In China alone, notes Dr. Sen, fifty million women are "missing," victims of female feticide, selective malnourishment of girls, lack of investment in women's health, and various forms of violence (Sen 1990).

## 2. Gender violence affects initiatives already high on the international health agenda.

*Safe Motherhood.* It is ironic that an international initiative on safe pregnancy and childbirth would include no mention of the "physical" safety of the mother and her child. Yet surveys suggest that pregnant mothers are prime targets for abuse. Preliminary results from a large, prospective study of battery during pregnancy in the United States indicate that one out of *every six* pregnant women are battered during their present pregnancy (McFarlane 1991). (The study, sponsored by the Centers for Disease Control, followed a stratified cohort of 1,200 white, African-American and Hispanic women for three years in Houston and Baltimore.) Other studies indicate that women battered during pregnancy run twice the risk of miscarriage and four times the risk of having a low-birth-weight baby compared with women who are not beaten (Stark et al. 1981; Bullock and McFarlane 1989) Low birth weight is a powerful predictor of a child's survival prospects in its first year of life (IOM 1985).

It is possible that battering during pregnancy would have an even greater impact on Third World mothers who are already malnourished and overworked. A survey of 342 randomly sampled women in Mexico City revealed that 20 percent of those battered reported blows to the stomach during pregnancy (Valdez Santiago and Shrader Cox 1991). Extrapolating these results to the rest of the population suggests that almost one million Mexican women are at risk for battering during pregnancy.[10] In another study of eighty battered women who sought judicial intervention against their partner in San Jose, Costa Rica, 49 percent report being beaten during pregnancy. Of these, 7.5 percent reported miscarriages due to the abuse (Ugalde 1988).

Violence may also be responsible for a sizeable, but yet unrecognized, portion of maternal deaths, especially among young unwed mothers. Fauveau and Blanchet (1989) report that in Matlab, Bangladesh, homicide and suicide—motivated by stigma over unwed pregnancy, beatings or dowry—accounted for 6 percent of all maternal deaths between 1976 and 1986.[11] The figure rises to 22 percent if one includes deaths due to botched abortions; many also related to shame over unwed pregnancies. Among all deaths of women aged fifteen to forty-four (not just maternal deaths), intentional injury accounts for 12.3 percent of deaths, with deaths due to homicide and suicide outnumbering those due to abortions.

*Child Survival.* Increasingly, UNICEF and other agencies involved with the Child Survival initiative are examining factors that affect the quality of children's lives, not just their mere survival. Family violence should be on this agenda. Children who witness wife abuse are at risk of being assaulted themselves and of developing adjustment problems during childhood and adolescence. In one study of battered women presenting to the Institute of Legal Medicine in Bogota, Colombia, 74 percent of those who had children said that their children were present during the attack. In 49 percent of cases the children were also injured (Berenguer 1984). Likewise, of eighty women presenting themselves to the Medico Forense of San Jose, Costa Rica, 40 percent said that their children were also beaten by their partner (Ugalde 1988).

Perhaps even more significant than physical injury, is the impact that family violence has on a child's sense of security and developing personality. Two recent studies (Davis and Carlson 1987; Jaffe et al. 1986) indicate that children who witness violence experience many of the same emotional and behavioral problems exhibited by abused children, including depression, aggression, disobedience, nightmares, poor school performance, and somatic health complaints.[12] There is also evidence that suggests that children who witness or experience violence are more likely to become abusive as adults (Stordeur and Stille 1989).

But violence may affect child survival in another, more subtle way. It is now well established that female education is significantly and independently related to child survival. (Blumberg 1989; Floro and Wolf 1990). But how does education work to affect child health? There is increasing evidence that schooling works not by imparting new health knowledge or skills, but by eroding fatalism, improving women's self confidence, and changing the power balance in the family (Lindernbaum 1985; Levine 1987; Caldwell 1979). In the words of Peter Adamson (1988), "Education erodes resignation and substitutes for it a degree of confidence, an awareness of choice, a belief that decisions can be made, circumstances changed, life improved." Using qualitative research techniques, Griffiths (1988) has identified some of the mechanisms by which maternal confidence and self-esteem operate to affect child health. Her research in Indonesia, Cameroon and India has demonstrated that mothers with higher self-esteem take a more assertive role in their child's feeding—they introduce weaning foods earlier, they take swifter action when a child is sick, and they persist in feeding even when a child refuses. Not surprisingly, more-confident mothers have better-nourished children.

If "education" is in fact a proxy for some intervening variable, like self-confidence or self-esteem, then anything that undermines confidence will affect child health. Acts of violence and society's tacit acceptance of them stand as constant reminders to women of their low worth. Where women's confidence and status is critical to achieving a development goal—such as improving child survival—violence will remain a powerful obstacle to progress.

*Family Planning and AIDS Prevention.* The family planning literature is replete with examples of women who would like to use family planning but are afraid to do so without their husband's permission (Greenstreet 1990). The unspoken reality behind this fear is that women can be beaten if they disobey.

Violence or the threat of violence is an all-too-common dimension of women's sexual decision making. Because of women's economic dependence and men's superior strength, women are often not free to decide with whom they have sex, when, how often, or with what kind of protection. Sometimes they are given no choice at all: In the United States, one out of every seven married women have been raped by their husband. (Russel 1982). In Seoul, South Korea, the figure is two out of every three (Shim Young 1991).

Women's relative powerlessness to negotiate sex or condom use is a fact rarely acknowledged by AIDS education programs. Until programs confront this reality, prevention strategies will be doomed to failure. As a woman from Buwunga, Uganda observed recently in a village discussion on AIDS, "If you advise your husband to use a condom, he may beat you and send you away. Where will you go then?" (Perlez 1990).

Similar fears plague low-income and minority women in the United States. According to Dooley Worth (1989), an anthropologist working with an AIDS education project in New York City, "Women engage in sexual risk-taking mainly because of perceived threats to their social and economic survival, and a lack of power in sexual decision making." Three-quarters of the women Worth surveyed had been physically abused as adults, primarily by their sexual partner. "Asking them to introduce condoms into their relationship," notes Worth, "can mean asking them to risk further abuse."

Clearly, fear of economic or physical reprisal increases women's vulnerability to AIDS in comparison to men's. Women desperately need a new option for protecting themselves against sexually transmitted diseases—one that will allow them to control the decision to use it. And for Third World women, much of whose social status depends on childbearing, the technology must also permit conception. As Kathryn Carovano (1991) notes, "To provide women exclusively with HIV prevention methods that contradict most societies' fertility norms is to provide many women with no options at all."

### 3. Health care workers are best positioned to identify, counsel and refer victims of physical abuse.

The health care system is the only institution that all women are likely to interact with sometime in their lives. Thus it is particularly well placed to identify and assist victims of violence. Regrettably, even in the United States, the health care system has not taken leadership on this issue.

Studies document that in a typical metropolitan emergency room in the United States, health care workers identify only one battered women in thirty-five, even though battered women have proven quite willing to admit abuse when questioned in private (Stark et al. 1981; Stark 1984).[13] With proper training and protocols, however, health care facilities can greatly improve their staff's sensitivity to battered women. At the emergency department of the Medical College of Pennsylvania, for example, the percentage of women found to be battered increased more than five-fold, from 5.6 percent to 30 percent, after training and protocols were introduced (McCleer and Anwar 1989).

Such reforms remain uncommon in the United States, primarily because institutions seldom change without outside pressure; and battered-women's advocates have invested most of their energy in opening shelters and working for justice-system reform. But recently, advocates successfully lobbied the U.S. Joint Commission on Hospital Accreditation to include training and emergency room protocols on family violence among the criteria used to evaluate hospitals for accreditation (Heise and Chapman 1991). This should encourage increased attention to domestic violence within the medical community.

Health and family planning workers in developing countries are also well-suited to identify and counsel victims of abuse. Especially in politically repressive countries, women are unlikely to seek help from the police or other governmental authorities. But they may admit abuse when questioned gently, in private, by a supportive health care provider. Providers can emphasize that no one deserves to be beaten or raped, and help women think through future options for protecting themselves (e.g. seeking safety at a friend's). And in large urban areas, there are a growing number of women's crisis centers to which providers can refer women for legal or psychological support. But even where no external support exists, having a sympathetic individual acknowledge and denounce the violence in a woman's life offers considerable relief from isolation and self-blame.

### 4. There is enormous pent-up demand for information and services related to gender violence.

In myriad ways, women around the world are saying that violence is a priority issue for them, but their voices are not being heard. At a recent twelve-country workshop on women's nonformal education held in China, participants were asked to name the worst aspect of being female: fear of male violence was the almost-unanimous answer (Bradley 1990). In 1988, MATCH International, a Canadian NGO devoted to assisting Third World women's projects, surveyed women's groups worldwide about their priorities. The number one concern expressed was violence against women (Carrillo 1991). And in 1990, when the Foundation for International Community Assistance (FINCA), a grassroots banking and credit scheme for women, decided to provide educational materials on health during its weekly meetings, women bankers identified domestic violence as one of the issues they most wanted to receive information on. Other priority themes identified in focus groups were alcoholism; drug detection and prevention in children; parasites; and women's infections, including STDs and AIDS (Salamon and Velazquez 1991).

Clearly, violence against women is of primary concern to Third World women, and they are acting on that concern—witness the 379 programs against violence in Latin America alone. But most of these groups are struggling to survive with little or no support from their own governments or mainstream health and development funders. Given both the indigenous demand for antiviolence programs and the links between violence and existing health and development priorities, there is a strong case for greater international investment in gender-violence research and services.

*5. Confronting gender violence pushes the women's health agenda beyond reproductive health.*

Historically, the international health community has been interested in women only as a means to an end, such as controlling population growth or saving children's lives—rather than as human beings with independent needs. Even Maternal and Child Health (MCH) programs have concentrated almost exclusively on children, leading some observers to ask, "Where is the M in MCH?"

The Safe Motherhood Initiative represents a first step toward focusing more on the health of women, as does recent advocacy to broaden "family planning" to include the full range of women's reproductive health needs (Germain and Ordway, 1989). But even these programs ignore elements of women's physical and emotional well-being that go beyond their reproductive anatomy. Putting violence on the women's health agenda gives value on the *quality* of women's lives. Preliminary data suggest that gender violence may be among the most significant causes of morbidity and mental distress among women. If involuntary pregnancy were recognized as a form of violence, this would most certainly be the case.

## Important First Steps

The international health community is well positioned to advance the fight against gender violence. The key is to identify opportunities to integrate training, information, and questions about violence into ongoing initiatives. For example, many countries are currently surveying individuals' sexual attitudes and practices to help design successful AIDS education campaigns. Several additional items could be added to the questionnaire to reveal the nature and extent of violence against women.

Likewise, training materials for family planning workers, health promoters, and refugee workers could include information about how to identify and respond to rape and abuse. More and more countries are using entertainment media, including soap operas, radio shows, or songs, to promote family planning, AIDS awareness, and child survival. Messages about violence could be woven among these other themes.

But most importantly, international NGOs and development agencies can actively support the growing number of local groups fighting violence at the grassroots. Funders capable of making small grants should make it known that they are receptive to proposals related to violence, and large-scale funders should consider funding umbrella organizations that make grants directly to Third World groups. Canada's bilateral-aid agency, CIDA, for example, funds Match International, which in turn manages an entire grant program focused on violence against women.

In this age of dwindling resources, programs against violence are apt to be dismissed as an unaffordable luxury. But it is precisely now, when the survival of many families hinges on the mother's emotional and physical strength, that antiviolence programs are most desperately needed. More importantly, it is time that the international community recognizes that women have a right to live free from physical and psychological abuse. Gender violence is crippling, both physically and emotionally. A health agenda that values women as women could not ignore this all-too-common reality of women's lives.

## Notes

1. This definition was inspired by one offered for domestic violence by Carmen Antony and Gladys Miller in their work, "Estudio Exploratorio Sobre el Maltrato Fisico que es Victima Mujer Panamena." Panama: ICRUP/Ministerio de Trabajo y Bienestar Social, 1986.

2. Levinson's (1989) analysis of ethnographic data from ninety peasant and small-scale societies indicates that 86 percent experience violence against wives by husbands. Only sixteen "can be described as essentially free or untroubled by family violence" (p. 452). In an analysis of ethnographic research on fourteen cultures by female anthropologists using female informants, Counts et al. (1992) identifies only one society, the Wape of Papua New Guinea, that have little or no woman abuse.

3. A recent study by the Addiction Research Foundation in Toronto found that battered women's use of sedatives was 74 percent higher and their use of sleeping pills 40.5 percent higher than nonabused women (Groenveld and Shane 1989).

4. Stark (1984) reports that fully 26 percent of female suicide attempts presenting to Yale University Hospital in 1979 were associated with abuse, as were 50 percent of attempts made by African-American women. The battered women also accounted for 42 percent of all traumatic attempts and were significantly more likely to attempt suicide more than once (20 percent versus 8 percent).

5. Fiji reference from Shamima Ali, Women's Crisis Centre, Suva, Figi Islands, private communication, June 6, 1991; Philippines reference from Nilda Ramonte, Center for the Pacific-Asian Family, Los Angeles, California, private communication June 7, 1991; Peru reference from Gina Cedamanos, Centro de la Mujer Peruana Flora Tristan, Lima, Peru, private communication, June 7, 1991; Mexico reference from Elizabeth Shrader Cox, Centro de Investigación y Lucha contra la Violencia Domestica, A.C. (CECOVID), Mexico City, private communication, September 27, 1991.

6. Bangladesh from Adanda and Shamim (1985). India data from Kelkar (1991). Malaysia data from Asian and Pacific Women's Resource and Collection Network (1989). South Africa from Russel (1991).

7. The South African estimate of rape incidence in 1988 was calculated using the following information: number of rapes committed = 386,160; population of women fifteen and older = 11,265,000. Population figures are from the United Nations, *Assessment of World Population 1990.* The U.S. rate is based on an estimate of rape incidence in 1986 made by Koss, Koss, and Woodruff, who surveyed more than 2,291 adult working women in Cleveland, Ohio and calculated the rape rate using the same definition of rape used in the National Crime Survey. The incidence of rape over a twelve-month period was 28 per 1,000 women, which they adjusted to 18 per 1,000 women to allow for telescoping (the documented tendency for people to recall events forward in time). For more details see Koss, Mary P. "Rape Incidence: A Review and Assessment of the Data," Testimony presented before the Senate Judiciary Committee, United States Congress, August 29, 1990.

8. **Developing Countries with Shelters**: El Salvador, Paraguay, Uruguay, Egypt, Malaysia, Puerto Rico, Korea, Thailand. **With Rape Crisis Centers**: South Africa, Malaysia, Mexico, Philippines, St. Lucia, Trinidad and Tobago, Guyana, Nicaragua, Panama, Puerto Rico, Venezuela, Korea. **With General Women's Crisis Centers**: Argentina, Brazil, Chile, Colombia, Costa Rica, Ecuador, El Salvador, Dominican Republic, St. Lucia, Uruguay, Fiji, Thailand, Japan, Hong Kong, India, Korea, Sri Lanka, China, Jamaica.

9. For a description of programs see "Linking Global Struggles to End Violence" 1990. Ottawa: Match International and "Violence Against Women: Confronting Invisible Barriers to Development." June 1991. New York: International Tribune Center.

10. The study by Valdez Santiago and Shrader Cox (1991) indicated that 25 percent of women surveyed had been in an abusive relationship with a male partner or ex-partner. Of these women 66 percent report physical violence, and of those, 20 percent report blows to the stomach during pregnancy. According to the United Nations *Assessment of World Population 1990,* the number of women in Mexico aged 15 years and older was 28,206,000. 28,206,000(.25) x (.66) x (.2). = 930,798 women at risk of battering during pregnancy.

11. The World Health Organization (WHO) defines maternal mortality as a death during pregnancy or within 42 days afterward, from causes related to or aggravated by the pregnancy or its management.

12. The Davis and Carlson (1987) study found that 90 percent of abused boys and 75 percent of those witnessing violence (compared to 13 percent for controls), had behavior-problem scores greater than one standard deviation above the norm.

13. When Planned Parenthood of Houston and Southeast Texas added four abuse-assessment questions to their standard intake form, 8.2 percent of women identified themselves as physically abused (Bullock, et al. 1989).

## References

Acasadi, George and Johnson-Acasadi, Gwendolyn. 1990. "Safe Motherhood in South Asia: Socio-cultural and Demographic Aspects of Maternal Health." Background paper prepared for the Safe Motherhood South Asia Conference, Lahore, Pakistan, March 24-28.

Adamson, Peter. 1988. "Two Powerful Sources for Child Survival." *People* 15(1).

Adebajo, Christine. 1991. "A Grassroots Project by Nurses and Midwives in Nigeria to Eradicate Female Circumcision." Paper presented at the 18th Annual NCIH International Health Conference, Arlington, VA.

Amaro, Hortensia, Fried, L., Cabral, H., and B. Zuckerman. 1990. "Violence During Pregnancy and Substance Use." *American Journal of Public Health* 80(5):575-579.

Adanda, Latifa and Shamim, Ishrat. 1985. *Women and Violence: A Comparative Study of Rural and Urban Violence Against Women in Bangladesh.* Dhaka, Bangladesh: Women for Women: A Research and Study Group.

Asian and Pacific Women's Resource Collection Network. 1989. *Asian and Pacific Women's Resource and Action Series: Health.* Kuala Lumpur, Malaysia: Asian and Pacific Development Centre.

Berenguer, Ana Maria. 1988. "Alternativas Desde la Medicina Legal y Experiéncias Sobre la Violencia Intrafamiliar." In *Violencia en la Intimidad.* Bogat, Columbia: Corporación Casa de la Mujer.

Blumberg, R.L. 1989. *Making the Case for the Gender Variable: Women and the Wealth and Well-Being of Nations.* Technical Reports in Gender and Development No. 2. Washington, D.C.: U.S. Agency for International Development, Office of Women in Development.

Bradley, Christine. 1988(a). "The Problem of Domestic Violence in Papua New Guinea." In *Guidelines for Police Training on Violence Against Women and Child Sexual Abuse.* London: Commonwealth Secretariat, Women and Development Programme.

Bradley, Christine. 1988(b). "How Can We Help Rural Beaten Wives? Some Suggestions from Papua New Guinea." Paper presented at the International Welsh Women's Aid Conference, Cardiff, Wales.

Bradley, Christine. 1990. "Why Male Violence Against Women is a Development Issue: Reflections From Papua New Guinea." Occasional Paper. New York, N.Y.: United Nations Fund for Women (UNIFEM).

Bhatia, S. 1985. "Status and Survival." *World Health.*

Browne, Angela. 1987. *When Battered Women Kill.* New York, N.Y.: Free Press.

Browne, Angela and Williams, Kirk. 1989. "Exploring the Effect of Resource Availability and the Likelihood of Female-Perpetrated Homicides." *Law and Society Review* 23(1).

Bullock, Linda F. and McFarlane, Judith. 1989. "The Birth-Weight/Battering Connection." *American Journal of Nursing.* Pp. 1153-1155.

Byerly, Carolyn. 1984. Contigo, Pan Cebollas..Y También Golpes?" in *VIVA*, newsletter of the Centro de la Mujer Peruana Flora Tristan. Lima, Peru. No. 2.

Caldwell, J.C. 1979. "Education as a Factor in Mortality Decline: An Examination of Nigerian Data." *Population Studies* 33(3):395-413.

CAMVAC. 1985. "Carpeta de Información Bsica Para la Atención Solidaria y Feminista a Mujeres Violadas." Mexico City: Centro de Apoyo A Mujeres Violadas (CAMVAC).

Canadian Centre for Justice Statistics. 1988. *Homicide in Canada 1987: A Statistical Perspective.* Ottawa: Ministry of Supply and Services Canada.

Cañas, Mercedes. 1990. "Maltrato Físico A La Mujer Salvadore:a." Unpublished thesis, San Salvador. (Available from author).

Carovano, Kathryn. 1991. "More than Mothers and Whores: Redefining the AIDS Prevention Needs of Women." *International Journal of Health Services* 21(1):131-142.

Carillo, Roxanna. 1991. "Violence Against Women: An Obstacle to Development." Center of Women's Global Leadership, Rutgers University, New Brunswick, New Jersey.

Chen, Lincoln; Huq, Emdadul and Stan D'Souza. 1981. "Sex Bias in the Family Allocation of Food and Health Care in Rural Bangladesh." *Population and Development Review* 7(1):55-70.

Consumers Association of Penang. 1988. *Rape in Malaysia.* Penang, Malaysia.

Counts, Dorothy. 1987. "Female Suicide and Wife Abuse: A Cross-Cultural Perspective." *Suicide and Life Threatening Behavior* 17(3):194-205.

Counts, Dorothy Ayers; Brown, Judith K. and Jacquelyn C. Campbell. 1992. *Sanctions and Sanctuary: Cultural Perspectives on the Beating of Wives.* Boulder, Colorado: Westview Press.

COVAC. 1990. "Evaluación de Proyecto para Educación, Capacitación, y Atención a Mujeres y Menores de Edad en Materia de Violencia Sexual, Enero a Diciembre 1990." Mexico City: Asociación Mexicana Contra la Violencia a las Mujeres, A.C. (COVAC).

Crossette, Barbara. 1989. "India Studying `Accidental' Deaths of Hindu Wives." *New York Times.* January 15.

Das Gupta, M. 1987. "Selective Discrimination Against Female Children in Rural Punjab, India. *Population and Development Review* 13(1):55-70.

Davis, Liane V. and Carlson, Bonnie. 1987. "Observation of Spouse Abuse: What Happens to the Children?" *Journal of Interpersonal Violence* 2(3):278-291.

Demographic and Health Survey (DHS Colombia). *Colombia: Encuestra de Prevalencia, Demografía y Salud.* Columbia, MD: Institute for Resource Development.

Fauveau, V. and Blanchet, T. 1989. "Deaths from Injuries and Induced Abortion Among Rural Bangladeshi Women," *Social Science and Medicine* 29.

Friedman, Amy. 1991. "Rape and Domestic Violence: The Experience of Refugee Women." Occasional Paper. Washington, D.C.: Refugee Women in Development.

Gelles, Richard and Cornell, Caire. 1990. *Intimate Violence in Families*. Newbury Park: Sage Publications.

Germain, Adrienne and Ordway, Jane. 1989. "Population Control and Women's Health: Balancing the Scales." New York, N.Y.: International Women's Health Coalition with the Overseas Development Council.

Greenstreet, M. "Education and Reproductive Choices in Ghana: Gender Issues in Population Policy." *Development* 1: 40-47.

Griffiths, Marcia. 1988. "Maternal Self-Confidence and Child Well-Being." Paper presented at the Society for Applied Anthropology Annual Meeting, Tampa, Florida, April 20-24.

Groeneveld, J. and Shain, M. 1989. *Drug Abuse Among Victims of Physical and Sexual Abuse: A Preliminary Report*. Toronto: Addiction Research Foundation.

Guenette, Louis and Heffeman, Tracy. 1989. "A Global Struggle Against Violence Against Women." *Vis-a-Vis*. Canadian Council on Social Development, Volume 7(1).

Haynes, R.H. 1984 "Suicide in Figi: A Preliminary Study." *British Journal of Psychiatry* 145:433-438.

Heise, Lori. 1989. "International Dimensions of Violence Against Women." *Response to the Victimization of Women and Children* 12(1):3-11.

Heise, Lori and Chapman, Jane Roberts. 1991. "Reflections on a Movement: The U.S. Battle Against Woman Abuse." In Margaret Schuler, ed., *Freedom from Violence: Women's Strategies from Around the World*. Washington, D.C.: OEF International. (Available through UNIFEM, New York, NY).

Hosken, Fran. 1988. "International Seminar: Female Circumcision Strategies to Bring About Change." *Women's International Network News* 14(3):24-37.

Illinois Coalition Against Sexual Assault. 1991. "Sexual Assault Statistical Report." Springfield, IL: Illinois Coalition Against Sexual Assault.

International Women's Tribune Center. "Violence Against Women: Invisible Barriers to Development." *The Tribune*. No. 46.

Isis International. 1990a. *Violencia en Contra de La Mujer en América Latina y El Caribe: Directorio de Programas*. Santiago, Chile.

Isis International. 1990b. *Violencia en Contra de La Mujer en América Latina y El Caribe. Informe Final*. Santiago, Chile.

Jaffe, P., Wolfe, D., Wilson, S., and L. Zack. 1986. "Similarities in Behavioral and Social Maladjustment Among Child Victims and Witnesses to Family Violence." *American Journal of Orthopsychiatry* 56:142-146.

Karkal, Malini. 1985. "How the Other Half Dies in Bombay." *Economic and Political Weekly*. p. 1424.

Kelkar, Govind. 1991. "Stopping the Violence Against Women: Issues and Perspectives from India." In Margaret Schuler, ed., *Freedom From Violence: Women's Strategies from Around the World*. Washington, D.C.: OEF International. (Available through UNIFEM, New York, NY).

Kilpatrick, Dean. 1990. "Testimony Before the House Select Committee on Children, Youth and Families," as cited by Congressional Caucus for Women's Issues, "Violence Against Women Fact Sheet," Washington, D.C.

Koop, C. Everett. 1989. "Violence Against Women: A Global Problem," Address by the Surgeon General of the U.S. Public Health Service at a conference of the Pan American Health Organization, Washington, D.C., May 22.

Koso-Thomas, O. 1987. *The Circumcision of Women: A Strategy for Eradication.* London: Zed Books Ltd.

Koss, M.P., Gidycz, C.A. and N. Wisniewski. 1987. "The Scope of Rape: Incidence and Prevalence of Sexual Aggression and Victimization in a National Sample of Higher Education Students," *Journal of Consulting and Clinical Psychology* 55:162-170.

Koss, M.P., Koss, P. and W.J. Woodruff. 1990. "Relation of Criminal Victimization to Health Perceptions among Women Medical Patients." *Journal of Consulting and Clinical Psychology.*

Levine, R.A., Levine, Sara E., Richman, Amy, and Clara Sunderland Correa. 1987. "Schooling and Maternal Behavior in a Mexican City: The Effects on Fertility and Child Survival," *Fertility Determinants Research Notes.* No. 16.

Levinson, David. 1989. *Violence in Cross-Cultural Perspective.* Newbury Park: Sage Publications.

Londono, Melba Arias. 1990. *Cinco Formas de Violencia Contra la Mujer.* Bogota, Colombia: Casa de la Mujer.

Lightfoot-Klein, Hanny, 1989. *Prisoners of Ritual.* Binghamton, New York: Harrington Park Press, Inc.

Mahajan, A. 1990. "Instigators of Wife Battering." In *Violence Against Women.* Edited by Sushma Sood. Jaipur, India: Arihant Publishers.

Mohammed, Asha. 1991. "Medical and Cultural Aspects of Female Circumcision in Somalia and Recent Efforts for Eradication." Paper Presented at the 18th Annual NCIH International Health Conference, Arlington, VA.

McCleer, S.V. and Anwar, R. 1989. "A Study of Women Presenting in an Emergency Department." *American Journal of Public Health* 79:65-67.

McFarlane, Judith. 1992. "Assessing for Abuse during Pregnancy: Severity and Frequency of Injuries and Associated Entry into Prenatal Care." *Journal of American Medical Association.* 267(23):3176-3178.

Mollica, Richard and Son, Linda. 1989. "Cultural Dimensions in the Evaluation and Treatment of Sexual Trauma: An Overview. *Psychiatric Clinics of North America* 12(2):363-379.

Moltedo, Cecelia, Clotiled, Silva, Orellana, Christina, Tarifeño, Antonia, and Clara Poblete. 1989. "Estudio Sobre Violencia Doméstica en Mujeres Pobladoras Chilenas." Santiago, Chile: CUSO.

National Committee for Injury Prevention and Control. 1989. *Injury Prevention: Meeting the Challenge.* New York: Oxford University Press.

Patel, Vibhuti. 1989. "Feminist Street Theatre in India." *DIVA: A Quarterly Journal of Asian women.* Vol. 2(1) as cited in *Linking Women's Global Struggles.* 1990. Ottawa: MATCH International Centre.

Pawar, M.S. "Women and Family Violence: Policies and Programs." In *Violence Against Women.* Edited by Sushman Sood. Jaipur, India: Arihant Publishers.

Perez, Amelia Marquez. 1990. "Aproximaci<n Diagn<stica a Las Violaciones de Mujeres en Los Distritos de Panam y San Miguelito." Centro para El Desarrollo de la Mujer, Universdad de Panam.

Perlez, Jane. 1990. "For the Oppressed Sex, Brave Words to Live By," *New York Times*, June 6.

Pitanguy, Jacqueline. 1991. "Brazil's Response to Violence Against Women." Presentation at the Ford Foundation, New York, NY, February 14.

Portugal, Ana Maria. 1988. "Crónica de una Violación Provocada?" *Revista Murjer/ Fempress*. Contraviolencia. Chile: FEMPRESS-ILET.

Raikes, Alanagh. 1990. *Pregnancy, Birthing and Family Planning in Kenya: Changing Patterns of Behavior.* Copenhagen: Centre for Development Research.

Ramaanamma, A. 1990. "Female Foeticide and Infanticide: A Silent Violence," In *Violence Against Women.* Edited by Sushman Sood. Jaipur, India: Arihant Publishers.

Rushwan, Hamid. 1990. "Female circumcision." *World Health.* April-May.

Russel, Diana. 1982. *Rape in Marriage.* New York: MacMillian.

Russel, Diana. 1991. "Rape and Child Sexual Abuse in Soweto: An Interview with Community Leader Mary Mabaso." Seminar presented at the Centre for African Studies. University of Cape Town, South Africa, March 26.

Salamon, Jill D. And Velazquez, Mary Luz. 1991. "Qualitative Needs Assessment of Women Village Bankers in Tijuana, Mexico and Development of a Self-Educational Guide on Domestic Violence." Paper presented at the 18th Annual NCIH International Health Conference, Arlington, VA.

Schei, B. and Bakketeig, L. 1989. "Gynecological Impact of Sexual and Physical Abuse by a Spouse: A study of a Random Sample of Norwegian Women." *British Journal of Obstetrics and Gynecology* 96:1379-1383.

Sen, Amartya. 1990. "More than 100 Million Women are Missing," *The New York Review of Books.* December 20.

Shim, Young-Hee,Yun, Seong-Eun, Park, Sun-Mi, Cho, Jeong-Hee, Kim, Sung-Young, and Young-Su Kang. 1991. "Sexual Violence and its Countermeasures in Korea: A Victimization Survey of Seoul Women." Summary of a report by the Korean Institute of Criminology as reprinted in the *Information Booklet of the Korea Sexual Violence Relief Center.* Seoul, Korea.

Shamim, Ishrat. 1985. "Kidnapped, Raped, Killed: Recent Trends in Bangladesh." Paper presented at the International Conference on Families in the Face of Urbanization, New Delhi, December 2-5.

Shrader Cox, Elizabeth. 1991. "Violence Against Women in Mexico: Legislative Reform and Service Innovations for Battered Women and Rape Survivors." Paper presented at the 18th Annual NCIH International Health Conference, Arlington, VA.

Sorensen, S.B., Stein, J.A., Siegel, J.M., Golding, J.M., and M.A. Burnam. 1987. "Prevalence of Adult Sexual Assault: the Los Angeles Epidemiologic Catchment Area Study." *American Journal of Epidemiology* 126(6):1154-1164.

Stark, E., Flitcraft, A., Zuckerman, B., Grey, A., Robinson, J., and W. Frazier. 1981. *Wife Abuse in the Medical Setting: An Introduction for Health Personnel.* Monograph #7. Washington, D.C.: Office of Domestic Violence.

Stark, E. 1984. "The Battering Syndrome; Social Knowledge, Social Policy and the Abuse of Women," (dissertation). SUNY-Binghamton.

Stark, E. and Flitcraft, A. 1991. "Spouse Abuse." In Rosenburg, Mark and Fenley, Mary Ann, eds. *Violence in America: A Public Health Approach*. New York: Oxford University Press.

Stewart, Denise. 1989. "The Global Injustice." *Vis-a-Vis*. Ottawa: Canadian Council on Social Development.

Stordeur, Richard and Stille, Richard. 1989. *Ending Men's Violence Against Their Partners: One Road to Peace*. Newbury Park, CA: Sage Publications, Inc.

Straus, M. and Steinmentz, S.K. 1980. *Behind Closed Doors: A Survey of Family Violence in America*. New York: Doubleday.

"Ten Facts about Violence Against Young Women," compiled by the Senate Judiciary Committee. U.S. Congress. August 29, 1990.

Ugalde, Juan Gerardo. 1988. "Síndrome de la Mujer Agredida." In *Mujer* no. 5. San José, Costa Rica: Cefemina.

UNICEF. 1986. *Statistical Review of the Situation of Children of the World*. New York: UNICEF.

Valdez, Santiago Rosario and Shrader Cox, Elizabeth. 1991. "Violencia Doméstica: Características y Alternativas de Solución en México." Paper presented at "Leading the Way Out," and international conference on violence against women sponsored by the Global Fund for Women, Menlo Park, CA.

Vogelman, Lloyd. 1990. "Violent Crime: Rape." In *People and Violence in South Africa*. Edited by Brian McKendrick and Wilma Hoffman. Cape Town: Oxford University Press.

Walker, Lenore. 1989. *Terrifying Love: Why Battered Women Kill and How Society Responds*. New York, NY: Harper & Row Publishers.

World Health Organization. 1985. *World Health Statistics Annual*. Geneva: WHO.

Worth, Dooley. 1989. "Sexual Decision-Making and AIDS: Why Condom Promotion Among Vulnerable Women is Likely to Fail." *Studies in Family Planning* 20(6):297-307.

Wu Han. 1986. United Nations Case Study of China. Proceedings of the Expert Group Meeting on Violence in the Family with a Special Emphasis on its Effects

# 9

# Women's Mental Health: A Global Perspective

*Freda L. Paltiel*

At the outset, I shall challenge several myths. The first is that mental health, particularly women's mental health, is a luxury concern, an issue for wealthy countries, to be addressed only after the solution of more basic problems. At Nairobi we learned that women were sick and tired of being sick and tired, that health and well-being of women and their children was so important that when Kenyan women wanted a community health clinic, they began by baking the bricks. Even in economically advanced countries, our understanding of women's mental health is so primitive or distorted that we, too, are still "making or rearranging the bricks."

The second myth is the dichotomy of interests between women of economically developed and developing countries. Geography, history, culture, politics and economics *do* count, but the International Women's Decade (IWD) revealed that everywhere women are overworked, overlooked and undervalued, and that poverty, discrimination, violence and powerlessness are pervasive features of women's lives. The Decade was the antidote to learned helplessness, as women collectively found common cause and placed their concerns on public agendas throughout the world.

The third myth is that attention to the health and well-being of women comes at the expense of children's well-being. Throughout the world, it is women who are preoccupied with the welfare of their children. UNICEF, the World Bank, WHO and others, as their child-survival initiatives mature, are recognizing that the quality of life of children is a function or reflection of the quality of life, of health, education, working and living conditions of mothers. This realization gave impetus to the Safe Motherhood Initiative.

The fourth common misconception is that, overall, mental disorder is more prevalent among women than men. This is not borne out by present epidemiological studies, which show that, overall, male prevalence is higher, but that male and female predominance differs for different disorders.

Early in the IWD, I developed a new paradigm to replace that of self-actualization and the hierarchy of human needs, as the latter never really applied to women socialized to the nurturing of others' aspirations. Evidence was mounting that social policy development required systematic gender-sensitive attention not only to the needs, but also the risks and tasks of persons at each life stage. This led to the postulate that adults at all ages need three anchors; *work, family* and *friends* (Paltiel 1981). Moreover, adequate guidance for children and life-skills apprenticeship for adolescents are necessary to assist individuals to build and secure these three anchors, for physical and emotional health and for coping with the tasks and risks at each life stage. It was gratifying to introduce these concepts into the Nairobi Forward-Looking Strategies for the Advancement of Women to the Year 2000 in clauses acceptable to all regions and political blocs.

Two anchors make it possible to function–optimally–but a single anchor constitutes high risk. The one-anchor workaholic is vulnerable to stress, redundancy, infarct, burnout or family breakdown. If the work anchor is threatened, adults can cope effectively with the support of family and friends. In cases of family breakdown, an adult with intact work and friendship anchors may be sustained, compensated, or reoriented. If friendship fails, the anchors of work and family may help maintain self-esteem and perspective. The housebound one-anchor married woman with small children is at elevated risk for mild or moderate depression, and particularly vulnerable to the entrapment of wife abuse.

In subsistence societies, friends, work, and family all interlock and social integration is high. However, life may also be short, nasty, brutish or limited by fatalism and lack of opportunities. Indeed, women in enmeshed societies may find themselves dominated, rather than supported, by the extended families of their husbands.

Despite obvious caveats regarding a universal generalization about the mental health of women, given the paucity and fragmentation of information, one is impressed by the functional mental health of most women, as demonstrated by their economic and social productivity. A global review for WHO on women and mental health concluded that women are excellent copers (Paltiel 1987). They are extraordinarily resourceful, creative members of their communities, despite their economic deprivation, subordination, and lack of support and control over their life circumstances. Economic downturns, environmental degradation, restructuring with rising food prices, and cutbacks in health and social services, have increased women's need for survival strategies, their burdens of care but not their authority or control (Paltiel forthcoming).

Moser, in a study for UNICEF, found increasing emotional distress associated with new austerity measures, which place increasing demands on women's time and energy (Moser 1989). We do not know precisely how these circumstances have affected their physical and mental health, since their lives remain largely unexamined and their experiences unreported. However, the UN Statistical Office has recently provided us with a global picture, a statistical trend analysis from 1970 to 1990 in 178 countries revealing gender gaps in health, power, wealth and opportunity (UN 1991). For example, in much of Africa and Asia, three-quarters of women aged 25 and over are illiterate. How does this affect their cognitive development?

In this paper, I apply a gender and cross-cultural perspective on mental health and mental illness, considering the conditions and factors associated with both at various life stages, and offering proposals for areas for investigation and action. I also will present a coping paradigm developed for an earlier paper on mental health.

Health For All 2000 (HFA-2000) defines a state of health as one which enables people to lead economically and socially productive lives. Missing is "personally satisfying lives," related to women's social, productive and reproductive roles. Freud's definition, to work and to love, also implies that the ability to work and love confers life satisfaction, but women know otherwise.

The absence of cognitive, emotional or behavioral dysfunction does not necessarily equate with mental health. A holistic view of mental health is offered by Aboriginal peoples, who include a spiritual dimension and harmony with one's self and the environment.

## Childhood: Gender and Mental Health Risks

Bowlby has postulated two lifelong needs–exploration and security. Are these the dividing lines in early gender socialization? There appears to be a gender-based differentiation in the satisfaction of these needs, with greater curtailment of exploration for females, a contributing factor to "learned helplessness." Moreover, to the extent that their security is derived from actual or presumed dependence on a male, their satisfaction of that basic need is also curtailed.

Risk factors for mental, developmental and behavioral disorders for children include biological and environmental deficits and/or insults. Gender discrimination in some countries of Asia and Latin America may be life-threatening and contribute to the excess mortality of girls aged two– five. WHO estimates that in some developing countries up to 20 percent of child contacts with primary health care agents are caused by psychological problems (WHO 1990). Mental health services for children are scarce in developing countries. Even in the U.S. only slightly over a quarter of the children and adolescents who suffer from mental disorders receive mental health treatment. Currently, more than 230 psychotherapeutic techniques conducted with individuals, groups or families are in use for treating children and adolescents with mental disorders (NIMH 1990). We know little about their efficacy and generalizability. Developing countries cannot afford such trial and error.

The rates for conduct disorder and hyperactivity for boys is two–three times the rates for girls. A substantial proportion with antisocial behavior will be physically violent or involved in illegal behavior as adults. Females may become their victims. So appropriate, early intervention is critical for all of society.

Emotional disorders are more frequent in adolescent girls but not in children. However, one Canadian study of school children found that 18 percent of the children, mostly female, met criteria for anxiety and/or depression. Low scores for self-esteem correlated with high scores for anxiety and depression (Stavrakaki et al. 1991). The sequelae of childhood and adolescent anxiety disorders are not well documented (Boyle 1991).

## Reproductive Life Cycle and Mental Health

From menarche to menopause women's reproductive cycle has been mystified by ritual, stereotype and medicalization. Lack of access to appropriate reproductive health information and services is a matter of major concern globally.

The course and duration of adolescence vary widely, with different role expectations by geographic area, culture, socioeconomic status, and gender. In many developing countries, cognitive and social development of girls is curtailed by the view that they can learn all they need for their restricted social roles. Many girls and young women receive inadequate schooling, provide unpaid family labor or work in public places subject to assault, sexual abuse and rape, or premature pregnancy (Sadik 1990). The lifetime mental health consequences of these life circumstances remain largely unexamined.

Menstrual-related mood disorders are listed in the *Diagnostic and Statistical Manual of Mental Health* (DSM) as late luteal phase disorder. Yet severe "premenstrual syndrome" (PMS), which receives considerable attention, affects only about 5 percent of the population. Studies have revealed an overlap between PMS and major affective disorders, particularly the latter. Depression, which affects large numbers of women, interfering with well-being and major life duties, deserves more emphasis. The physiological changes related to the reproductive life cycle may represent a biological dimension of the etiology of depression. One known contributing factor to depression has been the use of oral contraceptives (OCs), with depression reported in 50 percent of earlier users. Psychiatric side-effects have accounted for an estimated 30–50 percent of OC discontinuation (Hamilton et al. 1988).

It is surprising that the lowest incidence of depression occurs during **pregnancy**, the period of greatest hormonal change. Citing hormonal fluctuation and behavioral association in men, Hamilton has recommended gender-comparative and longitudinal methods to illuminate neuroendo-crinology in both sexes, as well as improved understanding of endogenous cycles in humans (Hamilton et al. 1988).

When **infertility** occurs in a couple, in developing and developed countries, the woman is blamed and socially isolated. In developing countries, infertility may occur not only as a result of sexually transmitted diseases or toxic exposures in either partner, but also from infections due to poor obstetric and gynecological practices or by untrained attendants in childbirth and abortion. Prevention of infertility is therefore an important dimension of Safe Motherhood. The psychosocial aspects of infertility and the social implications of new reproductive technologies in various societies require more study as a basis for sound and equitable policy development and practices to prevent, control, and treat infertility.

Postpartum appears to be a particularly high-risk period for women, yet **postpartum depression** is not listed in American or international psychiatric classification systems, with insufficient investigation into the etiology, diagnostic criteria, course, treatment, and outcomes of these "undefined" disorders (Hamilton 1989). The revised International Classification of Disorders, ICD-10, is scheduled to include postpartum depression. Three types usually cited are **transitory blues, moderate depression** and **postpartum psychosis.** Hamilton proposes five syndromes occurring at definite stages of the return of body chemistry and reproductive organs from pregnant to nonpregnant states. "Multidisciplinary multisite studies are needed to guide appropriate risk identification, treatment, care and support, and if possible, prevention measures of this neglected female-specific illness" (Paltiel forthcoming).

**Menopause,** the gradual cessation of ovarian function which culminates at approximately age fifty is a culturally-mediated universal physiological experience for women whose life expectation goes beyond that age. Premature menopause which occurs with hysterectomy has also been cited for disadvantaged populations. In Western countries, midlife women with dysphoric moods were often labelled as suffering from involutional melancholia or an "empty-nest syndrome." Psychoanalytic theory ascribed menopausal symptoms to a loss of femininity, or castration anxiety. Although Seiden (1989) observes that psychiatric symptoms during menoxpausal years are now rarely attributed to menopause per se, midlife women still receive more prescriptions for psychotropic drugs compared to women of other age groups and similarly aged men.

Women in nonindustrialized societies differ in onset of menarche, menses, diet, parity, age at first pregnancy, and a shorter interval between last pregnancy and climacteric, access to health care, medical diagnosis, and treatment. Some authors have concluded that differences in role status in post-child-bearing ages in nonindustrialized societies have resulted in positive menopausal experience. In some societies, postmenopausal women are no longer "impure"; are relieved of the travails of repeated pregnancies; and with the support of their sons and daughters-in-law, have achieved their life goals, security, and respect (Beyene 1989; Barnett 1988).

North American midlife women are experiencing the disappearance of the empty nest syndrome. Mental health statistics show a steady decline in their share of psychiatric hospitalization, at least in Canada. Recent studies also indicate that female sexuality remains strong after menopause. On the other hand, they experience role strain. The care of elderly parents and relatives often represents a major burden for midlife women whose own health is beginning to decline as they try to manage employment, household responsibilities, and care for adult, though not yet independent, children. In 1990 in the U.S., 32 percent of single males and 20 percent of single females aged twenty-five to thirty-four are still living with parents (Gross 1991). Midlife may be associated with role expansion rather than role constriction.

Postmenopausal women in some developing countries may expect to live another twenty years, while Western women may expect to live another thirty years. Physical and mental health, income, education, mental status, social integration, environmental stressors and supports, as well as attitudes towards aging and gender all affect the quality of life and ability to cope of older women. Improving their quality of life should be an important component of primary care and healthy public policy.

In developing countries, the migration of young family members, the weakening of age deference and of traditional family obligations, as well as urbanization, are altering the social structures of intergenerational societies, disrupting support systems or placing extra burdens on care-givers, usually grandmothers. This is true in developed and developing countries. Sometimes they must care for even older, senile relatives and for other children or grandchildren whose parents emigrated to seek work. The aging of societies should not be viewed in classical terms of dependency ratios or of increased personal consumption of health care. Current studies show that higher consumption of medical care occurs in the very last stage of life, and that older persons provide various services to kin and others.

## Gender Aspects of Mental Disorders

A review of prevalence rates of aggregate mental disorders and symptoms from community surveys conducted in thirty-three countries around the world revealed a range of from 5.5 percent to 34.5 percent for women and from 2.3 percent to 31.0 percent for men (Paltiel 1987). The NIMH Epidemiological Catchment Area Program (ECA) study of about seventeen thousand community residents in three sites (New Haven, Baltimore and St. Louis), found lifetime prevalence of any psychiatric disorder was 36 percent for men and 30 for women, for all disorders. However, more women received treatment than men: 23 percent versus 14 percent, particularly unmarried women. The rate for financially dependent persons was highest. The NIMH–ECA study confirmed that women are overrepresented in depression in a ratio of two to one, particularly major depressive episodes and dysthymia; in anxiety disorders, particularly agoraphobia and panic disorder, in somatization mainly for older women. For phobia disorders the strongest and most consistent gender differences were found among the Hispanic population, where female prevalence rates were more than twice the rates for males. Male-predominant disorders are alcohol abuse/dependency and antisocial-personality disorder. Some men with these disorders may be found in prisons rather than health care facilities.

The study pointed out the need for public education on recognition of disorders and information regarding effective treatment and improved access to care. It also dispelled the stereotype of the person with psychiatric disorder as a middle-aged, anxious or depressed woman (Robins and Regier 1991).

The NIMH–ECA also studied the prevalence of specific psychiatric disorders in Puerto Rico, where lifetime rates by sex were 34.0 percent male and 22.8 percent female, and female-predominant disorders were dysthymia, anxiety disorders, and psychosexual dysfunction. In Bland's Alberta study of six months' prevalence of disorders, an overall rate 17.1 percent was found. Here too, for all disorders combined, the prevalence rate for men exceeded that for women. Bland confirms the findings of most other studies that men clearly predominate in alcohol abuse/dependence, drug abuse/dependence and antisocial-personality disorder. The five most common disorders for women were: phobia, dysthymia, major depressive episode, alcohol abuse/dependence, and obsessive-compulsive disorder (Bland, Newman and Orn 1988).

In Caribbean countries and Central America, outpatient mental health services are used more frequently by females, and inpatient services are used more by males. American and UK studies show that most women are treated by general practitioners, while men receive specialized treatment.

As noted above, studies have suggested that women are at greater risk for disorders involving anxiety and depression or for "neurotic" disorders generally. Yet a computer search on a large medical data base revealed less than 1 percent concerning gender and *anxiety* disorders (Cameron and Hill 1989). Neurotic disorders per se were excluded from DSM-III, while ICD-9 includes anxiety states under neurotic disorders. Some believe that generalized anxiety, panic attacks, and phobias may be considered predisposing factors to an ultimate diagnosis of affective disorder (Paltiel 1987).

*Phobia*, a most common disorder in women, is lowest in the 65-plus age group. Women represent approximately 85 percent of reported cases of agoraphobia, the most pervasive form. According to Cameron and Hill, in clinical samples, social phobia is more common in males than in females (Cameron and Hill 1989). The relationship of symptoms of anxiety states or panic disorders to organic illnesses (e.g. thyrotoxicosis, pheochromocytoma, or hypoglycemia) as well as to the destabilizing perimenopausal vasomotor disturbances needs closer examination. What is considered agoraphobia in some women may have environmental rather than psychogenic explanations. Since women are justifiably fearful of rape and sexual or physical assault in unprotected and unfamiliar surroundings, as well as in some intimate relationships, these situations must be better understood. A Canadian public opinion poll revealed that 34 percent of Canadian women are afraid of walking alone at night in their own neighborhoods (Ottawa Citizen 1991).

Moreover women's round-the-clock caring responsibilities for partners, the infirm, children, and others places them in a state of "hypervigilance," which may be interpreted as a disorder, or may indeed lead to anxiety disorders, in the absence of relief or support. It is not surprising, therefore, to find that female phobias are more often diagnosed as generalized and male phobias as more discrete. Cameron and Hill also suggest that possible bias may exist in clinical definitions (Cameron and Hill 1989).

*Depression*, because of the prevalence, persistence, recurrence and interference with well-being and performance, is the single most serious mental problem for women, with a preponderance for females in every age group. Sartorius et al. (1980) found that the "core" symptoms of depression (e.g. sadness, worthlessness, lethargy, decreased interest and concentration) vary little from country to country. Depression and associated affective/ mood disorders have been estimated to affect approximately 8 percent of the U.S. population. An estimated two-thirds do not receive treatment. The age of onset of major depression is declining; the mean age of onset is twenty-seven years. In the U.S., young, poor, sole-support mothers, and young married women who work at dead-end jobs are particularly vulnerable.

The American Psychological Association (APA) Task Force on Women's Depression investigated the relationship to women's psychological characteristics, reproductive-related events, social roles, and life circumstances. Severe life strains associated with poverty, physical illness, family relationships, home and work circumstances, and losses were hypothesized. The personality traits hypothesized are low self-esteem, gender-role sensitization, women's orientation towards others, pessimistic explanatory style, less perceived life control, and devaluation of the female gender role. Studies show that employed wives with low marital strain and low employment strain have the lowest rate of depression, while nonemployed with high marital strain have the highest rate of depression. The Task Force calls for an improved understanding of neuroendocrinology—particularly the role of serotonin—within a social context and the need for a better clinical history taking. The Report suggests that diagnostic bias needs further exploration as disorder rates are higher for disorders congruent with society's idealized view of femininity, while other disorders (e.g. alcohol dependency) may be neglected, untreated, or misdiagnosed in women.

The relationship of psychosocial and economic factors such as stress, conflict in interpersonal relations, physical and sexual abuse, discrimination, and poverty to women's depression requires more systematic examination (APA 1990).

Immune failures may contribute to mental illness, as demonstrated in AIDS, as patients live longer and develop psychoneurological complications. Almost all known autoimmune diseases occur predominantly in females—SLE, 6-9:1; rheumatoid arthritis, 2:1; multiple sclerosis, 2:1. Diabetes and hypertension, which are also female-predominant diseases in Latin America and the Caribbean, produce changes in brain activity.

*Schizophrenia*, although equally distributed between the sexes, appears to have a different course in women, including differences in age of onset, intensity, chronicity, and recurrence. It was formerly diagnosed by its negative prognosis. Current evidence suggests that approximately 60 percent can achieve an outcome of significant improvement or full recovery with appropriate treatment and support, although the course is often complex with acute periods, remissions, and chronic phases (Thornton, 1989).

Table 9.1 synthesizes some salient features of significant, female-predominant, seemingly intractable disorders which shed increasing light on the personality-shattering consequences of sexual abuse presented as different disorders. We lack information on the occurrence of eating disorders, borderline personality disorder or post-traumatic stress disorder in developing countries. We have failed to look into these dark corners of the lives of girls and women.

TABLE 9.1 Selected Disorders/Female Predominant or Gender Implications

| Disorder | Prevalence estimate | Characteristics | Determinants/Etiology | Social Implications | Ref |
|---|---|---|---|---|---|
| Anorexia Nervosa | 1:200-250 young females; 90% female sex distribution | starvation; distorted body image; amenorrhea–reduced body thermostat | sex-role conflicts; ideal of thinness; ballet training locus of control/self esteem | elevated mortality risk; need for gender-sensitive treatment (G.S.T.) | 31,32 33,34 |
| Bulimia | up to 20% female college population; 95% female sex distribution | binge eating; vomiting; distorted body image; lability | sex-role conflicts; sexual abuse; self-esteem impairments; locus-of-control problem | symptom overlap with borderline; need for G.S.T. | 31,32 35,36 |
| Borderline Personality Disorder | prevalence unknown; 60-80% female sex distribution | dissociation; unstable intense relationship; identity disturbance; self-damage; intense anger; emptiness | history of sexual abuse/incest | formerly considered intractable; addressing sexual abuse key to recovery | 37,38 |
| Post-Traumatic Stress Disorder | Prevalence unknown | dissociation conversion reactions; flashback; depressed affect; agitation; numbness | survival of overwhelming experience (e.g. Holocaust, disasters), sexual abuse, torture, hostage | suspected elevated mortality rate; overlap with multiple personality disorder; need for G.S.T. | 31,37 39 |
| Schizophrenia | 1:100-150; even sex distribution; later female onset, age 25-44 | disassociation, disordered thought; aggressiveness; withdrawal; hallucination; stupor; inappropriate affect; major cause of psychiatric hospitalization | etiology unknown; genetic/toxic/psychosocial factors unknown; neurotransmitter impairment | risks include stigma, chronic tardive dyskinesia, poverty, homelessness, 'bag-lady' syndrome | 31,40 41,42 43 |

Source: Paltiel, F.L. "Women and Mental Health in the Americas." In *Women, Health and Development in the Americas.* Washingon D.C.: Pan American Health Organization. Typescript.

## Suicide

While men have higher rates for death by suicide (2–3:1), women predominate for attempted suicides, which occur more frequently than completed suicides. Weissman notes that depression and suicide are highly related disorders; however, whereas the typical depressed woman is a married person between twenty-five and forty years of age, the typical suicide attempter is a single woman under the age of twenty-five, often as young as fifteen (Weissman 1986). Nonfatal attempters have been found to have personality disorder, chemical dependence, or "situational disorder" (Blumenthal 1988). Suicide rates also vary by age, occupation, race, immigrant status, physical and mental conditions, and marital status. The greatest risk for suicide is among the widowed, divorced, and those who live alone. Black persons appear to be at lower risk, although it is rising among the young; while aboriginal persons, especially youth, are at elevated risk. Physicians have twice the risk for committing suicide as the general population. Among women, suicide risks are elevated for chemists, nurses, medical students, and pharmacists. This has important implications for workplace mental health within the health sector. Psychiatric disorders are highly predictive of completed suicides (Blumenthal 1988). Significant physical illness, mainly serious malignancy, are determining factors. Unemployment is an established risk factor, but for the long-term unemployed this may be confounded by the presence of a mental or personality disorder.

Blumenthal's risk assessment provides some useful clues to gender differences in suicidal behavior. Lethality is one of the confirmed factors that separates the completers, mainly male, from the attempters, mainly female. Over 50 percent of male suicides use firearms; however, a disturbing fact is that one-half of American young women now use firearms (Blumenthal 1988). Suicide incidence is 20 percent greater for drug users than for the general population. One factor cited by Blumenthal as a precipitant is a humiliating life event. The combination of aggressiveness, alcohol abuse, sociopathic tendencies, and the perception of an event as humiliating may differentiate males from females. The hypotheses related to these differences need to be studied. Social-integration theories in relation to the high rates of suicide among indigenous persons, particularly the young also require further study.

Earlier explorations of gender differences cited hysterical acts and attention-getting behavior of female attempters. Current concepts of "parasuicide" similarly differentiate intent. Ambivalence is always present. This author hypothesizes that women are held back from completing the act by their empathy for survivors, even when the latter are the cause of their despair.

## Substance Use and Abuse

There is ample evidence that women are more likely than men to receive prescribed psychotropic drugs, including antianxiety agents, sedatives and hypnotics, antipsychotic agents and antidepressants, in an estimated ratio of 2:1. Even when type of medical condition is controlled, women are more likely than men to receive prescription in doctor visits. Divorced, separated or widowed women receive more prescriptions (Cafferata and Meyers 1990).

Gender-specific studies on addictions are recent and sparse, but of growing importance and concern as the continuing and increasing use and abuse of substances such as alcohol, drugs and tobacco among younger women becomes more evident. Sociocultural pressures, psychic and physical distress, a quest for instant gratification regardless of the long-term adverse consequences have all been advanced as determinant factors by a WHO Expert Committee of Drug Dependence (Johnson 1986). Moreover, since women are more likely than men to have cross-addictions, a single-substance approach is not productive.

Despite increasing alcohol use and abuse among women, little is known about the determinants, circumstances and consequences of female drinking. A review article by Blume noted differences in women for "peak blood alcohol levels, patterns of drinking, effects of drinking on sexual functioning, onset of alcohol-related diseases, and demographics and clinical characteristics of patients" (Blume 1986).

Alcohol consumption contributes significantly to etiology and/or to cause and outcome of various physical, psychological and behaviorial problems. Moreover, it is difficult to disentangle life events caused by drinking and drinking caused by lifeevents. Even consumption at levels below the thresholds of alcohol-dependence may increase adverse health consequences, including cirrhosis of the liver. Risks include injury, debilitating or lethal medical complication of the gastrointestinal, nervous, cardiovascular and respiratory systems as well as adverse pregnancy outcomes and fetal abnormalities (Ashley and Rankin 1986). The lack of intimacy and or a confiding relationship have been identified as contributing factors to women's alcohol dependency.

One study comparing younger with older women in treatment found startling differences in age of onset of substance abuse. Four times as many younger women began drinking before age sixteen, while nearly half of the young women, compared with just 3 percent of the older women, began using drugs by age fifteen, with intravenous drug use six times as common among the younger group (Harrison 1989). A Trinidad and Tobago study notes that female admissions for alcoholism increased between 1970 and 1980 from 2.4 to 10.0 percent of all female admissions, while admissions for women with drug dependencies increased 300 percent from 1970 to 1984 (Sharpe 1986).

Women with higher rates of tobacco use tend to be young, poor, less educated, indigenous, institutionalized, or otherwise disadvantaged. Cross-dependency of tobacco and alcohol is generally overlooked by researchers.

## Gender Bias in Research

The inadequacy of existing scientific knowledge for understanding gender differences in mental disorders and treatments is beginning to receive systematic attention, with the NIMH currently developing a women's mental health agenda (Russo 1990). We need a much clearer understanding of the psychosocial aspects of chronic disease while not dismissing symptoms as psychogenic in origin. Many if not most chronic diseases cannot be cured, are slow and insidious in onset, are difficult to diagnose, and are characterized by mysterious exacerbations and remissions resulting in multiple referrals to various specialists and the prescription of various mood-altering drugs. On the other hand, we must avoid the medicalization of social problems experienced by women. Gender- and culture-sensitive mental health research is still a neglected area.

An examination of leading medical journals found pervasive examples of an androcentric perspective, generalization to both sexes from male-only studies, gender-insensitivity, and a double standard for judging identical behaviors, traits or situations (Eichler et al. 1988). This is extended to medical practice. For example, a recent multi-center study conducted in Canada and the U.S. concluded that, despite the fact that coronary artery disease (CAD) is the leading cause of death in women, physicians pursued a less aggressive management approach to coronary disease in women than in men, despite greater cardiac disability in women (Steingart et.al. 1991). Another study found that women hospitalized for coronary heart disease undergo fewer major diagnostic and therapeutic procedures than men (Ayanian and Epstein 1991).

Research samples may consist of males and females to meet requirements of granting agencies. Findings, however, are reported for sexes aggregated or for males only, suppressing or ignoring information on females. This is particularly glaring in gerontological studies, where females are the majority. Critical knowledge is curtailed when clinical trials are performed on young males for medications to be used for diseases which occur mainly in older women, who metabolize drugs differently. Bias is also evident in the choice of research topics, as women are underrepresented in the policy-making levels of research organizations, as faculty in universities or as gatekeepers in research establishments. Current Congressional scrutiny in the U.S. should influence future research practices.

## Shifting the Paradigms and Practices

The Parsonian assumptions of instrumental men and expressive women as functional in industrial societies, continue to guide sociological and psychological observations and inferences regarding sex-appropriate male and female behavior, including the concept of sick role behavior for women. The normative views of male providers and women dependents continues to be operant, despite women's rising participation rates and support of dependents.

"On the threshold of the twenty-first century, we are hobbled by nine-teenth century psychological theory linked to biological determinism. The basic scaffolding of psychodynamic thought is still sexist, viewing women as inadequate, irrational or incomplete humans with unstable superegos and penis envy. A coherent, fully elaborated psychological theory of women's development does not yet exist" (Paltiel forthcoming).

In the past twenty years the women's movement has questioned and altered precepts and practices and has challenged the applicable categories and terms to women's depression and fears (Fedele and Miller 1988). New insights are emerging of how women think, feel and behave, which challenge traditional assumptions of health, pathology, maturity, and sex-stereotyped care-giving allocations.

Women are caught in a double bind as their mental-illness burden is ascribed to their help-seeking behavior, while their sensitivity to others is interpreted as weakness. We need more and better studies on the health and mental-health effects of women's help-giving, rather than help-seeking, behaviors as others rely on their strengths and sense of responsibility—to the detriment of their own well-being, including burnout, a form of physical and emotional exhaustion.

## Effective Mental Health Policy: Programs and Practices

We need mental health systems which promote, protect, and restore the mental health of females and males of all ages in culturally appropriate ways. Mental health is crucial to women's well-being and performance of life's tasks. Girls' and women's overwork, exhaustion, and undervaluation saps their energy and damages their self-esteem. Women's unsupported and taken-for-granted caring functions affect their physical and mental health. With cutbacks in health and social services their caring burdens are increased.

Women's health advocates, researchers, and health providers are developing new paradigms and practices to address women's health needs:

- primary health care, to be effective, must include attention to psychosocial aspects of health and disease;
- healthy public policy should promote women's mental health by building supportive environments reducing inequities and enhancing coping and control;
- health providers require a better understanding of women's life circumstances and their effects on mental health;
- gender bias in research and practice should be identified and eliminated;
- care-givers' functions should be more equitably shared and rewarded;
- women must participate more fully in all the decision making which affects them, their families and societies.

Mental health workers must participate in those policies which develop and resource mental health. But mental-health professionals must prepare themselves for these tasks by altering perspectives, and by ridding themselves of class-bound, culture-bound, and gender-bound assumptions about appropriate thoughts, feelings and behaviors, as well as paternalistic, patronizing methods of treatment.

In recent years, mental health professionals have developed principles and guidelines for therapy and counseling to reduce gender and culture bias and sex-role stereotyping. Feminist therapists have adopted approaches to counter the paternalistic features of traditional doctor-patient relationships and replace them with:

- a more egalitarian, less authoritarian therapeutic alliance with shared responsibility;
- the recognition of cultural and socioeconomic determinants of feeling, self-esteem and expression;
- the enhancement of healthy social relationships and the nourishment of aspirations; and
- therapy aimed at strengthening and empowering the woman seeking help.

More systematic training in psychosocial aspects of health for all health workers would ensure that they recognize threats to mental health, factors which promote mental health, and signs of mental illness and disorder, and acquire competence for effective surveillance, treatment, management, advice and rehabilitation. Mental health policy should also ensure that health workers have a better understanding of the different situations, resources, demands and power relations of women and men, and understand the needs for care of care-givers.

FIGURE 9.1 Paltiel Positive Coping Schema

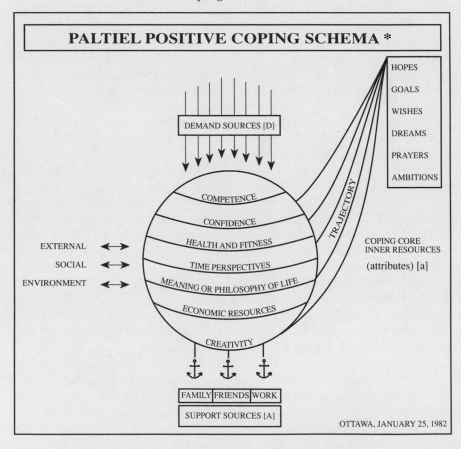

*Source:* Paltiel, F.L. "Is Being Poor a Mental Health Hazard?" *Women & Health,* vol. 12 no. 3/4, pp. 189-210.

## Stress, Social Support, and Coping

Economic security is a basic and necessary, but insufficient, condition for mental health. Discrimination is an overlooked stressor in the lives of all women. We have empirical evidence from various studies that the support gap is a significant contributor to women's depression. Lennon, Wasserman and Allen found that women with more than one child under three, regardless of others' involvement, are significantly more depressed if their husband's involvement in auxiliary child care is low (Lennon et. al. 1991).

Life-events research is not useful for understanding women's risks, yet Cohen and Wills report that 90 percent of studies of stress, social support, and well-being, use cumulative-event measures. They also found that support may maintain health, attenuate or prevent a stress-appraisal response, alleviate the impact of stress through a problem solution, reduce the perceived importance of the problem, tranquilize the neuroendocrine system, or facilitate healthful behaviors. A single confidant may buffer stress by influencing feelings of self-esteem and self-efficacy, with women showing more benefit than men (Cohen and Wills 1985).

Examples of groups in possible double jeopardy and with special needs for supportive environments, enhanced coping and control, and specific measures for the reduction of inequities are poor women, women with disabilities, visible minorities, immigrants and refugee women, and aboriginal women.

The author's three-anchor needs/supports postulate has been incorporated into a positive coping schema and coping formula in which these three anchors serve as support sources, balanced against an inventory of demands and mediated by both external environmental factors which favor or hinder the attributes or inner resources of the individual—with all of these related to a person's aspirations (See Figure 9.1). The Formula is: Anchors (A) plus attributes (a) minus Demands (D) equals the Coping Quotient (A+a-D=CQ). This formula can be tested and applied within programs which seek to enhance individual coping and control, in the realization that personality is only one of the factors to be considered; and that even personal attributes can be acquired only when discriminatory obstacles to their attainment are removed—positive action promotes their acquisition and aspirations can be nourished.

*The views expressed are those of the author and not necessarily those of Health and Welfare Canada or the Government of Canada. The material in this paper has been addressed more extensively in a chapter prepared for the Pan American Health Organization's forthcoming edition of Women, Health and Development in the Americas.*

# References

American Psychological Association (APA). 1990. *Women and depression: risk factors and treatment issues*: final report of the American Psychological Association's National Task Force on Women and Depression. Edited by E. McGrath et al., Washington, D.C.

Ashley, M.J. and Rankin, J.G. Alcohol-related Health Problems and their Prevention. In: *Public Health and Preventive Medicine*. Last, J.M. (ed.) Norwalk, Conn: Appleton-Century-Crofts, 1986.

Ayanian, J.Z., and Epstein, A.M. 1991. "Differences in the Use of Procedures between Women and Men Hospitalized for Coronary Artery Disease." *NEMJ*, Vol.325 no.4, July 25 pp. 221-225.

Barnett, E.A. 1988. La edad critica: The positive experience of menopause in a small Peruvian town. In: Patricia Whelehan, *Women and Health: Cross cultural perspectives*. Massachusetts, Bergin and Garvey.

Beyene, Y. 1989. *From Menarche to Menopause: Reproductive lives of peasant women in the cultures*. Albany, State University of New York Press.

Bland, R.C., Newman, S.C. & Orn, H. 1988. "Period Prevalence of Psychiatric Disorders in Edmonton." *Acta Psychiatrica Scandinavia*, 77 (suppl. 338): 33-42.

Blume, S.B. 1986. "Women and Alcohol: A Review" *JAMA* Sept. 19, Vol. 256, no.11, pp.1467-1470.

Blumenthal, S.J. 1988. "Suicide: A guide to risk factors, assessment, and treatment of suicidal patients." *Medical Clinics of North America*, 72 (4): 937-971.

Boyle, M.H. 1991. Children's Mental Health Issues. In: Johnson, L.C. and Barnhorst, D. (eds), *Children, Families and Public Policy in the 90s*, Toronto, Thompson Educational Publishing, Inc.

Bryer, J.B., et al. 1987. "Childhood Sexual and Physical Abuse as Factors in Adult Psychiatric Illness." *American Journal of Psychiatry*, 144: 1426-1430. Cited in: Sexual traumata among eating-disordered, psychiatric, and normal female groups by H. Steiger and M. Zanko (Journal of interpersonal violence, 5 (1): 74-86, 1990).

Cafferata, G.L. & Meyers, S.M. 1990. "Pathways to Psychotropic Drugs: Understanding the basis of gender differences." *Medical Care*, 28 (4): 285-300.

Cameron, O.G. & Hill, E.M. 1989. "Women and Anxiety." *Psychiatric Clinics of North America*, 12 (1): 175-186.

Cohen, S. & Wills, T.A. 1985. "Stress, Social Support, and the Buffering Hypothesis." *Psychological Bulletin*, vol.98 (2): 310-357.

Duchmann, E.G, Williamson, D.A. & Stricker, P.M. 1989. "Bulimia, Dietary Restraint, and Concern for Dieting." *Journal of Psychopathology and Behavioral Assessment*, 11 (1): 1-13.

Eichler, M. et al. 1988. *Gender Bias in Medical Research*. Presented at Day on "Gender, Science and Medicine." University of Toronto, November.

Fedele, N., and Miller, J.B. 1988. *Putting Theory into Practice: Creating Health Programs for Women*, work in progress, Stone Center for Development of Services and Studies.

Garner, D.M. & Garfinkle, P.E. 1980. " Socio-cultural Factors in the Development of Anorexia Nervosa." *Psychological Medicine* 10: 647-656. Cited in: Women and Mental Health: A post Nairobi perspective, Freda L. Paltiel, WHO Stat. Q.

Gross, J. 1991, More young single men hang onto apron strings. New York Times, June 16, p.1.

Hamilton, James A. 1989. "Postpartum psychiatric syndromes." *Psychiatric Clinics of North America*, 12 (1): 89-103.

Hamilton, Jean A., Parry, B.L., & Blumenthal, S.J. 1988. "The menstrual cycle in content, I: Affective syndromes associated with reproductive hormonal changes." *Journal of Clinical Psychiatry*, 49 (12): 474-480.

Hamilton, Jean A. et al. 1988. "The menstrual cycle in context, 11: Human Gonadal steroid hormone variability." *Journal of Clinical Psychiatry*, 49 (12):480-484.

Harrison, P.A. 1989. "Women in Treatment: Changing over Time." *Int. J. of the Addictions*, Vol. 24. no. 7. pp. 655-673.Conn: Appleton-Century-Crofts, 1986.

Herman, J.L. & Van der Kolk, B.A. 1987. "Traumatic Antecedents of Borderline Personality Disorder." In: *Psychological Trauma*. Washington, American Psychiatric Press Inc.

Johnson, A. Prevention and Control of Drug Abuse. In: *Public Health and Preventive Medicine*. Last, J.M. (ed.) Norwalk, Conn: Appleton-Century-Crofts, 1986.

Lennon, M.C., et. al. 1991. "Infant Care and Wives' Depressive Symptoms". *Women and Health*, Vol. 17 No.2, pp. 1-24.

McCarthy, M. 1990. "The Thin Ideal: Depression and Eating Disorders in Women." *Behavior Res. Ther.*, 28 (3): 205-215.

Mills, C. & Ota, H. 1989. "Homeless Women with Minor Children in the Detroit Metropolitan Area." *Social Work*, 34, (6): 485-486.

Moser, C. 1989. "The Impact of Recession and Adjustment Policies at the Micro-level: Low-income women and their households in Guayanquil, Ecuador" in UNICEF, Regional Office for Latin America and the Caribbean, *The Invisible Adjustment: Poor Women and the Economic Crisis*, Santiago, Chile, pp. 137-166.

National Advisory Mental Health Council (NAMHC). 1989. *Approaching the 21st century: Opportunities for NIMH Neuroscience Research*. Report to Congress on the Decade of the Brain. Rockville, National Institute of Mental Health.

National Institute of Mental Health (NIMH). 1990. *National Plan for Research on Child and Adolescent Mental Disorders*. A report requested by the U.S. Congress submitted by the National Advisory Mental Health Council, Maryland.

Ottawa Citizen, p.1., May 23, 1991.

Paltiel, F.L. 1981. "Shaping Futures for Women." *Women's Studies International Quarterly*, 4, No. 1:13-25.

Paltiel, F.L. 1987. "Women and Mental Health: A Post-Nairobi Perspective." *World Health Statistics Quarterly*, 40: 233-266.

Paltiel, F.L. 1987a. "Is Being Poor a Mental Health Hazard?" *Women and Health*, vol. 12 no. 3/4, pp. 189-210.

Paltiel, F.L., "Mental Health of Women in the Americas." In *Women, Health and Development in the Americas*, Pan American Health Organization (in press).

Robins, L.N. and Regier, D.A. 1991. An overview of psychiatric disorders in America. In: *Psychiatric Disorders in America*. (The Epidemiologic Catchment Area Study). New York, The Free Press.

Rothblum, E.D. 1990. "Women and Weight: Fad and Fiction." *Journal of Psychology*, 124 (1): 5-24.

Russo, N.F. 1990. "Overview: Forging research priorities for women's mental health." *American Psychologist*, 45 (3): 368-373.

Sadik, N. 1990. "The UNFPA Contribution: Theory to Action Programmes." *Development, Journal of the Society for International Development*, 1:7-12.

Sartorius L., et al. 1980. "WHO Collaborative Study: Assessment of Depressive Disorders." *Psychological Medicine*, 10: 743-749.North America, 12 (1): 175-186.

Seiden, A.M. 1989. "Psychological Issues Affecting Women Throughout the Life Cycle." *Psychiatric Clinics of North America*, 12 (1): 1-24.

Sharpe, J. 1986. *The Mental Health of Women in Trinidad and Tobago*. Report submitted to PAHO as part of Mental Health of Women in the Caribbean.

Stavrakaki, C. & Williams, E., 1990. "Eating Disorders in Adolescents: Anorexia Nervosa and Bulimia." *Canadian Journal of Pediatric*. February: 7-20.

Stavrakaki, C. et al. 1991. "Pilot-study of Anxiety and Depression in Prepubertal Children." *Canadian Journal of Psychiatry*, 36 (5): 332-338.

Steingart, R.M. 1991."Sex Differences in the Management of Coronary Artery Disease." *NEMJ*, Vol 325. no.4, July 25, pp.226-230.

Thornton, J. F. 1989. "Schizophrenia: Courses and Outcome." Clarke Institute of Psychiatry, University of Toronto, Toronto (issued by Professional Services Department, Merrell Dow, Canada).

United Nations (UN), Department of Economic and Social Affairs Statistical Office. 1991. *The World's Women 1970-1990: Trends and Statistics*, United Nations, New York.

Van der Kolk, B.A. 1987. "The Psychological Consequences of Overwhelming Life Experiences." In: *Psychological Trauma*. Washington, American Psychiatric Press Inc.

Weissman, M.M. "Being Young and Female: Risk Factors for Major Depression." In: G.L. Klerman, ed. *Suicide and Depression Among Adolescents and Young Adults*. American Psychiatric Press Inc., 1986.

World Health Organization (WHO). 1990. *WHO's Activities in the Field of Child and Adolescent Mental Health and Psychosocial Development*. WHO/MNH/PSF/90.2

# 10

## Access to Care: More Than a Problem of Distance

*Judith Timyan, Susan J. Griffey Brechin,*
*Diana M. Measham, and Bisi Ogunleye*

Significant progress has been made over the past few decades in providing health care to populations in developing countries. But this progress has been uneven; women, in particular, have not had an equal share. The availability of care in pregnancy and childbirth provides an example: Of the 130 million deliveries that take place each year in the developing world, only 50 percent are attended by trained personnel (Petros-Barvazian 1991). Women's inadequate access to health care is also reflected in mortality statistics: While infant mortality rates have declined significantly over the past few decades, maternal mortality levels remain stubbornly high, despite the fact that "maternal health" has received the most attention within the complex of women's health needs.

The elements required for women to have effective access to care are myriad and complex. While ensuring the availability of facilities and personnel within reasonable distance is indeed a primary requirement, effective access to care can only be ensured if that care is considered affordable, appropriate and acceptable by the women it aims to serve. The 18th International Health Conference of the National Council of International Health, held in Arlington, Virginia in June 1991 on the theme "Women's Health: The Action Agenda for the '90s" was notable for highlighting the complexity of issues that restrict women's access to care, many of which relate to demand rather than supply. To be sure, such factors as distance from the site of care, lack of availability of equipment and supplies at the site, and lack of money to cover the costs of transportation and treatment were mentioned often by both panelists and participants. In many cases, however, the key constraints to access were identified as being of a sociocultural or informational nature, including lack of awareness of

217

health issues, the low social and legal status assigned to women in most cultures, lack of self-esteem and sense of control, religious restrictions, and perceived inappropriateness of care.

As a result, the discussion of supply and demand factors that follows emphasizes the determinants of women's utilization of services rather than the health system's supply of services. Thus, service factors are primarily considered from a demand-side perspective—that is, how these factors affect women's ability or decision to seek health care.

## Supply-Side Determinants: Service Factors

### Physical Infrastructure and Service Organization

According to the World Bank, the single most important obstacle the poor face in gaining access to health services remains the lack of physical infrastructure (World Bank 1991). This is certainly still true for the majority of women in developing countries, where there are major inequities in the distribution of health facilities and personnel, and where transport and communication infrastructure is inadequately developed. Scarce health sector resources are often disproportionately spent on urban-based hospital care rather than rural primary care. Where strategies have been implemented to increase access to primary care in rural areas they have resulted at times in additional and unexpected rural/urban inequities. The use of community health workers (CHWs) provides an example. In some settings, this approach has imposed a disproportionate burden on rural communities, which are typically obliged to provide personal resources in support of the CHW, while urban families continue to use government-supplied and subsidized health services free of charge (Ogunleye 1991).

Women's health care is often channeled through maternal and child health (MCH) services. Because these services are typically limited to reproductive health, representing only a subset of women's health needs, MCH services have in fact restricted access to care for many women. Indeed, MCH services usually address only a subset of women's reproductive health needs. The needs of young, unmarried women, women seeking pregnancy termination, women suffering from reproductive-tract infections and infertility, and women past childbearing age have been largely neglected (Leslie and Gupta 1989; Kurz 1991; Burdman 1991). In addition, MCH services have historically focused on the needs of the child. This can result in conflicts between maternal and child health needs, a situation that must be better understood if a balance between maternal and child health care is to be achieved (Heymann 1991).

The roots of women's health problems are often found in a lack of adequate access to care in infancy, childhood and adolescence. In many countries, female children are less likely to be fed adequately or to receive medical attention than male children. In India, for example, boys are fifty times more likely to be hospitalized for treatment of protein-energy malnutrition, though this condition is four to five times more common among girls (Gupta 1987 as cited in Starrs and Measham 1990). In some societies, preferential feeding practices in favor of male children continue through adolescence and into adulthood, resulting in chronic micronutrient deficiencies among girls and women (Kurz 1991). Existing health services rarely focus on this issue in any systematic fashion.

A primary focus on the *physical* dimensions of women's health has resulted in poor access to mental health care for women in both developed and developing countries (Paltiel 1991). Finally, there is an urgent need to address the health needs of women who are elderly (Burdman 1991), handicapped, terminally ill, or physically abused (Heise 1991). This neglect of women's general health needs is, in fact, reflected in the content of this chapter, which highlights data on maternal care, given the paucity of information on other areas. (For extensive bibliographies on factors affecting women's access to and utilization of maternal health care, see Leslie and Gupta 1989 and Thaddeus and Maine 1990).

## Location of Services

Distance limits women's willingness and ability to seek care, particularly when appropriate transportation is in limited supply, communications difficult, and terrain and climate inhospitable. In Mexico, for example, the existence of a "good road" was associated with a 30 percent increase in prenatal care utilization (Leslie and Gupta 1989). While women are more likely to overcome distance barriers when faced with emergencies, the emergency itself compounds the difficulties involved. Transporting a woman facing pregnancy-related complications is a formidable task, particularly when terrain is rough and transport options limited. In India's Ananthapur District, of women transported to the hospital with serious pregnancy-related complications, 69 percent went by public bus and 19 percent by animal-drawn carts (Bhatia 1986 as cited in Thaddeus and Maine 1990). One Chinese study found that 15 percent of recorded maternal deaths occurred en route to the hospital (Lingmei and Ding 1988 as cited in Thaddeus and Maine 1990). These logistical difficulties are compounded further still by cultural restrictions on women's mobility.

A survey in rural Uganda found that among the minority of women who deliver in health facilities, most walk or use a bicycle for transport. The survey also confirmed that men often control the necessary cash for transport to and use of services, yet they lack understanding of the risks of pregnancy and need for care. The prohibitive cost, or sheer lack, of transport was identified as a significant barrier to access. In one district, the family of a woman suffering from obstructed labor had to butcher two goats to pay village men to carry her to the nearest facility (Kasolo 1991).

A study in rural West Java also found that deficiencies in communication and transportation were major barriers to access to maternal care. Based on the study findings, a regional care system is being developed to link health facilities and providers. "Maternal and Child Huts," staffed by nurse midwives and traditional birth attendants (TBAs), will provide prenatal care, routine delivery, and other services at the village level. The huts will be linked to health centers and hospitals via a communications network and improved transport between health service levels. They will also be located near both the community and a road, and will have access to four-wheel-drive vehicles (Alisjahbana 1991).

A recent study in Senegal makes it clear that even small increments of distance can have a discernable effect. A network of health huts was established, each one to serve four to six villages, based on the theory that making the full range of primary care services available at the village level would provide universal access. Differences in utilization remained, however, primarily between those residing in the village where the health hut was located and those defined residing in a peripheral village. Service utilization among both men and women in peripheral villages was significantly lower than that among those in health hut villages, In addition, women in the peripheral villages were affected more than men. The results of this study imply that we must move beyond generalizing about socioeconomic groups and "peripheral" populations. Identifying target populations within a generally disadvantaged population is necessary to ensure maximum program impact (Leighton 1991).

Bringing services closer to women—through the provision of mobile services or home-based care, for example—would overcome many of the distance and transport constraints currently affecting access to care. Other creative solutions include the establishment of maternity waiting homes close to hospitals, where women can be transferred prior to the onset of labor, or ensuring the availability of transport by setting aside community funds or making arrangements with community members with access to vehicles (Thaddeus and Maine 1990).

## Availability, Use, and Distribution of Personnel

Constraints related to the availability of health personnel stem as much from their inefficient use within the health care system as they do from inadequate numbers and inequitable distribution. Significant factors include lack of appropriate training, reluctance among medical professionals to grant greater responsibility to the nursing and midwifery corps, and lack of coordination between levels of health personnel.

For instance, the important role of traditional care providers is often not recognized, despite documented community preferences for such care, particularly during pregnancy and childbirth. TBAs assist 60–80 percent of all births in developing countries (Leslie and Gupta 1989) and yet they have not been incorporated into formal community-level maternal care in many instances. Formal services should supplement rather than supplant such care, ensuring appropriate training, supervision, and access to referral services.

Trained midwives, who serve as the bridge between communities, TBAs and clinical resources, are key to improving access to maternal care in most developing countries. Unfortunately, their absolute and relative numbers are declining in many settings. In Tanzania, for example, the midwife-to-live-birth ratio has declined by 50 percent in the last ten years. Strong voices were raised at the NCIH Conference urging not only an increase in the number of midwives but that they also be trained in essential obstetric functions, which would enable them to handle emergencies more effectively in the absence of specialist care (Kwast 1991). Posting midwives trained to handle common obstetric problems at the community level can improve currently limited access to obstetric care, with significant corresponding mortality reductions. In Matlab, Bangladesh, where trained midwives were posted at two health outposts and given responsibility for attending home deliveries, detecting and managing obstetric complications, and/or referring and accompanying patients to the project maternity center, maternal mortality was reduced by 68 percent in only three years (Fauveau 1991). Other examples of the benefits of recognizing the role and enhancing the skills of this important cadre of health workers are outlined below.

In Grenada, where the maternal mortality ratio is now only 120 deaths per 100,000 live births, prenatal and delivery care are provided by nurse-midwives who are given significant responsibility and are trained to use well-defined protocols to recognize and refer women with signs of complications. Training and delegation of responsibility must be complemented by appropriate logistical changes to ensure effective interaction between the levels of the maternal health care system; in Grenada, improved telephone communications between the nurse-midwives and higher-level facilities has been essential to its smooth functioning (Laukaran 1991).

In Ghana, life-saving skills were taught to midwives when it became clear that they were widely and effectively utilized in the private sector, though poorly integrated into the government health care system. Ghana-ian midwives have close, mutually respectful relationships with the community and traditional practitioners. With training in advanced midwifery skills and supportive obstetrical backup and supervision, they have been able to provide life-saving therapy in rural areas, with significant corresponding mortality reductions. Emergency cases are referred to formal care facilities when available. When specialist care is not available, however, the midwives are able to deal with emergencies that would have previously gone unattended (Marshall 1991).

As noted above, a healthy relationship between different cadres of health workers is essential to ensuring access to care. While greater attention is perhaps being paid to the relationship between midwives and the medical community, less has been paid to that between midwives and TBAs. In Nigeria, for example, TBAs and midwives have a traditionally poor relationship; midwives are reluctant to accept TBA clients, and women themselves are sometimes reluctant to seek midwifery care, fearing a reprimand from the midwife for having relied on the TBA. A program is currently being implemented to improve this relationship, which should enhance access to midwifery care significantly (Okafor 1991).

The gender of health care providers is also a significant factor affecting women's use of services. Egypt provides a classic example of the problems inherent in the male doctor–female patient relationship in many settings. While trained providers are available throughout the country, most are male physicians from whom women cannot accept or do not want treatment due to the widely-held belief that women should not be seen after puberty by any male other than close relatives. Often, women need permission from their male guardian to seek care, even in emergencies. Any independently initiated association with a male who is not a close relative puts the woman at risk of being accused of sexual misconduct, which would cause irreparable damage to her reputation and that of her family. As a result, women's experience in talking to men who are not close relatives is limited; this in itself may negatively influence the efficacy of the client-provider relationship and thus the efficacy of care (Krieger 1991).

Islamic northern Cameroon provides another example. Men in that region are not allowed to touch other men's wives, even for medical examinations or emergency treatment, without the husband's authorization. Women themselves say they would prefer to die rather than seek unauthorized care in their husband's absence (Alexandre 1991).

Unfortunately, increasing the numbers of female physicians does not always solve problems of access. Indeed, the cultural and religious barriers that limit women's access to male providers also limit the ability of female providers to practice in those areas where they are most needed. There are many female physicians in Egypt, for example, but they are rarely assigned to rural areas where they are needed for the above-stated reasons, because they would be isolated and away from the protection of their families. In addition, some Egyptians feel that female physicians are less competent than male physicians (Krieger 1991).

## Impact of Economic Crisis and Structural Adjustment

On a macroeconomic level, the global economic crisis has engendered multiple inequities. Africa provides an example: Low and stagnant demand for the continent's non-oil exports, coupled with growing protectionism in the developed world, reduced its share of international trade from 2.4 percent to 1.7 percent. Many countries borrowed from the industrialized world to cushion the blow to their economies; the continent's debt now equals its gross national product, and it cannot meet its obligations. Internal economic distortions compound the effects of these external factors. Many countries instituted structural-adjustment programs in an effort to eliminate these internal distortions and promote sustainable growth, often at the urging of the International Monetary Fund and other donors (UNICEF 1990). In the forum entitled "What We Want–Voices from the South," some NCIH conference participants emphasized the deleterious effects of structural-adjustment policies. They called for radical solutions regarding the transfer of resources from North to South and changes in the way multilateral and bilateral funds are administered, as alternative solutions to economic crisis.

It is clear that the gains that have been made in enhancing health service availability over the past few decades are being eroded by the impact of economic crises and structural-adjustment programs. While the latter cannot always be blamed for the crises they aim to stabilize, care needs to be taken to cushion vulnerable sectors of the population from the effects of adjustment policies, many of which have implications for access to care on both the demand side, through declines in real wages—and the supply side, through social-service cutbacks (UNICEF 1990).

Cutbacks in public sector services have led to increased reliance on private facilities for health care, a situation that has disproportionately affected access to care for the poor. A study of the effects of structural-adjustment policies on poor women in Guayaquil, Ecuador showed that the decline in real wages resulted in an increase in women's employment as households worked to maintain their previous income levels. The increased burden on women's time reduced their health care utilization, although there is also evidence that the women's increased income and independence resulted in increased respect from male family members and increased self-esteem. In addition, it was found that women are attempting to compensate for health service cutbacks by playing greater community management roles and filling service gaps (Moser 1991).

*The Cost of Services*

The evidence on the effect of costs on demand for health care is mixed, showing demand to be uninfluenced, negatively influenced, and even positively influenced by cost levels (Leslie and Gupta 1989). In Tunisia, for example, individuals were found to associate higher fees with better quality (Auerbach 1982 as cited in Thaddeus and Maine 1990). More recent analyses have shown, however, that costs are more likely to deter than enhance utilization among the poor; again, this indicates the importance of stratifying populations, both within target groups and by gender, when assessing the impact of service or policy changes on utilization. It is likely, given women's absolute and relative poverty and lack of control over household income in most developing countries, that their demand for health care is influenced even more significantly than men's by cost. In Senegal, for example, where communities are involved in financing and managing primary health care, changes in utilization in response to rising costs were found to differ within socioeconomic groups, with the ultra-poor affected more significantly than the moderately poor, and women more affected than men (Leighton 1991).

Most developing-country governments can no longer afford to provide health care to all their citizens free of charge. Cost sharing programs, which can involve direct fees for services, employment-based pre-payment schemes, and a host of other mechanisms (Hoare and Mills 1986) present a promising possibility for raising revenue and thus, theoretically, improving the scope and quality of services. Indeed, cost sharing is now a reality in much of the developing world. Policy makers must make sure, however, that cost sharing does not reduce access to care among vulnerable groups.

The rural poor, and particularly women, are among the most vulnerable. The Country Women's Association of Nigeria (COWAN) uses a traditional credit system as the vehicle for assuring adequate health care for its members, regardless of their ability to pay. Members have access to health emergency loans for critical events, such as obstetrical emergencies. COWAN provides its members with a membership card that entitles them to immediate medical attention at the referral hospital or clinic; this is a critical element of the program, as many doctors are reluctant to treat rural patients who are unable to pay their fees. COWAN membership cards are recognized as a guarantee that all service and drug fees will be paid. To date, this program has helped ensure positive outcomes for forty-eight documented obstetrical emergencies; without appropriate care, these women would probably have died.

Two alternative fee-for-service models currently dominate the debate: fee collection at urban hospitals, with reallocation of revenue to underfunded rural and primary care programs, and community level financing, with local control of generated revenues. Each of these models behaves differently in terms of its ability to raise revenue, improve efficiency, reallocate expenditure in favor of primary care, and protect the poor (UNICEF 1990).

A well-considered balance between these models, based on an understanding of their differential gender impacts and consideration of other contextual issues, is likely to be optimal. The effect of financing reform and the imposition of user fees should be considered in the context of the increasing monetization of economies and continuing transition from subsistence to cash-crop farming, for example. This evolution has further lessened women's control over family income (given men's greater involvement in the cash economy) and increased demands on their time (Burns 1991).

The institution of user fees makes it all the more important that deficiencies in service efficiency and quality be recognized and addressed to enable users to see the benefits of the financial burden they have assumed and to minimize drops in utilization. A recent study of a Khmer community in the United States clearly illustrates that women were willing to pay more to find care that was culturally and linguistically comfortable (Frye 1991). Again, issues of cultural appropriateness and quality of care, as defined by the user, often override physical convenience and financial accessibility.

An important aspect of the cost of obtaining care is the opportunity cost of time spent traveling to, waiting for, and receiving care. The typically high time cost borne by women using health care services, both for themselves and for their children, was cited often during conference presentations as a significant deterrent. It was emphasized that, while continued research into new technologies and strategies for health care is necessary, those implementing these new technologies and strategies must take into account the burdens on women's time.

## Quality of Services

Many of the key components of the quality of health care that directly affect women's utilization of services relate to provider-client interaction: information given and information asked for, respect for the client, and confidentiality. Other factors include privacy, service hours, range of services available, fragmentation of services, availability of supplies, and equipment. Quality of care issues are discussed at length in the "Quality of Care" chapter. It is important to keep in mind the demand-side perspective of the quality of care issue. Ensuring that the services offered are competent, complete, and supported by a well-equipped infrastructure is not sufficient to ensure quality services as perceived by the client. Health care considered to be inappropriate will not be used. Health care planners must listen to women and guage their perceptions of quality care if services are to be truly appropriate.

## Demand-Side Determinants: User Factors

Many of the factors that influence women's *demand* for health care are related to the *supply* factors discussed above. Service fees become a deterrent to use when the client cannot afford them. The distance to a service becomes a constraint when the woman does not have time or transportation. Health care provider attitudes are an obstacle when the client perceives disrespect or indifference. Other demand-side determinants are specifically associated with user beliefs, knowledge, attitudes, and practices.

### Informational Barriers

Women's lack of knowledge and awareness, which can range from not knowing the location of a health care delivery site to a lack of understanding of the danger signs or gravity of a condition, have a profound impact on health care utilization. Often women do not perceive themselves as having a problem or of being at risk. In a Zimbabwe study, for example, the main reason behind delay in seeking care among patients with cervical cancer was that they they did not recognize the seriousness of their condition (Stein and Muir as cited in Thaddeus and Maine 1990). In addition, particular conditions may not be associated with a need for care, particularly care from the formal system. A condition may be so prevalent in the community, or the woman may have suffered its symptoms for so long, that it is not recognized as problematic. Classic examples include women who suffer chronic back pain from a young age, and women with multiple, chronic reproductive-tract infections. Having felt pain, discomfort, and/or fatigue for many years, they assume that these are normal states and never seek medical attention. Other conditions, such as sexually transmitted diseases, may be hidden because they are seen as shameful or stigmatizing.

Pregnancy provides another example. In many contexts, pregnancy is not viewed as a condition requiring care, unless complications arise. In addition, women may not want to know or admit that they are pregnant early in their pregnancy. In many West African societies it is considered impolite and to invite bad luck to admit to being pregnant before it is visually obvious (Pillsbury et al. 1990). In Jamaica, women often delay their first prenatal care visit until late in the second trimester, both because they are unaware of or ignore the need for care and because they may be ashamed of and want to deny their pregnancy (Wedderburn 1991). Another study in Jamaica found that although the women surveyed recognized the need for prenatal care, this implied a single consultation rather than regular interaction, a finding that must be built into continuing health education efforts (Sargent and Rawlins 1990).

## Low Self-Esteem

Lack of knowledge and awareness are linked to women's lack of self-esteem, particularly in those regions of the world where women's status is widely recognized as inferior. Low self-esteem leads to the belief that suffering is women's lot, discouraging them from seeking, and others from taking them or encouraging them to seek, care when problems arise or persist. Multiple reproductive-tract infections, chronic fatigue, and back pain, which are extremely common among women in developing countries, provide examples. As stated above, many women do not perceive their permanent exhaustion and discomfort, even their pain, as out of the ordinary or worthy of complaint or attention. A study of slum mothers in India found that treatment was sought only when symptoms became truly debilitating, and was discontinued once symptoms disappeared (Kanani 1991).

Low self-esteem and embarrassment are often at the root of women's hesitancy to seek care for domestic violence, or "gender violence," defined as violence committed against women because of their sex. Gender violence causes a sense of isolation in women, and makes them unlikely to report that they have been beaten and to seek care. The chapter on "Violence Against Women" discusses gender violence in more detail.

## Decision-Making Dynamics

Decisions to seek health care take place in a complex web of relationships; tracing the relevant communication patterns and decision-making process is never a simple matter. Decisions to seek health care can be made by the woman herself, or by the husband, the village elder, and/or other family or community members. Understanding these complexities is essential to determining the appropriate target audience for health education and the content of health messages. The fundamental principle in community education should be that the entire family and community at large need to learn about women's health needs, preventive behavior, and therapeutic choices. A project in rural Papua New Guinea, for example, provides community health classes in female reproductive anatomy and health to all married men (Brabec 1991). A project in Nepal educated mothers-in-law on proper care in pregnancy and delivery, for which they are largely responsible (Dali 1990 as cited in Starrs and Measham 1990).

Household data from a study in India show that the younger, more educated women in the family were more outspoken and adamant about the need to improve the quality and appropriateness of health care (Harding 1991). General education and leadership training could do much to further women's control over their own health by increasing their ability to challenge traditional authority structures. Education also improves access to care by increasing women's access to information, enhancing their self-esteem, and increasing their ability to adopt new health concepts and practices and participate as equals in client-provider interactions (Thaddeus and Maine 1990). In Guatemala and Panama, for example, use of modern prenatal and postpartum care was found to be positively associated with women's educational status (Leslie and Gupta 1989).

## Cultural Barriers

An important barrier to health care utilization relates to the conflict between biomedical and traditional explanations for health phenomena. This includes notions of disease causation, grouping of symptoms into syndromes or diseases, and perceptions of appropriate treatments and medications, anatomical make-up and functions, and appropriateness of care. These issues have received considerable attention in the literature. (For an extensive bibliography on traditional health care practices, particularly those related to maternal health, see Pillsbury et al. 1990). Cultural beliefs and preferences surrounding pregnancy and childbirth are particularly strong and resistant to change. In parts of Africa, for example, prolonged labor is believed to be punishment for a woman's infidelity (Kargbo 1984 in Thaddeus and Maine 1990). In others, it is believed that delivering without assistance is a sign of courage.

The reticence of a Khmer community in the United States to use modern care facilities has been attributed to the fact that their concepts of health and illness, and particularly pregnancy and childbirth, are completely alien to American care providers, and vice versa (Frye 1990). Similar cultural gaps between women and the health sector are found in Jamaica, where the most important factor influencing the selection of a birthing site among both rural and urban women is the social support of family and friends, followed by medical support, and then privacy and comfort. Capitalizing on these findings, the government of Jamaica agreed to a pilot project that will establish alternative childbirth locations to allow women privacy and comfort, the participation of their social-support network, and access to trained care, usually provided by nurses, nurse-midwives or nurse practitioners, whom the women tend to prefer (Wedderburn 1991).

It is widely recognized that making health care as culturally appropriate as possible is an important component of quality care. This includes evaluating cultural practices and beliefs on an individual basis to determine their medical significance. If they are beneficial or benign (neither medically beneficial nor harmful) every effort should be made to incorporate them into health care delivery services if so doing will enhance the perceived quality of care (Pillsbury et al. 1990).

## Recommendations for Policy, Research, and Programs

- Recognizing that there is no panacea for improving women's access to care, which relates to a complex set of service-related factors, as well as an equally, if not more, complex set of factors related to women's knowledge and attitudes, and their cultural, religious and legal milieu.
- Recognizing that physical convenience and financial accessibility are often less important than cultural appropriateness and perceived quality of care. Women are often willing to travel further and pay more for care they consider appropriate and of high quality.

### Service Factors

Expanding and re-organizing services:

- Increasing the availability of trained workers and facilities in underserved or unserved rural areas, and involving women in their design and implementation.
- Moving away from the traditional focus on women's health as it relates to childbearing and the needs of the child. This includes:
- Broadening the focus of traditional maternal and child health (MCH) to ensure adequate attention to maternal health;
- Ensuring that attention is paid to broader reproductive health needs, including STDs, pregnancy termination, infertility, and the special needs of adolescents and women in menopause; and,
- Addressing nonreproductive health needs, including those of female children, the elderly, women who are handicapped or terminally ill, and the victims of gender violence.

Overcoming distance barriers:

- Recognizing that the effects of physical distance are exacerbated by cultural and financial restrictions on women's mobility, as well as lack of awareness of the need for care and signs of danger or potential problems.
- Ensuring that all of women's basic health needs can be attended to at the community level, including front-line management and referral of emergencies.
- Improving communications and transport systems for effective operation of the referral system, including effective interaction of the many levels of the health system.

- Exploring and evaluating creative ways to bring services closer to women (including home-based care, mobile services, and maternity waiting homes) as well as ensuring the availability of transport in emergencies (including setting aside community funds and making arrangements with local vehicle owners).
- Recognizing that even small increments of distance may have a discernible effect on utilization; peripheral areas have their own peripheries.

## Increasing access to trained personnel:

- Taking advantage of the services of traditional care providers, providing them with appropriate training, and granting them additional responsibility; the medical community, through its reluctance to recognize the significant roles of and, in many cases, women's preferences for traditional care and non-medical health cadres, has severely limited women's access to care.
- Increasing the numbers and responsibilities of midwives, who serve as the critical link between communities, TBAs and clinical resources in most developing countries, and posting them at the community level.
- Ensuring that midwives are trained and equipped to undertake all essential obstetric functions, including the management of emergencies.
- Ensuring adequate communication and healthy relations between levels of health personnel; this includes not only the relationship between physicians and the nursing and midwifery corps, but also that between midwives and traditional care providers.
- Increasing the availability of female health personnel, while recognizing that some of the same barriers that prevent women from using male health personnel make it difficult to station female personnel where they are most needed.

## Understanding and minimizing the impact of economic crisis:

- Ensuring that vulnerable sectors of the population are cushioned from the simultaneous impact of falling real incomes and service cutbacks.
- Recognizing that women's access to care is likely to be affected disproportionately by service cutbacks, while keeping in mind that in some settings their increasing importance as additional bread-winners may increase their status and independence, and thus their ability to seek care.

## Ensuring that services are affordable:

- Evaluating the effects of alternative cost-sharing models, not only in terms of their ability to raise revenue, but the degree to which they can reallocate expenditure in favor of primary care and protect the poor.
- Determining the effects of cost-sharing programs by gender and by substrata of disadvantaged populations; evidence suggests that women's demand is more affected than that of men's, and that the demand of the ultra-poor is affected more than that of the poor.

- Recognizing that the effect of fees on women's demand for and use of care will vary according to their control over income and the demands on their time. The increasing monetization of developing economies tends to lessen the former, and increase the latter.
- Ensuring that service quality and efficiency improvements go hand in hand with cost-sharing programs to minimize drops in utilization.
- Implementing creative programs—such as traditional community credit systems—to ensure access to care regardless of ability to pay.
- Recognizing that an important aspect of the cost of obtaining care is the opportunity cost of women's time, which should be built into the service design process.

Improving quality of care:

- Ensuring that services are provided at convenient hours, in a comprehensive, nonfragmented manner, and with privacy, confidentiality, and respect—all of which should be evaluated from the perspective of the woman, not the service provider.

## *User Factors*

Overcoming informational barriers:

- Increasing women's knowledge and understanding of:
  - the need for and availability of care
  - the risks they face, symptoms of illness, and signs of danger
  - their right to be healthy—and not in pain or exhausted

Improving women's self-esteem

- Providing women with education and leadership training to enhance their sense of self-worth and their right to good health, and enabling them to assert themselves in health-care decision making.
- Educating women and the general public that gender violence is not acceptable, to ensure that women seek care without fear of the consequences, and providing them with all necessary support.

Reaching the decision-makers:

- Gaining an understanding of family decision-making dynamics prior to launching health education programs to ensure that messages reach those who actually make the decisions, including mothers-in-law, men, and community or religious leaders.

Overcoming cultural barriers:

- Recognizing the conflict between biomedical and traditional explanations for health phenomena, particularly those related to pregnancy.
- Evaluating traditional beliefs and practices on an individual basis and incorporating beneficial and benign practices into formal health services, if doing so will enhance their quality from the users' perspective.

## References

Alexandre, Marie. 1991. "The Role of Gender, Socio-economic, Cultural, and Religious Pressure on the Health of Women in Cameroon." Paper presented at the 18th Annual NCIH International Health Conference. Arlington, VA.

Alisjahbana, Anna. 1991. "Regionalization of Perinatal Health Care in a Rural Area in West Java." Paper presented at the 18th Annual NCIH International Health Conference. Arlington, VA.

Brabec, Joan. 1991. "The Importance of Education Men in Women's Health Issues: Surprising Findings from a Pilot Project to Train Birth Attendants in Rural Papua New Guinea." Paper presented at the 18th Annual NCIH International Health Conference. Arlington, VA.

Burdman, Geri Marr. 1991. "Women, Aging, and Health Promotion: An International Perspective." Paper presented at the 18th Annual NCIH International Health Conference. Arlington, VA.

Burns, M.J. 1991. "Financing Accesible Health Care: Issues in Family Decision Making and Resource Allocation." Presentation at the 18th Annual NCIH International Health Conference. Arlington, VA.

Fauveau, Vincent. 1991. "Mortality Impact of a Community-Based Maternity Care Program in Rural Bangladesh." Presentation at the 18th Annual NCIH International Health Conference. Arlington, VA.

Frye, Barbara. 1990. "The Process of Health Care Decision Making among Cambodian Immigrant Women." International Quarterly of Community Health Education 10(2):113-124.

Frye, Barbara. 1991. "The Impact of Belief Structures on the Health Behavior of Cambodian Refugee Women in America." Paper presented at the 18th Annual NCIH International Health Conference. Arlington, VA.

Harding, Anna K. 1991. "Women's Role in the Family Choice of Health Care: A Study Conducted in Tamil Nadu." Paper presented at the 18th Annual NCIH International Health Conference. Arlington, VA.

Heise, Lori. 1991. "Violence Against Women." Presentation at the 18th Annual NCIH International Health Conference. Arlington, VA.

Heymann, Jody. 1991. "Addressing the Potentially Conflicting Health Needs of Mother and Child." Presentation at the 18th Annual NCIH International Health Conference. Arlington, VA.

Hoare, Geoff, and Ann Mills. 1986. Paying for the Health Sector: a Review and Annotated Bibliography of the Literature on Developing Countries. Evaluation and Planning Centre for Health re, London School of Hygiene and Tropical Medicine, EPC No. 12.

Kanani, Shubhada. 1991. "Application of Ethnographic Research to Understand Women's Perceptions of Health and Disease in Slums of Baroda, India." Presentation at the 18th Annual NCIH International Health Conference. Arlington, VA.

Kasolo, Josephine. 1991. "Women's Use of Health Services: A Survey in Rural Uganda." Paper presented at the 18th Annual NCIH International Health Conference. Arlington, VA.

Krieger, Laurie. 1991. "Male Doctor, Female Patient: Access to Health Care in Egypt." Paper presented at the 18th Annual NCIH International Health Conference. Arlington, VA.

Kurz, Kathleen. 1991. "Adolescent Girls: Nutritional Risks and Opportunities for Intervention." Paper presented at the 18th Annual NCIH International Health Conference. Arlington, VA.

Kwast, Barbara. 1991. "Safe Motherhood—A Midwifery Challenge." Paper presented at the 18th Annual NCIH International Health Conference. Arlington, VA.

Laudaran, Virginia Hight. 1991. "Maternity Care in Grenada, West Indies." Paper presented at the 18th Annual NCIH International Health Conference. Arlington, VA.

Laukaran, Virginia and Adity Bahattacharya. 1991. "Maternity Care in Grenada, West Indies: A Comprehensive Study." Paper presented at the 18th Annual NCIH International Health Conference. Arlington, VA.

Leighton, Charlotte. 1991. "The Impact of Health Financing Policy Reform on Women's Access to Primary and Preventative Health Services." Paper presented at the 18th Annual NCIH International Health Conference. Arlington, VA.

Leslie, Joanne and Geeta Rao Gupta. 1989. Utilization of Services for Maternal Nutrition and Health Care. Maternal Nutrition and Health Care Program, International Center for Research on Women.

Marshall, Margaret. 1991. "Life Saving Skills Workshops for Ghanian Midwives." Paper presented at the 18th Annual NCIH International Health Conference. Arlington, VA.

Moser, Caroline. 1991. Presentation at the 18th Annual NCIH International Health Conference. Arlington, VA.

Ogunleye, Bisi. 1991. "Using Our Own Resources as an Alternative Way of Improving Women's Health." Paper presented at the 18th Annual NCIH International Health Conference. Arlington, VA.

Okafor, Chinyelu. 1991. "Women Helping Women: Incorporating Women's Perspectives into Community Health Projects." Paper presented at the 18th Annual NCIH International Health Conference. Arlington, VA.

Paltiel, Freda. 1991. "The Mental Health of Women." Presentation at the 18th Annual NCIH International Health Conference. Arlington, VA.

Petros-Barvazian, Angele. 1991. "Changing Priorities in Women's Health—No Longer Last With Least." Presentation at the 18th Annual NCIH International Health Conference. Arlington, VA.

Pillsbury, Barbara, Ann Brownlee, and Judith Timyan. 1990. Understanding and Evaluating Traditional Practices: A Guide for Improving Maternal Care. Maternal Nutrition and Health Care Program, International Center for Research on Women.

Sargent, Carolyn and Joan Rawlins. 1990. "Factors Influencing Pre-Natal Care Use Among Low-Income Jamaican Women." Report for Maternal Nutrition and Health Care Program. ICRW. Washington, D.C.

Starrs, Ann, and Diana Measham. 1990. Safe Motherhood in South Asia: Challenge for the Nineties. Report of the Safe Motherhood South Asia Conference, Lahore, Pakistan, March 1990. The World Bank and Family Care International.

Thaddeus, Sereen and Deborah Maine. 1990. Too Far to Walk: Maternal Mortality in Context. Prevention of Maternal Mortality Program, Center for Population and Family Health, Columbia University.

UNICEF. 1990. Economic Crisis, Adjustment, and the Bamako Initiative: Health Care Financing in the Economic Context of sub-Saharan Africa. Bamako Initiative Technical Report–Background Document for the Pan-African Conference on Community Financing in Primary Health Care, Kinshasa, Zaire, June 1990.

Wedderburn, Maxine. 1991. "Understanding the Childbirth Choices of Jamaican Women." Paper presented at the 18th Annual NCIH International Health Conference. Arlington, VA.

World Bank. 1991. World Development Report 1990: Poverty. New York: Oxford University Press.

# 11

## Quality of Care:
## A Neglected Dimension

*Barbara Mensch*

Despite widespread agreement on the value of providing health services of adequate quality, the care available to women in the developing world is thought to be far from satisfactory. While men may also receive poor services, women are presumed to suffer disproportionately, reflecting pervasive gender discrimination and their marginal status in many societies (Das Gupta 1989; United Nations 1991). However, very little is actually known about the quality of health care in most developing countries.

Perceiving quality to be a luxury in resource-poor settings, international donors, national policy makers, and local providers have directed their attention to expansion of services, ignoring, for the most part, the nature of those services. Not surprisingly then, researchers investigating the health sector in developing countries rarely focus explicitly on the assessment of existing services.[1]

Recently, however, those involved with the delivery of health care have recognized that evaluation of program effort should consider not only the quantity, accessibility and distribution of services, but also the quality. With that goal in mind the World Health Organization has outlined approaches and developed protocols for the assessment of the quality of primary health care services in developing countries.[2] Within the specific arena of family planning, a Subcommittee on Quality of Care Indicators in Family Planning Service Delivery has been formed with representatives from international agencies, universities, and governmental and nongovernmental organizations. Their stated goal is to establish guidelines for measuring quality of care in the provision of family planning services (Subcommittee on Quality Indicators in Family Planning Service Delivery 1990).

Reflecting this intensified interest, the 18th International Health Conference of the National Council on International Health included quality of care as one of the focal themes in its action agenda for women's health.

This chapter will examine the current state of thinking on quality of care as it pertains specifically to women's health. It will review attempts to conceptualize quality of care, discuss approaches to its assessment, and offer suggestions for future work.

## Culturally Appropriate Care

In the years since the Alma-Ata Conference in 1978, medical anthropologists involved in the effort to expand and improve primary health care in developing countries have been concerned with the nature of health services (Coreil 1990). They have emphasized that in order to understand the cultural context in which health programs operate, it is necessary to conduct ethnomedical studies. Such studies investigate the social construction of illness, including local terminology, disease etiology, and health-seeking behavior (Kendall 1990; Nichter 1990).

However, while anthropologists have consistently argued for culturally appropriate care and community involvement when introducing Western medicine to societies where traditional medicine has held sway (Mull and Mull 1990), they have less frequently discussed outright the quality of existing services. In part this may reflect the anthropologist's role as "cultural broker" (Donahue 1990) rather than evaluator of care. Nonetheless, their work has laid the groundwork for much of the ensuing work on quality.

## Defining Quality

While the notion of quality of care is implicit in much of the work of medical anthropologists and public health specialists, explicit attention to the definition and measurement of quality of care on the part of the international health community can be attributed to the widespread dissemination of the writings of Bruce and her colleagues, who have initiated activities to operationalize what had previously been thought a rather elusive concept (Bruce and Jain 1990; Bruce 1990; Kumar et al. 1989). Bruce's work, which is a crystallization of ideas that have been bandied about for quite some time, has drawn heavily on the writings of Donabedian and Simmons.

### A Patient-Centered Focus

Reflecting the emphasis in Western health systems on advanced technology and specialized training, quality of care had been defined largely in terms of the clinical aspects of services, neglecting the patient-provider interaction. Donabedian's contribution to the assessment of health care is his emphasis not only on the technical domain (defined as knowledge, judgment and skill of providers), but also the interpersonal. In his model, the interpersonal domain consists of patient communication to the physician for purposes of both diagnosis and the determination of preference for treatment, and physician communication to the patient for purposes of information on the nature and management of the illness. He notes that the relationship between patient and provider should be characterized by "privacy, confidentiality, informed choice, concern, empathy, honesty, tact [and] sensitivity," arguing that the "interpersonal process is the vehicle by which technical care is implemented and on which its success depends" (Donabedian 1988).

Among those involved in research on health care delivery in developing countries, Simmons, whose work has been confined to family planning, has been the primary force in the movement to focus on transactions between client (or patient) and provider. She claims that the provider-client interface should be at the nucleus of any examination of the determinants of contraceptive behavior, mediating the effect of service-supply factors on the demand for family planning.

Based on field work in South Asia, she and her colleagues argue that program functioning hinges on the way clients are treated by the system providing services (Simmons et al. 1986; Simmons and Phillips 1990; Simmons 1991).

## A Quality-of-Care Framework for Family Planning

Bruce has been influenced by Donabedian and Simmons in developing a conceptual framework which defines quality of care for family planning and related reproductive services.

Her aim is to describe the service transaction from the vantage point of the individual client, asserting that family planning programs exist to assist women in the fulfillment of their own, and not just the larger community's, reproductive goals.

In large part Bruce's model is designed to sensitize the family planning community, whose overriding concern has been demographic, to the importance of quality of service delivery. While she feels that improvement in the quality of care is desirable in and of itself, she maintains that it should also have an impact on contraceptive use. The argument is that the better the quality, the more sustained the use. Indeed, it has been shown, albeit with limited empirical information, that the level of care provided is an important determinant of contraceptive acceptance and continuation (Jain 1989).

The Bruce framework defines quality in terms of the following six elements and associated indicators (Bruce 1990; Kumar et al. 1989):

1. *Choice of methods*—methods for significant client groups (based on age, breast-feeding status, health profile, reproductive intentions, etc.) and provider biases towards, and restriction on, methods;

2. *Provider-client information exchange*—information given to clients on (a) method options, (b) contraindications, (c) use, and (d) side-effects; and understanding clients by obtaining information on their (a) background, (b) preferences, (c) contraceptive history, (d) reproductive intentions, and (e) health;

3. *Provider competence*—technical competence and proficiency in (a) screening for contraindications, (b) providing "clinical" methods, and (c) handling complications; and qualifications: (a) training, (b) knowledge, and (c) experience;

4. *Interpersonal relations*—treatment of client by staff, including (a) privacy, (b) respectful and responsive provider behavior, (c) waiting time, and (d) time spent with client;

5. *Mechanisms to encourage continuity*—follow-up procedures including (a) promotion of continuity through community media, and (b) specific mechanisms, such as reminders stipulating when to return, future appointments, and home visits; and

6. *Appropriate constellation of services*—configuration of family planning services so they are responsive to the broader health needs of clients.

The Subcommittee on Quality Indicators accepted the framework virtually in its entirety, only expanding the sixth element, **appropriate constellation of services**, and renaming it **appropriateness and acceptability of services**. This new element includes constellation of services as well as location of services, days and hours of operation, privacy arrangements, physical facility, staffing patterns and client flow (Subcommittee on Quality Indicators in Family Planning Service Delivery 1990).

## A Framework for Women's Health Services

Emphasizing women's perspective on the service experience, the feminist health movement has been instrumental in drawing attention to the quality of care provided to women. Although their critique of women's treatment by the medical system is clearly oriented to developed countries, much of what they have to say is relevant in developing-country settings.

*Our Bodies, Ourselves*, one of the most popular feminist volumes on women's health, claims that medical personnel have:

> not listened to [women] or believed what they said; withheld knowledge; lied to them; treated them without their consent; not warned of risks and negative effects of treatments; ... [and] experimented on them or used them as a teaching material... (The Boston Women's Health Book Collective 1985:556).

These statements by women have informed the work of many of those concerned with women's health. However, to engage policy makers in developing countries and attract donor notice, a more systematic assessment of quality of women's health care is required.

Within the field of family planning, the Bruce framework has served an important political, programmatic and research purpose. Since its dissemination, the issue of quality of care has begun to gain legitimacy as an important area of concern for those involved in the provision and evaluation of services. Because there is now some consensus as to what is meant by quality of care, the foundation has been laid for assessing and improving family planning programs.

To encourage a more comprehensive and systematic examination of women's health services, it would be worthwhile to specify the components of a quality-of-care framework within the larger domain of women's health.

Here, women's health is broadly defined to include counseling, where relevant, and treatment or services for: problems or concerns related to sexuality, physical abuse, reproductive-tract infections, other diseases of the reproductive organs, abortion, infertility, prenatal care, childbirth, problems or concerns with lactation, other postpartum care, and problems or concerns related to menopause.[3] While the definition has been restricted to problems or conditions that are unique to or much more common in women, it can be broadened to include problems or conditions for which the risk factor and/or interventions are different for women (Task Force on Women's Health Issues 1985; Ward 1989).

Most of the elements from the Bruce family planning framework are transferable to a woman's health care framework, although the indicators differ. The following is a suggested list of elements and their corresponding indicators:

1. *Provider-woman information exchange*—conveying information to women, i.e. (a) explanation of the diagnosis, (b) information, where medically appropriate, on treatment options, (c) information on the therapeutic regime, (d) information on contraindications to and side effects of all medications and drugs; and listening to and understand

ing women, including their (a) background, (b) preferences for treatment, and (c) medical history;

2. *Provider competence*—(a) accurate knowledge about the disease, problem, or condition, (b) technical proficiency in providing safe and appropriate clinical treatment known to produce an impact on mortality, morbidity or the existing condition,[4] and (c) knowledge of procedures for referring cases which cannot be adequately managed;

3. *Interpersonal relations*—sensitive treatment of women including (a) privacy, (b) respectful and responsive provider behavior, (c) encouragement of women's participation in decision making, (d) avoidance of moral judgments, (e) confidentiality, (f) limited waiting time, and (g) adequate amount of time spent with woman; and

4. *Mechanisms to encourage continuity of medical care*—(a) information about when to return and, if possible, other locations where services and medications can be obtained, and (b) specific follow-up procedures including, when deemed necessary, future appointments and home visits.

## Constellation of Services and Quality of Care

The framework described above excludes **constellation of services**, but not without some hesitation. Bruce and her colleagues ultimately eliminated this element from their family planning framework because they believe that there is no one model or context for service delivery. In some settings, having family planning stand on its own might work perfectly well; in others, integrating family planning with maternal and child health services might work better.

In the broader domain of women's health, it is also not possible to state unequivocally what the "best" constellation of services is. It is only possible to make some judgments as to which types of delivery systems and service paradigms generally produce the best outcome in certain situations. For example, it has been claimed that one major impediment to the delivery of postabortion family planning services in many developing countries is the fact that reproductive health services are often vertically integrated. Because access to legal safe abortions is limited, women wanting to terminate an unwanted pregnancy frequently end up in acute obstetrical/gynecological wards or emergency rooms where family planning services are unavailable. If postabortion family planning were made a priority, services would be redesigned so as to make contraception easily accessible to women regardless of how they entered the formal health system (Leonard 1991). On the other hand, if safe abortion services were freely available, it would not necessary to provide family planning counseling in emergency rooms.

In contrast to current postabortion family planning services, standard postpartum family planning services have as their goal the provision of contraception immediately after pregnancy termination, which in this case is childbirth. This approach assumes that women are most highly motivated to use contraception as soon after delivery as possible, and will not or can not return to a service delivery point at some later date. The question that arises is whether this type of service paradigm is always in the best interests of the mother and child. The response depends on the setting and is determined by breast-feeding behavior, duration of contraceptive use, ability to return to a service delivery point, and the types of services available.

In societies where contraceptive continuation rates are low and where breast-feeding is extensive and of long duration (or, if on the wane, where it can be reversed), child morbidity and mortality might be reduced and the average interval to the next pregnancy lengthened if postpartum family planning services were redesigned to encourage later initiation and integration with well-baby and maternal care. (Winikoff and Mensch 1991).

Designing health services for women around the concept of reproductive risk is another example of a paradigm that might work well in some settings (i.e. those with rich resource systems), but not in others. In the absence of basic reproductive health services, identification of women who are at greatest risk of labor and delivery complications for treatment at secondary or tertiary centers is often beyond the capability of the system (Winikoff 1991; Bruce and Winikoff 1990).

In sum, constellation of services is excluded from a quality of care framework not because it is unimportant—indeed it can have fundamental consequences for women's health—but because it is not possible to make judgements as to which service delivery system or service paradigm always produces the best outcome. Whether a given system or approach to services is maximally functional depends on the circumstances and context.

## Access to Services and Quality of Care

While the Subcommittee on Quality of Care included service location in its version of the quality-of-care framework, it is excluded here. Accessibility is considered here to be conceptually distinct from quality, although (as documented in the chapter "Access to Care") it is clearly of fundamental importance in any examination of the supply of services. Accessibility in its narrow sense is usually defined in terms of density of outlets, distance, travel time, and cost of travel and services (Tsui 1991; Wilkinson 1991), while quality is defined in terms of what happens once one arrives at an outlet. As the discussion in the chapter on "Access to Care" points out, ther are also broader notions of accessibility which include appropriateness and acceptability of care as perceived by the client. Maine, in her analytical model of maternal mortality, places quality of care under the "access to health services" rubric. The justification for this is that the existence of facilities is not sufficient to reduce maternal deaths; the facilities need to be providing adequate services which are acceptable to women (Maine 1991).

Interestingly, what has motivated much interest in quality within the family planning field is the finding that clinic accessibility does not always show a significant or uniform association with contraceptive behavior either within or between countries.[5] If women do not always go to the nearest family facility to obtain services, then, by implication, the outlet they do select may depend on the type of services available and the treatment received there. Jacobson, in her recent summary of the literature on women's reproductive health, asserts that quality of care is a "... vital determinant of the share of women who seek medical treatment," (1991:24); and Leslie and Gupta (1989) in their analysis of women's demand for services point to the patient-provider interaction as a crucial factor in explaining women's use of medical services. A number of problems are mentioned as reasons for underutilization of available facilities, namely, "poor relationships between health care professionals and their clients, long waits, . . . administrative red tape, . . . lack of emotional support and privacy, differences in language and culture between health professionals and their clients, a rude medical staff, and the often-expected 'gift' for medical attention. . . ." (Jacobson 1991:25).

While the papers cited above suggest that inadequate quality is a primary cause of women's underutilization of health services, more field studies have to be undertaken before this can be definitively concluded. While logically one would expect that poor care should affect women's willingness to visit a health facility, if demand for services is high and/or expectations low, it is possible that quality may not turn out to be the crucial factor influencing use.

### Establishing Quality-of-Care Standards

Inevitably, in a discussion of quality of care the issue of standards arises. There are some who might argue that in defining quality of care, universal standards are implicitly established. Given the enormous variability in medical systems, cultures, and economic conditions throughout the world, mandating such standards is problematic and potentially self-defeating. Where resources are limited, attempts to adhere to an exalted level of care are destined to fall short. Rather than attempting to define some universal notion of quality, policy makers should be encouraged to specify a normative standard of care—that is, a standard which is acceptable and achievable within the context of the individual country.

In resisting the establishment of international standards one is, however, taking a somewhat disingenuous position. Clearly there are, in the language of Donabedian, "certain limits" in service provision which should not be "transgressed" (Donabedian 1968:183). For example, because of the risk of infection, asepsis should be adhered to at all times when performing clinical procedures. In the interpersonal dimension, even when staff are overwhelmed by the volume of patients, rudeness and disrespectful behavior, however locally defined, should not be condoned.

Thus, while there are no optimum standards, there are some very basic minimum standards which need to be articulated.[6]

### The Use of Outcome Measures to Assess Quality

Undoubtedly because evaluation at the level of the service delivery point is rarely conducted, quality of care, if it is considered at all, is assessed in terms of its effect on some outcome. That is, without any attempt at documentation, the state of women's health is attributed, at least in part, to the poor condition of existing services for women. Indeed, it has been observed that most studies of prenatal health services use "the changes in the health condition of the mothers, the neonate or both" to evaluate health care programs rather than "obtain[ing] data on the process of health care" (Villaroman-Bautista et al. 1990:6).

Although problems with reliability and completeness remain, epidemiological data on maternal morbidity and mortality indicate that in developing countries there are considerable numbers of women who die or are disabled due to hemorrhage, sepsis, toxemia, obstructed labor, abortion, hepatitis, and anemia (Boerma 1987; Jacobson 1991; Maine 1991; United Nations 1991). Indeed, pregnancy-related mortality is the primary explanation for the lower life expectancy of women compared to men in many South Asian countries and the smaller than expected female advantage in other developing regions (Heligman 1983; Ruzicka and Lopez 1983).

Many of the same studies which document the substantial risk associated with pregnancy ascribe maternal illness and death to, among other factors, the inadequate quality of health services. References to deficient medical care abound in the literature with such phrases as "poor quality of services," and "improper treatment" extremely commonplace, and pleas for "improved health care services" standard policy recommendations (Maine 1991; United Nations 1991; Barns 1991; Kamel 1983; International Center for Research on Women 1989). Yet attempts to describe the "poor" and "im proper services" in a systematic fashion, and then link them to morbidity and mortality, are rarely undertaken. Indeed, there is more detail available on traditional health behaviors and customs, especially those surrounding childbirth, and their deleterious consequences for maternal well-being, than there is on the quality of more formal medical services (Bhatia 1983).

The use of outcome data to assess the quality of health services available to women has practical consequences for both policy and research. In the absence of on-site visits, it is not possible to identify what aspects of service delivery and which facilities are most in need of improvement. Nor is it possible to pinpoint which aspects of service delivery are most responsible for the recognized outcomes.[7]

### Assessing Services: Infrastructure and Quality of Care

In attempting to upgrade services for women, it is important to describe both the structure and process of care-giving. As outlined here, quality of care is rather narrowly defined. Although the frame work does not include the health infrastructure, this dimension clearly cannot be ignored when evaluating services.

There are, then, two parts to a comprehensive assessment of services.[8] The first is a description of program elements which are considered part of the infrastructure (i.e. equipment and facilities, staff and training, supervision, record-keeping, and supplies). If all of these are functioning, the necessary, although not sufficient, conditions for adequate services can be said to be in place. In other words, a facility might be clean, reasonably equipped, and staffed with trained personnel, but still treat women poorly both from a medical and personal standpoint. Similarly, a family planning clinic might have a decent contraceptive logistics system with an adequate range of supplies, but not provide balanced information or a full range of methods. The existence of a large supply of any one method may simply indicate that that particular method is rarely offered.

Limited field studies suggest, however, that the necessary conditions for adequate services are probably not in place in most developing countries. In the few places where the health infrastructure has been investigated, it is generally judged deficient. A review of the literature on maternal health services documents the inadequate supply of drugs and equipment in facilities devoted to reproductive health (Leslie and Gupta 1989).

The second part of the assessment of health services is a description of the care-giving process. As with the description of the infrastructure, to determine the quality of care which is actually being provided, it is necessary to ͻ to the service delivery point. There are few studies in which this has been undertaken. Those that have are either not comprehensive, in that they examine only some aspects of services, and/or they are not generalizable, in that they are restricted to one hospital or health center.

A PRICOR systems analysis conducted in fifty-four villages in Niger observed seventeen prenatal and thirty postnatal patient/matrone visits. Matrones are traditional birth attendants who are trained to assist deliveries and provide postnatal care and health education. While it is not clear to what extent these observations accurately represent the level of maternal care available in rural Niger, they do indicate inadequate knowledge about, and supplies and techniques for, safe childbirth. For example, "only 40 percent [of matrones] stated the need to wash their hands, and less than half the delivery kits had clean razor blades in them." (Franco et al. 1991:2). The analysis described only the technical competence of the provider, either overlooking, or not reporting on, the interpersonal dimension.

Another study of the quality of prenatal care examined the "use pattern, process, and effectiveness" of health workers in a Filipino province. Four different types of health workers–public doctors, private doctors, licensed midwives and traditional care-givers ("hilot") were interviewed and observed in interaction with clients. While traditional workers scored highest on interpersonal dimensions, they scored lowest on the technical aspects of health care. That is, they were significantly less likely than the other types of health workers to obtain a medical history and perform a physical and laboratory examination. On the other hand, doctors and midwives, particularly public doctors, were less attentive to the emotional well-being of clients. In summarizing the results, the investigators emphasized that, in general, health workers (with the exception of traditional care-givers) were "perfunctory" in physical examinations, spent minimal time in "rapport-building conversation" and did not "encourage clients to participate actively in consultation sessions." Given this low level of quality, it is not surprising that women failed to come for regular check-ups (Villaroman-Bautista et al. 1990).

Similarly, a comprehensive examination of studies evaluating the client-provider interface in maternal and child health and family planning clinics in Latin America reported that, in general, interactions were "short, impersonal and brusque" with limited sharing of relevant information with the client and few opportunities for questions (Gay 1980). Although this monograph is over ten years old, there apparently are no data available which suggest that the situation has changed dramatically.

While there are few studies of the quality of care of fixed facilities, there are even fewer which evaluate the quality of outreach efforts. The notable exception is the observation of care-giving provided by female field workers to women in the MCH/FP Extension Project in rural Bangladesh. While "the range of functions performed by [these women] . . . transcends the boundaries of what is conventionally implied by the concept of supply," in that they are "agents of change" in a society that values the tradition of purdah, workload pressure undermines the quality of care which can be offered (Simmons et al. 1988:36). Health and family planning information was frequently not provided to clients and screening for method suitability, assessment of side-effects, and, "screening and assessment of pregnant and postnatal women were almost never done" (Koblinsky et al. 1989:230).

While studies describing the health facilities and the nature of care-giving are rare, the limited research that has been undertaken suggests that the quality of care which apparently exists for many women in developing countries is less than adequate.

## Recommendations for Action: Policy and Research

### Articulating and Implementing Minimum Standards

If the quality of women's health care in developing countries is to improve, it is essential that policy makers and donor agencies make this an explicit item on their agendas. Without their commitment, it is difficult to envision how services can change for the better.

The first step in improving quality of care is an articulation of the minimum standards that are acceptable and affordable. Policy makers must then provide a clear statement of the level of services they are able and willing to offer, which in most settings will be identical to the minimum acceptable standards, given the severe constraints under which health systems are currently operating. This should include all elements of care, interpersonal and informational, as well as clinical.

As was argued earlier, each country or program should specify its own standards, intentions, and plans for implementation. There should not be universals, only locally formulated guidelines.

Judith Wasserheit has developed a step-wise approach to the management of reproductive-tract infections (RTIs) in developing countries, which illustrates the process of standard-setting for a clinical procedure. If resources permit, treatment for RTIs should include a pelvic examination plus a laboratory evaluation. However, it is the rare developing country that can afford the equipment and training necessary for "gold-standard" microbiological tests, let alone simpler lab tests. If laboratory evaluation is not possible then a pelvic examination along with treatment algorithms which utilize findings from the examination along with patient symptoms and community epidemiological data must suffice. In the absence of a pelvic examination, the practitioner must rely on the patient's history and the community epidemiological data (Wasserheit 1989).

The same process should be undertaken for interpersonal dimensions of care. While the "gold standard" might include lengthy provider-patient interaction, complete privacy, thorough taking of patient medical history, encouragement of patient participation in decision making, complete information on treatment options, and home visits for follow-up, the minimum acceptable standards might be considerably less stringent.

At the very least, health providers, who are often socially and economically removed from the women they serve, must be trained to be supportive and understanding regardless of the underlying reason care is being sought. In short, as the chapter on "Health Women's Way" advocates, health workers must, in the broadest meaning of the phrase, learn to "listen to women." Women who have been victims of physical abuse (see Chapter 8), who have developed complications from unsafe abortions (see Chapter 6), who present with chronic pelvic pain and vaginal discharge (see Chapter 4), who desire contraception, although young and unmarried (see Chapter 5), must be counseled and treated with particular sensitivity given their concerns about social stigmatization, economic vulnerability, and/or physical reprisal.

By specifying standards and developing program guidelines, policy makers are acknowledging that services should attempt to reach a certain minimum level. This is a necessary step in upgrading quality.

### A Research Agenda: Ethnographies, Situation Analyses, and Impact Studies

In order for policy makers and program managers to improve service delivery it is necessary for them to be aware of what is happening at individual hospitals, health centers, and other sites where care is provided. To that end, there is a dire need for both quantitative and qualitative studies. Information collected through these studies can then be used to determine if the articulated standards are being met, and if not, where they fall short.

An ethnographic approach would be particularly valuable in a small number of communities. Qualitative data can contribute useful insights into the cultural milieu in which care-giving is provided as well as produce a more complete description of quality. Research on women's and providers' perceptions of RTIs in Egypt (Khattab 1991) and India (Bang 1991) demonstrates the importance of an interdisciplinary orientation to uncover the social context of ill health. Indeed, medical anthropologists have called for ethnographic studies prior to extensive quantitative-data collection t improve the utility of structured survey instruments (Pelto et al. 1990).

Large-scale survey efforts which attempt to describe the quality of care have begun to incorporate some of the data-gathering techniques developed by anthropologists. One innovative design which has done so and proven useful in the evaluation of family planning services is known as "situation analysis." This approach to family planning program assessment is unique for a number of reasons: (1) a representative sample of service delivery points is examined rather than a single clinic; (2) the research team, which consists of a nurse and a social scientist, actually observes the situation rather than relying on knowledgeable observers; and (3) a comprehensive investigation of the service delivery point is undertaken, including the major family planning subsystems (logistics, facilities, staffing, training, supervision, IEC, and record keeping) as well as the elements of quality (Miller et al. 1991; Fisher et al. 1991).

This methodology could be used to assess the quality of other medical services for women in a more systematic manner than has heretofore been undertaken. The basic instruments developed for family planning assessment could be modified for (1) evaluating the inventory of supplies, equipment, and facilities; (2) interviewing patients; (3) interviewing nurses, doctors, and other health providers; and (4) observing patient-caregiver interactions. One limitation of the situation analysis design as it has recently been used for family planning program analysis is that the investigator remains at the service delivery point for a short time, typically one day. Providers tend to be affected by the presence of outsiders and, thus, the quality of care observed on that day is undoubtedly better than what is usually provided. It would be worthwhile for investigators to spend much more time at the service delivery point and in the community. Not only would this result in a more accurate assessment, it would also provide a more detailed picture of quality of care.

Having described the health subsystems and quality of care which exists in a country, region or community, research could then be undertaken to evaluate the programmatic impact of the quality of service provision on one or more of the following outcomes: (1) morbidity, (2) mortality, (3) patient compliance, (4) patient satisfaction, and (5) utilization of services. The objective of such research is to identify aspects of program functioning and quality of care which influence community and individual health and well-being, independent of individual and contextual characteristics.

However, when evaluating the impact of quality on these outcome indicators, one must keep in mind that they may not prove equally useful. Implicit in the concept of "patient compliance" is the notion that the woman may share some of the responsibility for the success or failure of treatment. Rather than "blaming" women for not following the treatment, the hope is that ethnographic research will identify what individual characteristics contribute to the woman's inability to comply and where the process of communication went awry. Patient satisfaction may also be a problematic outcome measure. Courtesy bias is thought to be very common in developing countries; just because a woman claims she is satisfied with the services provided does not mean that she actually is. Furthermore, if expectations are low, a woman may say she is satisfied even though the quality of care is inadequate.

## A Final Word

As the title of this chapter indicates, quality of care has been a neglected dimension of policies, programs, and research concerned with women's health in developing countries. It is hoped that with donor support, managers will realize the importance of assessing the quality of care that is currently provided and will introduce and evaluate new approaches and programs which will improve services available to women.

## Notes

1. A MEDLINE database search using the key words "quality of health care" and "developing countries" for literature published in the last five years came up with eighteen citations, only one of which had anything to do with the assessment of quality. This is in contrast to a search not restricted to developing countries, which produced hundreds of citations.

2. The monograph published under the auspices of WHO focuses on "the adequacy of resources—staffing, training, equipment, and supplies—and the correctness of technical procedures," devoting little space to the evaluation of the interpersonal aspect of quality. This is in direct contrast to the family planning literature on quality of care. However, to the best of our knowledge, the WHO volume is the only publication which discusses the assessment of quality of care in developing countries. (Roemer and Montoya-Aguilar 1988).

3. Family planning is excluded because the Bruce framework specifically focuses on it.

4. The definition of technical competence is based on the Roemer and Montoya-Aguilar (1988) publication on quality assessment produced for WHO.

5. For an examination of the association between accessibility and contraceptive use, see Tsui (1991) and Wilkinson (1991). For a discussion of the limitations of accessibility studies see Jain (1991).

6. For an argument against the setting of "absolute" standards, see Roemer, M.I., and C. Montoya-Aguilar (1988). They assert that standards should have a "scientific basis," be regionally "relevant," be "measurable and implementable," and be "changed" as conditions change.

7. There are instances in which outcome measures can theoretically be used to indicate the quality of care being provided. Nosocomial infection rates are commonly used to evaluate the quality of hospital care in developed countries. The incidence of hospital-induced infection is thought to reflect proper aseptic techniques, appropriate use of antibiotics and other drugs, and adequate patient monitoring. However, failure to adjust for patient risk may limit the utility of even this kind of ostensibly objective indicator (Larson and Hendrick 1988).

8. This section incorporates ideas from ongoing work at the Population Council to assess the quality of family planning services (Population Council 1991).

## References

Bang, Rani and Abhay Bang. 1991. "Reproductive Tract Infections: Rural Women's Point of View." Paper presented at the 18th Annual NCIH International Health Conference, Arlington, VA.

Barns, Tom. 1991. "Obstetric Mortality and Its Causes in Developing Countries." *British Journal of Obstetrics and Gynecology* 98(4):345-348.

Bhatia, Shushum. 1983. "Traditional Practices Affecting Female Health and Survival: Evidence From Countries of South Asia," in Lado T. Ruzicka and Alan D. Lopez, eds., *Sex Differentials in Mortality: Trends, Determinants and Consequences* Pp. 165-177. Canberra, Australia: Australian National University Department of Demography.

Boerma, J. Ties. 1987. "Levels of Maternal Mortality in Developing Countries." *Studies in Family Planning* 18(4):213-221.

Bruce, Judith and Beverly Winikoff. 1990. *Executive Summary - Findings from the Seminar on "Reassessment of the Concept of Reproductive Risk in Maternity Care and Family Planning Services," February 12-13, 1990, The Population Council.* New York: The Population Council.

Bruce, Judith. 1990. "Fundamental Elements of Quality of Care: A Simple Framework." *Studies in Family Planning* 21(2):61-91.

Bruce, Judith and Anrudh K. Jain. 1990. "Improving the Quality of Care Through Operations Research." Paper prepared for the TVT/MORE Conference on Operations Research in Family Planning, Arlington, VA.

Coreil, Jeannine. 1990. "The Evolution of Anthropology in International Health," in Jeannine Coreil and J. Dennis Mull, eds., *Anthropology and Primary Health Care* Pp. 3-27. Boulder, CO: Westview Press.

Das Gupta, Monica. 1989. "The Effects of Discrimination on Health and Mortality." in *Proceedings of the International Population Conference* 3:349-365. Liege, Belgium: International Union for the Scientific Study of Population.

Donabedian, Avedis. 1968. "Promoting Quality Through Evaluating the Process of Patient Care." *Medical Care* 6(3):181-202.

Donabedian, Avedis. 1988. "The Quality of Care: How Can It Be Assessed?" *Journal of the American Medical Association* 260(12):1743-1748.

Donahue, John M. 1990. "The Role of Anthropologists in Primary Health Care: Reconciling Professional and Community Interests," in Jeannine Coreil and J. Dennis Mull, eds., *Anthropology and Primary Health Care* Pp. 79-97. Boulder, CO: Westview Press.

Fisher, Andrew A., Barbara Mensch, Robert Miller, Ian Askew, Anrudh K. Jain, Cecilia Ndeti, Lewis Ndhlovu, and Placide Tapsoba. 1991. *Standard Protocol and Guidelines for Situation Analysis and Related Impact Studies.* New York: The Population Council Africa Operations Research and Technical Assistance Project and Ebert Program.

Franco, Lynne Miller, Theresa Hatzell, Wayne Stinson and Tisna Veldhuyzen Van Zanten. 1991. "Local Financing and Community Mobilization for Improving Quality of Maternal Care in the Third World." Paper presented at the 18th Annual NCIH International Health Conference, Arlington, VA.

Gay, Jill. 1980. "A Literature Review of the Client-Provider Interface in Maternal and Child Health and Family Planning Clinics in Latin America." Report prepared for the Pan American Health Organization and World Health Organization.

Heligman, Larry. 1983. "Patterns of Sex Differentials in Mortality in Less Developed Countries," in Lado T. Ruzicka and Alan D. Lopez, eds., *Sex Differentials in Mortality: Trends, Determinants and Consequences* Pp. 7-32. Canberra, Australia: Australian National University Department of Demography.

International Center for Research on Women. 1989. *Strengthening Women: Health Research Priorities for Women in Developing Countries.* Washington, D.C.: International Center for Research on Women.

Jacobson, Jodi L. 1991. "Women's Reproductive Health: The Silent Emergency." *Worldwatch Paper* No. 102. Washington, D.C.: The Worldwatch Institute.

Jain, Anrudh K. 1991. "Quality and Supply of Services." Paper presented at the Expert Meeting on Measuring the Influence of Accessibility of Family Planning Services in Developing Countries, Committee on Population, National Research Council, Washington, D.C.

Jain, Anrudh K. 1989. "Fertility Reduction and the Quality of Family Planning Services." *Studies in Family Planning* 20(1):1-16.

Kamel, Nahid M. 1983. "Determinants and Patterns of Female Mortality Associated with Women's Reproductive Role," in Lado T. Ruzicka and Alan D. Lopez, eds., *Sex Differentials in Mortality: Trends, Determinants and Consequences* Pp. 179-91. Canberra, Australia: Australian National University Department of Demography.

Kendall, Carl. 1990. "Public Health and the Domestic Domain: Lessons from Anthropological Research on Diarrheal Diseases." in Jeannine Coreil and J. Dennis Mull, eds., *Anthropology and Primary Health Care* Pp. 173-195. Boulder, CO: Westview Press.

Khattab, Hind. 1991. "Research Methods to Elicit Information From Women." Paper presented at the 18th Annual NCIH International Health Conference, Arlington, VA.

Koblinsky, Marjorie A., Susan J. Griffey Brechin, Samuel D. Clark and M. Yousuf Hasan. 1989. "Helping Managers to Manage: Work Schedules of Field-Worker in Rural Bangladesh." *Studies in Family Planning* 20(4):225-234.

Kumar, Sushil, Anrudh K. Jain and Judith Bruce. 1989. "Assessing the Quality of Family Planning Services in Developing Countries." *Programs Division Working Paper* No. 2. New York: The Population Council.

Larson, Elaine Lucia Oram and Eddie Hendrick. 1988. "Nosocomial Infection Rates as an Indicator of Quality." *Medical Care* 26(7):676-684.

Leonard, Ann. 1991. "Post-Abortion Family Planning." Paper presented at the 18th Annual NCIH International Health Conference, Arlington, VA.

Leslie, Joanne and Geeta Rao Gupta. 1989. *Utilization of Formal Services for Maternal Nutrition and Health Care in the Third World.* Washington, D.C.: International Center for Research on Women.

Maine, Deborah. 1991. *Safe Motherhood Programs: Options and Issues.* New York: Columbia University School of Public Health, Center for Population and Family Health.

Miller, Robert A., Lewis Ndhlovu, Margaret M. Gachara and Andrew Fisher. 1991. "The Situation Analysis Study of the Family Planning Program in Kenya." *Studies in Family Planning* 22(3):131-143.

Mull, Dorothy S. and J. Dennis Mull. 1990. "The Anthropologist and Primary Health Care," in Jeannine Coreil and J. Dennis Mull, eds., *Anthropology and Primary Health Care* Pp. 302-322. Boulder, CO: Westview Press.

Nichter, Mark. 1990. "Vaccinations in South Asia: False Expectations and Commanding Metaphors." in Jeannine Coreil and J. Dennis Mull, eds., *Anthropology and Primary Health Care*     Pp. 196-221. Boulder, CO: Westview Press.

Pelto, Pertti J., Margaret E. Bentley, and Gretel H. Pelto. 1990. "Applied Anthropological Research Methods: Diarrhea Studies as an Example," in Jeannine Coreil and J. Dennis Mull, eds., *Anthropology and Primary Health Care* Pp. 253-277. Boulder, CO: Westview Press.

Roemer, M.I. and C. Montoya-Aguilar. 1988. *Quality Assessment and Assurance in Primary Health Care.* Geneva: World Health Organization.

Ruzicka, Lado. T. and Alan D. Lopez. 1983. "Sex Differentials in Mortality: Conclusions and Prospects," in Lado T. Ruzicka and Alan D. Lopez, eds., *Sex Differentials in Mortality: Trends, Determinants and Consequences* Pp. 477-492. Canberra, Australia: Australian National University Department of Demography.

Simmons, Ruth. 1991. "Methodologies for Studying Client Interactions." Paper presented for the Seminar on Client Relations and Quality of Care, The Population Council.

Simmons, Ruth. and James F. Phillips. 1990. "The Proximate Operational Determinants of Fertility Regulation Behavior. *Research Division Working Paper* No. 15. New York: The Population Council.

Simmons, Ruth, Laila Baqee, Michael A. Koenig and James F. Phillips. 1988. "Beyond Supply: The Importance of Female Family Planning Workers in Rural Bangladesh." *Studies in Family Planning* 19(1):29-38.

Simmons, Ruth, Marjorie A. Koblinsky and James F. Phillips. 1986. "Client Relations in South Asia: Programmatic and Societal Determinants." *Studies in Family Planning* 17(6):257-268.

Subcommittee on Quality Indicators in Family Planning Service Delivery (Judith Helzner, Chair). 1990. "Report of the Subcommittee on Quality Indicators in Family Planning Services." Report submitted to the Task Force on Standardization of Family Planning Program Performance Indicators.

Task Force on Women's Health Issues. "Report on the Health Service Task Force on Women's Health Issues." *Public Health Reports* 100(1):73-105.

The Boston Women's Health Collective. 1985. *The New Our Bodies, Ourselves: A Book By and For Women*. New York: Simon and Schuster, Inc.

Tsui, Amy Ong. 1991. "Review of the Effects of Accessibility on Contraceptive Use and Fertility Behavior." Paper presented at the Expert Meeting on Measuring the Influence of Accessibility of Family Planning Services in Developing Countries, Committee on Population, National Research Council, Washington, D.C.

United Nations. 1991. *The World's Women 1970-1990: Trends and Statistics*. Social Statistics and Indicators Series K, No. 8. New York: United Nations Department of Discrimination on Health and Social Affairs.

Verme, Cynthia Steele. 1991. "Contraception During the Postpartum Period: Perspectives From Clients and Providers in Three Regions." Paper presented at the 18th Annual NCIH International Health Conference, Arlington, VA.

Villaroman-Bautista, Violeta, Aurorita Tan Roldan and Monina Basco. 1990. "A Comparison of Use Patterns, the Health Care Process, and the Effectiveness of Four Prenatal Health Services in a Provincial Community of the Philippines." *Maternal Nutrition and Health Care Program Report No. 9*. Washington, D.C.: International Center for Research on Women.

Ward, Jeannette. 1989. "Women's Health: Just One Question?" *Australian Family Physician* 18(2):81.

Wasserheit, Judith N. 1989. "The Significance and Scope of Reproductive Tract Infections Among Third World Women." *International Journal of Gynecology and Obstetrics Supplement 3, Women's Health in the Third World: The Impact of Unwanted Pregnancy* Pp. 145-168.

Wilkinson, Marilyn. 1991. "The DHS Service Availability Questionnaire." Paper presented at the Expert Meeting on Measuring the Influence of Accessibility of Family Planning Services in Developing Countries, Committee on Population, National Research Council, Washington, D.C.

Winikoff, Beverly and Barbara Mensch. 1991. "Rethinking Postpartum Family Planning." *Studies in Family Planning* 22(5):312-325.

Winikoff, Beverly. 1991. "Maternal Risk." Paper presented at the XXIII Berzelius Symposium, Swedish Society of Medicine, Stockholm, Sweden.

# 12

## Health Women's Way:
## Learning to Listen

*Susan Brems and Marcia Griffiths*

If women are indeed to benefit from actions to improve their health, we in the health care community must first benefit from women's voices. To do this we must make listening and talking with women a fundamental organizing principle of women's health programs.

This imperative arises on both developmental and pragmatic grounds. From a development perspective, programs that derive from community women's concerns and that work to strengthen women's ability to address those concerns are more likely to be programs that translate into long-term gains for women without disproportionate dependence on donor resources. Such programs can truly improve the quality of life—the goal of development. From a pragmatic perspective, women-centered programs are likely to be more effective, because they appropriately address local needs, as well as more cost-effective, because they draw on local resources.

Few people who have worked in or studied development closely would dispute these statements. Yet listening and talking with women is far from a standard activity in program design and implementation. We as health professionals can offer many rationalizations for this. Most of them stem from assumptions we make, implicitly or explicitly, albeit with the best of intentions.

First, we assume that health can be divorced from the everyday lives of women and acted upon with purely technical solutions. Therefore, we consider that we as international health professionals, because of our worldwide perspective and technical expertise, can best identify the priority problems and points of intervention, almost holding constant the environment in which women live.

Second, we assume that women who are illiterate, of low socioeconomic status, and with little or no economic or political power are reluctant or

255

unable to analyze their problems and speak about their health and health needs—particularly regarding a sensitive subject such as reproductive health. Therefore, it follows that we should design the programs that we assume women would want.

Third, we assume that the biomedical model of health, disease and health care is, if not universal, at least universally desirable. At best, we tend to see folk practices as interesting vestiges of traditional societies in which we are trying to effect change. At worst, we view such practices as products of ignorance and superstition that should be easily discarded for "rational" health beliefs. Therefore, we proceed to mount programs based on the biomedical model and discourage folk practices.

But if we are to take seriously the imperative of making listening and talking with women an organizing principle of our work, we need to: (1) dispel our assumptions and put a greater value on local knowledge; (2) understand how listening and talking to women as an organizing principle can benefit programs; (3) increase our efforts to work with women collectively; and (4) become familiar with the different ways that women's voices can reach policy makers, planners and managers. Many of the papers presented at the 1991 NCIH Conference offer guidance on these points, while underscoring the urgency of embracing the imperative.

## Local Knowledge

Unfortunately, too often health services for women that fit well within the biomedical agenda of global intervention priorities are inappropriate at the local level and are, therefore, underutilized, ineffective and unsustainable. Many conference papers underscore the importance of opening our ears and learning to listen to and talk with women, of being guided by what the anthropologist Clifford Geertz calls "local knowledge"—seeing broad principles in parochial facts (1983:167). Listening to and talking with women offers the best way to find common ground between what we as health professionals think is best and what local women want and will accept.

### Health First?

The first assumption—that health can be acted upon alone—is repudiated by a clear message we heard repeatedly at the conference: Health is an integral part of the political-economic and sociocultural milieu in which women live, as Letelier, Matembe and da Silva emphasized in the forum on "Voices from the South." In session after session presenters offered testimony on how women's health is strongly conditioned by the political and economic environment in which they live, the society of which they are a part, and the cultural belief system that organizes and gives meaning to their lives.

Mataka, for example, spoke of how young women in Zambia may place themselves at risk of HIV infection because of economic need, despite their knowledge of how AIDS is transmitted. Shamima Islam recounted the case of a Bengali woman whose own mother resisted all attempts to seek hospital care for her during a difficult labor because of the loss of prestige the family would suffer with this violation of *purdah*. Krieger and ElFeraly similarly reported that in Egypt the sex of the doctor affects access to health care because of strong social norms that govern correct behavior between males and females. Patel showed how social and cultural notions of white vaginal discharge affect health-seeking behavior in India. And Bang and Bang reported how in India reproductive-tract infections are not just microbiology, but are surrounded by a complex cultural universe. Consequently, health programs that are to be effective must take these nontechnical, environmental factors into account.

Because local women understand the many factors that affect their quality of life, when given a choice they might not even choose a health program as a high priority. In Haiti, for example, Maternowski found that village women considered hunger, landlessness, lack of water and fear of political persecution as more important than their lack of access to family planning. And Beaton and Robinson found that women in Nepal put a higher priority on literacy, day care and income-generation than on health as we might narrowly define it. But these "non-health" programs can have health effects. In Bangladesh, women who joined together to form a savings group were more likely, after a period of participation, to accept contraception than women who did not join, according to Amin Islam. And, also in Bangladesh, Gomes reported that as women's incomes increased, so did their demands for health services.

A corollary to this assumption of the separability of health from the environment is the assumption of the separability of actions *within* health; that is, that certain single actions have catalytic effects in the sense that they can precipitate development almost single-handedly. Often referred to as the "silver bullet" proponents, those who hold this assumption usually advocate one particular intervention as the spearhead to development. The underlying logic is that resources are not adequate to address all problems so a lead intervention must be identified. Unfortunately, the intervention is typically chosen by health planners based on what is in vogue or has been successful in other contexts. The type of intervention thus recommended changes over time as development programers try one "bullet" after another. This results in donor programs that seldom have lasting impact.

Many of the conference papers gave evidence that local women reject silver bullet approaches to development, favoring synergism over catalysis. In synergism, different types of interventions can work together to produce an effect—development—that none can do alone. As Bang and Bang put it, "women's lives know no such compartments" (1991:11). Thus, in Haiti, Maternowski reported that, in accordance with the wishes of local women, a comprehensive project that considers women's health within a larger developmental standpoint took the place of the original donor-intended family planning program. And, as Amara Singham pointed out, women should not have to choose between maternal and child health or women in development programs, but should be able to participate in the synergistic approach that was envisioned under "Health for All" strategies almost fifteen years ago.

Another reason to work within a development model that considers the broader socioeconomic context is that as change occurs it might not always be in the direction that donors expect. Though some observers characterize health development as a type of convergence model, in which non-Western societies adopt more and more of biomedicine as its efficacy for particular ailments becomes evident (e.g. Foster 1978: 252), the opposite can also occur: Krieger and ElFeraly report that the revival of fundamentalist Islamic movements has limited the acceptability of biomedically-based perinatal care among Egyptian women who previously accepted it because of the predominance of male doctors in service delivery. In such cases, there is little point in assuming a gradual attrition of the environmental factors that affect health.

### Who's Listening?

The second assumption—that of women's reluctance or inability to speak—is contradicted by the abundant data in the conference papers that showed that poor, illiterate women do speak eagerly and eloquently about their bodies and health needs—if they are given the chance and their views are respected. The problem may not be so much their inability to speak as our inability to listen. Baker had little difficulty finding Nairobi women willing to discuss abortion experiences. Franco stated that women in Niger had a lot to say about the quality of health services. The women said they had not spoken out earlier because they had not been asked their opinion. Maternowski found that poor women in urban Haiti were very forthcoming about wanting education on the relative merits of the gamut of contraceptive methods, not just a "how-to" booklet on oral contraceptives.

Moreover, we may not be asking women about the problems they wish to discuss. Bang and Bang, Patel, and Kanani et al. all found many Indian women who would speak at some length about their priority problem of white discharge, a problem that an expatriate expert had dismissed as an "innocuous symptom" (Bang and Bang 1991). And Sanchez et al. in Bolivia found that usually reserved women spoke freely when involved in a process that allowed them to select and prioritize their problems.

It is also important that women understand why they are being sought out and that they see a possible benefit in making disclosures. Yacoob and Brieger told of prostitutes in Gambia who fictionalized their life stories until the reasons were explained for all the questions being put to them. And Gomes related how in her first attempt to work with destitute rural women in Bangladesh she was rejected because they could not understand why she was interested in them. But when, in a second attempt, she entered their world directly through participant observation, they opened their "hearts and lives" to her (1991:2).

Finally, the type of person who is asking the questions can greatly influence how candidly women speak. Women may say things to other women that they will not say to men, as Krieger and ElFeraly point out. Or they may communicate more freely with someone who is not in their social control network. Mataka spoke of Zambian teenagers who, close-mouthed in health education class, opened up when the teacher left the room and they were able to speak freely with an HIV-positive person from distant Nairobi. And Whitney et al. found peer counseling an effective strategy for reaching young women in the Philippines.

Moreover, those doing the listening must be sensitive to how notions are expressed. We need not always accept initial statements on face value but should continue to talk and listen to learn what else is intended. This was brought home in two independent pieces of research done in India by Bang and Bang and by Patel. Both studies reported that women with white discharge may speak of their problem obliquely, in symbolic terms, because of the social stigma attached to the health problem. They may speak of a generalized weakness or backache rather than of the discharge itself. Medical practitioners may take this weakness to mean anemia, when women are really saying something else. In other words, many times it takes a sensitive *listener* to hear what women are saying.

In summary, reports of women not wishing to speak to health researchers must be measured against the conditions under which the research was done. The success of listening to and talking with women is largely conditioned by *our willingness* to open our ears and *our ability* to learn how to listen.

## Meanings and Contexts

The third assumption—that of the universality of the biomedical model—is vitiated by the many research findings in which women's notions of how bodies work, diseases originate, and cures are sought contrast with the dominant paradigm of biomedicine.

Biomedicine, which underlies Western health and health care, divides the human being into the somatic body and the intangible mind. It then deals primarily with diseases that are discernible via empirical symptoms. It seeks organic, proximate causes of disease and treats these proximate causes. This model favors disaggregation, specialization, and categorization, and so feeds into the previous two assumptions: Just as it divides people into bodies and minds and divides bodies into systems, organs and smaller components, biomedicine has a similar tendency to divide health from the setting that produces it. And just as it emphasizes areas of specialization, laden with experts, biomedicine tends to have little confidence in lay or generalized knowledge—knowledge that is not the domain of an expert.

In many other cultures, however, the biomedical model coexists or is dwarfed by an ethnomedical model of health, disease, and health care. This point is critical, because we very often presume that local people, when they do not have the health education knowledge we would like them to have, are ignorant in the sense of knowing nothing about a topic. Clearly there are times when people are uninformed or misinformed. But more than likely they know very much about the particular topic, albeit in very different terms—their own ethnomedical terms. In the same way that biomedicine is a product of Western culture and is consonant with our faith in positivist science, disaggregation, and specialization, ethnomedical models reflect other cultural values. As Yacoob and Brieger explained in their work on guinea worm in Nigeria, discovering ethnomedical perceptions furnishes the *meaning and context* necessary to understand the disease in the culture at hand.

Examples abound in the conference papers. In Patel's work in India, the explanations women gave for the causes of their illnesses incorporated elements of a personalistic ethnomedicine, in which a being outside the sufferer can be responsible for the illness. In such a system, unity prevails: not only are mind and body not divided, but the person herself is not completely separable from other persons. In the Bang and Bang and Kanani et al. studies, disease causes cited by women reflected belief in a naturalistic, equilibrium model that seeks a balance between hot and cold humors. In the equilibrium model there is again an importance on wholeness, unity, and balance, in contrast to biomedicine's propensity to separate. Similarly, in Africa, Yacoob and Brieger found that women suffering from guinea worm see the worm as part of the body—not as a separable outside organism that invades the body, as our biomedical model describes it. And one reason Anderson gave for Indian women's reluctance to eat more during pregnancy is that they consider their stomach and uterus to be one. Increasing food intake deprives the baby of space.

One implication of the existence of health and medical models other than the biomedical one is that people who are not served by "modern" health programs nevertheless have a health system to which they have recourse. This may include home remedies and care that are part of generalized cultural knowledge diffuse in the community, as well as specialized knowledge and care by such traditional health personnel as healers, diviners, and birth attendants. Zigirumugabe found, for example, that in Rwanda births may be attended by any experienced woman or man and that birth attendants, in the sense of someone with specialized knowledge from whom everyone seeks help, don't exist. Birthing babies is generalized knowledge. In speaking with women, Bang and Bang learned of nearly forty types of indigenous treatments for white discharge—certainly not a limited pharmacopoeia.

## Reconciling Agendas

If indeed women know best what they need and have an alternative health system in place, what should be the role of donor-assisted programs in women's health? Clearly biomedicine, with its effective drugs, surgical techniques and hygienic practices, has much to offer, particularly in the realm of life-saving treatment. But women seem to be saying through the conference papers that health programs should not be exported in an unqualified way; they need to be tempered with an interest in and respect for local knowledge of needs, appropriate types of programs and resources, and should be designed, delivered and managed in an acceptable manner. In short, we need to reconcile the agenda of international health experts with that of the local women international health programs propose to serve.

One case in point is maternal mortality. The high rates of maternal death in many developing countries are unacceptable, and many women around the world live in the fear that pregnancy or childbirth may result in that fate for them, as Zigirumugabe cited in her work in Rwanda. There is no undermining the seriousness of that problem. The Safe Motherhood Initiative was launched in 1987 to apply creative thinking and large-scale resources to reduce maternity-related death, and certainly deserves a high priority in all countries.

At the same time, it appears equally clear that many Third World women do not consider maternal mortality their only problem, or perhaps even their most important problem. While maternal mortality presents a risk for all women who become pregnant, it is still a relatively infrequent occurrence and one over which some women may think they have little control. Therefore, they may put a higher priority on less dramatic but more chronic and frequent ailments that undermine the quality of their daily lives—illnesses in which both incidence and duration are high, translating into high prevalence.

This appears to be the case in both Patel's and Bang and Bang's research on gynecological morbidity in India, where women chose white discharge as their most serious health problem; the reason they gave for that priority was its painful and chronic nature. Few international health experts would have anticipated this response, perhaps because in Western culture we have such easy access to effective cures that we tend to dismiss these ailments a priori. And, Sanchez et al. pointed out that when women in the Altiplano of Bolivia prioritized maternal health problems and needs, they put family planning services first, then problems that relate more directly to maternal death.

Reconciling the two health agendas primarily means making services more appropriate. This requires considering the local ethnomedical system in service design. Zigirumugabe reported that women in Rwanda prefer to give birth at home because of the warm, supportive environment home birth affords. Incorporating this element of the ethnomedical ambiance might make institutional deliveries more appealing in situations like this, which abound in the Third World. Another alternative is to take selected aspects of biomedical delivery to the home or to maternity homes, which is what was proposed after Wedderburn's research in Jamaica indicated that women looked first for social support and secondarily for medical support when describing the ideal delivery situation.

Services and messages must also be socially appropriate. Mataka reported the conflicting messages Zambian adolescents receive when their social upbringing prepares them to be submissive to their husbands in marriage, while AIDS health education programs ask them to be assertive in practicing safe sex. Should they listen to their grandmothers or their teachers? With careful thought, some middle ground can certainly be struck here.

Timing of certain services must also be appropriate. Though childbirth is one of the major times that women come into contact with the biomedical health system, women in the three countries of Verme's research felt strongly that labor was an inappropriate time to discuss family planning.

## An Organizing Principle

For listening and talking to women to be an organizing principle in women's health, we must always have our ears and minds open and learn from and build on what we hear. Communication and collaboration with local women is essential—not only in the early stages of project design, but throughout project implementation and evaluation. Only though a continuing dialogue with local women do short-term health projects have the possibility of translating into sustainable, long-term development advances. The conference papers demonstrate the many uses and benefits that listening and talking to women can bring.

Listening and talking to women *heightens women's awareness* of their health needs and resources for addressing those needs. In Bolivia, Sanchez et al. showed how the process of self-diagnosis of health needs made women more conscious of their health. With the aid of local women in Mexico, Salamon developed an education guide on domestic violence that helped women analyze the problem and its possible solutions.

Listening and talking can allow women to realize that some problems of high prevalence need not be accepted as normal or as women's fate, but are amenable to treatment. Kanani et al. cited an Indian woman: "What to tell you, after marriage and childbearing it is natural for women to have weakness. All women around here have these problems in some degree or other" (1991:10). And Bang and Bang also cited: "Like every tree has flowers, every woman has white discharge, only thing is, it's not soothing like flowers" (1991:2).

Communication with women is essential to *identifying and prioritizing health needs* as women perceive them, as discussed above. Maternowski, Beaton and Robinson, and others stated women's preference for programs that take a broader view of health than do most experts. Yacoob and Brieger did some interesting impact case studies, in which the toll of guinea worm disease was not measured in such macro indicators as days lost to agricultural production or school days missed, but in micro, women-centered indicators, such as inability to perform household chores and to care for themselves, as well as negative effects on nutrition and prenatal care. This type of analysis can point to some different intervention points for the disease.

Local women can be effective in *advocating policy* that favors their health development. Bang and Bang asserted that by rejecting contraception, poor women of the Third World are sending signals to policy makers in the capitals of international donor assistance that no contraception is acceptable without gynecological care. In Nigeria, Okafor reported using seminars as a forum for policy input by community-based women's groups to city-based groups that controlled outside resources. And in both Uganda and Tanzania, according to Kasolo and Kamba, women's organizations are advocating appropriate policies for national Safe Motherhood Initiatives to government.

Services are likely to be more appropriate if community women help *plan interventions*. Based on discussions with community women, Krieger and ElFeraly gave the example of deploying mobile units of female doctors and nurses to address the problem of underutilization of care in Egypt.

Collaboration in planning by women in Nepal and Haiti, among other sites, resulted in more broad-based health programs. Wedderburn showed how women's opinions can be used to design birthing facilities that are an alternative to hospitals.

Where women themselves *implement programs*, those programs are more likely to benefit women's long-term development and to be sustainable in the absence of large donor inputs. The women's agents in Haiti were poor women native to the communities in which they worked; their training and development feeds into the development of the whole community. And the model in Uganda and Tanzania of implementing Safe Motherhood programs through women's organizations allows those groups to be strengthened at the same time that the limited resources of government are not overly taxed.

By collaborating in *measuring improvements in health*, community women see tangible benefits to health actions, further strengthening their belief in the value of health programs. Gomes described how women in Bangladesh collected data during the day and analyzed them at night to decide in which directions they should next move. And Maynard-Tucker provided an example of training local women in the mystery client method to get a true picture of what is happening in health services.

### Strengthening Women Collectively

The experiences documented in the conference papers support the notion that the most effective way to help improve the health of individual women in an ongoing way is to work with women collectively. This process means:

*Strengthening women's networks*. Most women have networks of kin and friends, diffuse contacts they maintain to seek and give advice or aid. These networks can be further strengthened to coalesce into formal groups able to act more concertedly for women's development. Beaton and Robinson spoke of "creation of organization" with women in Nepal, in which the formation of interest groups led to viable community organization that now brings pressure "from below" to bring about change. And Amin Islam described the main thrust of Save the Children women's programs in Bangladesh as organizing women in groups.

*Heightening awareness of shared feelings and reducing isolation and shame.* Gomes described how a group of women of which she was a member traveled to villages in Bangladesh to listen to other women's tales of poverty and exploitation. During these gatherings, the visiting women told their own stories of suffering and explained how their lives had changed since banding together. Whitney et al. provided the example of peer counseling in the Philippines, in which teenagers felt less shame in approaching other teens for advice. Participants in the Bolivian's women's groups described by Sanchez et al. spoke openly about very intimate things so they could grow to know each other and realize that their problems were shared by others. The confidence of these women increased to the point that they were able to talk to women they didn't know about maternal health problems.

*Helping channel demands collectively.* In many instances, aspects of community social organization may thwart women's attempts to effect changes in their lives. For example, Amin Islam reported opposition among Bengali villagers who feared loss of family status if their kinswomen participated in activities outside the home. But if women organize into strong groups, they can bring greater pressure to bear by voicing their demands collectively. Beaton and Robinson presented examples of pressure "from below": videos made by illiterate women to document their areas of concern; visits by group representatives to government officials to press demands and to other villages to strengthen solidarity; and greater female participation in village meetings.

*Encouraging non-hierarchical relations.* In programs where local women's skills are increased through participant-based activities, such as the Haitian project's women agents and the groups in Bolivia, women's strengthened expertise often confers greater status and acceptance and hence self-confidence and self-esteem. As women gain strength through their collectivity, they bring new confidence to their relations with other women and with other groups. Noorani describes how, through work in a women's group, "active" women were able to help more "passive" women and give them confidence and motivation to, for example, go to the health center. Okafor told of a program in Nigeria that sought to promote a good working relationship between traditional birth attendants and trained community midwives. Lack of confidence between the two groups of women health workers stemmed from disparagement of the traditional attendants' role. By analyzing their needs and problems together, women can understand more completely their social relations with men, the medical community and other segments of society. Indeed, Danforth and Karefa-

Smart, and Brabec caution that men need to be a target audience of women's health programs in instances where they are decision makers regarding health (the case in Brabec's work in Papua New Guinea) or participate in women's health care (the case in birthing in Bolivia, per Sanchez et al., and Rwanda, per Zigirumugabe).

*Strengthening women's resource base.* Working with women's groups facilitates pooling of resources at the same time that it adds to the collective resource base for the benefit of all. These additions may be in the form of knowledge, new linkages, materials, technical expertise or financial support. In Gomes' work in Bangladesh, different women in the group trained in different areas, increasing the resources of all. One area included legal aid because of the many problems women had with domestic violence and marriage status. Many other papers cited how loan funds have increased women's financial resources and provided seed money for income-generation; as Amin Islam pointed out, this in turn has had its effects on child survival, nutrition and acceptance of family planning.

*Making sustainable change more likely because it is effected at the group, rather than individual, level.* When women work for their health development in groups, the success of their efforts is not dependent on any one person. Further, because of the additional resources number confer, the content of the development can be wider. Gomes spoke of how women's groups in Bangladesh have evolved from an initial focus on savings for income-generation to encompass education, legal aid, health education, growth monitoring, collective kitchens, community sanitation, community health assessments and other areas. Similar broadening was reported by Maternowski, Beaton and Robinson, and Amin Islam.

## Methods for Listening to and Talking with Women

To hear women truly, we must come to them without fixed agendas and as free of cultural bias as possible. This means the methods we use and the information we obtain must principally be qualitative in nature. When research is of a quantitative nature, the questions and the categories for possible responses are a given. This research is appropriate once we have allowed women to define some of the question and response categories. However, at this stage in the development of women's health programs, so little is known and so much of the subject matter sensitive that survey instruments will not allow us to hear what women really want to say.

Whether the information was gathered in an informal way through women's groups or under a structured qualitative research protocol, the data presented in conference papers all showed the importance of taking time early in a project planning phase to allow women to talk, prioritize needs and work on solutions. While the methodologies are not always fully described in the papers, they cover the range of available qualitative methods. In addition, some useful techniques for assisting women in their analysis and prioritization of problems have been used as part of these methods.

The methods represented in the conference papers range from time-intensive observation, to structured in-depth interviews, to focussed group discussions conducted by skilled professionals and, in other cases, by trained local workers, to group interviews and less formal group discussions. The choice of methods depended on the purpose of information gathering and type of information required, and on whether the research was done as part of an ongoing development program with established women's groups.

Gomes and Salamon both used *participant observation* techniques to bring them closer to the reality of the women with whom they were working. Salamon lived with the family of one of the female bankers in the project. For Gomes, participant observation meant actually taking up the life of the women she hoped to help. These time-intensive experiences yielded tremendous insights and, in the case of Gomes, a life's work. Patel described the use of *direct observation* in her research. This is less time-intensive but yields some of the richness of participant observation because the researcher pauses during interviewing or discussion and actually watches— an important corollary activity to listening.

*Open-ended in-depth interviewing* was a commonly used method of gathering information on women's perceptions of problems and needs, and perceptions of solutions. The Indian researchers (Bang and Bang, Patel and Kanani) used this method with community women, key informants such as traditional birth attendants and community leaders, and health professionals. Through these interviews, the researchers were able to understand the range of health problems women experience, the priority they give these problems, and the treatments they pursue. Kattab described the usefulness of in-depth interviews in highlighting the differences in women's and health workers' perceptions of problems. She went on to use the interview results to develop a screening tool for gynecological infections. Baker described her in-depth interviews on abortion with volunteers in Nairobi, and Yacoob and Brieger's interviews illustrated the importance of understanding the etiology of disease from the perspective of the sufferers in order to understand their behavior and pinpoint intervention.

Two other specific types of interviewing were mentioned in the papers. The first, *verbal autopsy*, was used in Inquisivi, Bolivia, by Sanchez et al. Here the family of any woman who died during pregnancy, delivery or immediately postpartum was interviewed to ascertain what happened, what the family/woman did and why they believe she died. The other type of interviewing is *mystery-client interviewing*. This method was used by Maynard-Tucker in Haiti to evaluate health services. Here, local women were trained to be observer-clients at selected health services. After visiting, they evaluated the service based on their level of satisfaction, the competence and attitudes of the health care providers, and the physical environment.

Finally, other common methods involved group interviews or discussions. These were of three types: The first, focussed group discussions (in which specially recruited groups of people are asked their views on specific talking points) were used for a variety of purposes. Kanani and Yacoob and Brieger used them for initial exploration of topics to be probed further via in-depth interviews. Krieger and ElFeraly, Zigirumugabe, Franco and Wedderburn all used focussed group discussions as their main research method. The work of Krieger and Elferaly in Egypt explored gender issues in health service utilization. Zigirumugabe in Rwanda used focussed group discussions to learn more about women's felt needs relative to starting a family planning program. In Niger, focussed group discussions helped to learn more about women's attitudes toward utilization of health services. Wedderburn used focussed group discussions in Jamaica to inform policy makers on the design of appropriate out-of-hospital birthing facilities.

The second type of research in a group setting was *group interviews*, conducted by Noorani and Bang and Bang. These differ from focussed group discussions in that the questioning is more directed, the group is not specially recruited ahead of time, and the group may be much larger than the six–ten participants recommended for a focussed group discussion. Bang and Bang used the group utterances to prioritize health problems suggested by women. In Noorani's work in Bangladesh, they were used to learn about coping strategies of "active" and "passive" women.

The third type of group work was an *informal, semi-structured discussion* held among women in organized community groups. The Save the Children projects in both Bolivia (Sanchez et al.) and Bangladesh (Amin Islam) used this method, as did Beaton and Robinson in Nepal. These group discussions were called a self-diagnosis by the Bolivia team because women explored their own, collective attitudes toward pregnancy and maternal health problems, they discovered what they know and do about the problems, and they prioritized the problems for the group. These discussions are distinct from focussed group discussions because, again, the participants are not recruited, the group is often larger than that recommended for the focussed group discussions and there is a pre-existing and continuing relationship with the group, (i.e. the discussion functions to assist the group's development).

As part of the above-described methods, a number of techniques were used to help order or structure the information gathering:

*Picture analysis.* Sanchez et al. and Wedderburn used this projective technique in which women are asked to describe what they see in a picture or what they believe happens to the woman in the picture. This allows women to project their feelings and thoughts to someone else, often making it easier to discuss sensitive subject matter. Both researchers caution that the pictures should be pretested carefully.

*Free listing.* This was done by the Indian researchers Kanani, Patel, Bang and Bang, and by Sanchez et al. Here women are asked to list, for example, all health problems they experience, all the symptoms associated with a disease, or all its cures. This process allows the parameters of the discussion to be defined by the participants.

*Pile sorting.* Again, this was used by the Indian researchers Patel and Kanani. Once women have discussed major health problems, each problem is depicted on a card. The women in the group then sort the problems by prevalence and severity. This allows them to prioritize problems.

*Illness narrative.* Here women and others are asked to describe fully what they did during a specific illness or event. This technique was used by Yacoob and Brieger and by Kanani to better understand particular behaviors and decision making.

*Hypothetical scenarios.* Kanani used made-up situations ("What would you do if ...") in her interviews with health professionals to determine their level of competence and empathy with their patients.

While other techniques may have been used but not described by the researchers, it is clear that the repertoire is limited. It is in the development of techniques to help women discuss their feelings (often referred to as projective techniques), rank or prioritize problems and solve problems that more creative work is especially needed. Ways to explore women's self-confidence and esteem have barely been touched upon, but are mentioned constantly by researchers and programers as an important factor in improving the health of women.

As well as showing the variety of ways to explore attitudes, perceptions and practices with women, what is abundantly clear from the papers and from the discussions that took place with several authors is that the methods and techniques require additional creative work to allow more depth and scope to be achieved. It will only be when the lifestyle context for women's health programs is truly appreciated that real advances for women will be made. This means women's hopes, fears, inner-most ideas, perceptions of esteem and self-confidence need to be articulated and translated by women into workable solutions and brought out for policy makers, program planners, implementors, and other community members to hear and believe. For this, more time, patience, and creativity is required.

## Recommendations for Policy, Programs, and Research

The conference data on listening to and talking with women argue convincingly for a bottom-up approach to development that takes full account of the milieu in which women live. Yet, in contrast, much of the effort in development programing at the international donor level has been devoted to the identification of successful model programs which are then blueprinted and replicated around the globe, often in a top-down manner that tends to hold the local environment constant.

At the international donor level the top-down approach has a certain logic because it represents theoretical cost-effectiveness: Once a successful program is hammered out, subsequent programs do not have to begin the process all over again. The "goods" can be delivered, whether they be food supplements, prenatal contacts or tetanus-toxoid immunizations. But this thinking in turn assumes that the important part of the development process is the *product*, the "goods" we deliver. What many of the papers here suggest is that the *process* of encouraging women to articulate and act on their own needs may be more helpful to development than meeting quantifiable targets of goods delivered. Further, the blueprint approach assumes that successful programs can be extracted from the environment in which they were successful, when indeed it may have been precisely their close fit with environmental factors that made them successful.

The realities of international assistance, however, temper the feasibility of purely bottom-up programming. Nor is it desirable to ignore the many "lessons learned" that so abound in the development literature—especially when probably the major lesson learned is that development programs cannot be cut out like cookies. Clearly there has to be a balance between the *sui generis* grassroots approach and the culture of donor organizations. That culture calls on the front end for policy formulation based on current scientific knowledge, epidemiological priorities and field implementation experiences, while requiring accountability on the back end for resources expended via measurable entities such as improvements in nutrition status, maternal lives saved, and births averted. Pure process will never be a satisfactory indicator. To content ourselves with process indicators would be political suicide for donor-financed health programs that must compete with other types of programs for limited development dollars.

But what we can strive to do is to tailor standard packages to the local setting exactly by making listening to and talking with women an organizing principle for actions in women's health—by valuing local knowledge. This means that before project implementation begins, formative research should be conducted. This research should guide the tailoring of standard packages to highlight project components most suited to local needs, desires, and resources. It also means that during project implementation, local women should collaborate in an ongoing way, with latitude for mid-course alterations in project design. Local women should be in both management and service delivery positions and should be strengthened in their ability to carry out the programs, both through personal development and through expansion of the resource base available to them.

## Note

The authors gratefully acknowledge the collaboration of Joan Russ, who joined them as rapporteur for this topic.

## References

Amara Singham, Saha. 1991. "Women in Development or Mothers in Child Survival." Paper presented at the 18th Annual International Health Conference, Arlington, VA.

Anderson, Mary Ann. 1991. "Undernutrition During Pregnancy and Lactation in India." Paper presented at the 18th Annual International Health Conference, Arlington, VA.

Baker, Jean. 1991. "The Impact of Induced Abortion on Women's Health in Kenya." Paper presented at the 18th Annual International Health Conference, Arlington, VA.

Bang, Rani and Abhay Bang. 1991. "Reproductive Tract Infections: Rural Women's Point of View." Paper presented at the 18th Annual International Health Conference, Arlington, VA.

Beaton, Susan and Sheila A. Robinson. 1991. "Women and Health in Mehlkuna, Nepal." Paper presented at the 18th Annual International Health Conference, Arlington, VA.

Brabec, Joan. 1991. "The Importance of Educating Men in Women's Health Issues: Surprising Findings from a Pilot Project to Train Birth Attendants in Rural Papua New Guinea." Paper presented at the 18th Annual International Health Conference, Arlington, VA.

Danforth, Nick and Karefa-Smart, John. 1991. "Where Are the Men in Women's Health?" Paper presented at the 18th Annual International Health Conference, Arlington, VA.

Foster, George M. and Barbara Gallatin Anderson. 1978. *Medical Anthropology*. New York: Alfred A. Knopf.

Franco, Lynne Miller. 1991. "Local Financing and Community Mobilization for Improving Quality of Maternal Care at Village Level in Niger." Paper presented at the 18th Annual International Health Conference, Arlington, VA.

Geertz, Clifford. 1983. *Local Knowledge: Further Essays in Interpretive Anthropology*. New York: Basic Books.

Gomes, Angela. 1991. "Women Working for Change." Paper presented at the 18th Annual International Health Conference, Arlington, VA.

Islam, Amin. 1991. "The Impact of Women's Empowerment through Savings' Groups on Women's Contraceptive Behavior." Paper presented at the 18th Annual International Health Conference, Arlington, VA.

Islam, Shamima. 1991. "Women and Health: Migrant Workers Speak in Bangladesh." Paper presented at the 18th Annual International Health Conference, Arlington, VA.

Kamba, Kate. 1991. "The Relationship between Government Agencies and NGOs in Implementing Women's Health Projects at the Community Level." Paper presented at the 18th Annual International Health Conference, Arlington, VA.

Kanani, Shubhada, K. Latha, and Mona Shah. 1991. "Application of Ethnographic Research to Understand Perceptions of Women and Health Practitioners regarding Specific Health Disorders in India." Paper presented at the 18th Annual International Health Conference, Arlington, VA.

Kasolo, Josephine. 1991. "Women's Use of Health Services: A Survey in Rural Uganda." Paper presented at the 18th Annual International Health Conference, Arlington, VA.

Khattab, Hind Abou. "Research Methods to Elicit Information from Women to Develop Programs and Policies on RTIs." Paper presented at the 18th Annual International Health Conference, Arlington, VA.

Krieger, Laurie and Mohamed ElFeraly. 1991. "Male Doctor, Female Patient: Access to Health Care in Egypt." Paper presented at the 18th Annual International Health Conference.

Mataka, Elizabeth. 1991. "AIDS and the Zambian Adolescent." Paper presented at the 18th Annual International Health Conference, Arlington, VA.

Maternowski, Catherine M. 1991. "Our Project, Ourselves: A Case Study in Haiti." Paper presented at the 18th Annual International Health Conference, Arlington, VA.

Maynard-Tucker, Gisele. 1991. "The Mystery Client: A Method of Evaluating Quality of Care of the Family Planning Services in the Haitian Private Sector". Paper presented at the 18th Annual International Health Conference, Arlington, VA.

Noorani, Salina Aziz. 1991. "What Distinguishes Active Versus Passive Behavior Women from the Same Social Background." Paper presented at the 18th Annual International Health Conference, Arlington, VA.

Okafor, Chinyelu B. 1991. "Women Helping Women: Incorporating Women's Perspectives into Community Health Projects." Paper presented at the 18th Annual International Health Conference, Arlington, VA.

Patel, Pallavi. 1991. "Illness Beliefs and Health-Seeking Behavior of the Bhil Women of Panchamahal District of Gujarat State." Paper presented at the 18th Annual International Health Conference, Arlington, VA.

Salamon, Jill. 1991. "Qualitative Needs Assessment of Women Village Bankers." Paper presented at the 18th Annual International Health Conference, Arlington, VA.

Sanchez, Elsa, D. Rogers, and L. Howard-Grabman. 1991. "Researching Women's Health Problems Using Epidemiological and Participatory Methods to Plan the Inquisivi MotherCare Project." Paper presented at the 18th Annual International Health Conference, Arlington, VA.

Verme, Cynthia Steele. 1991. "Contraception during the Postpartum Period: Perspectives from Clients and Providers in Three Regions." Paper presented at the 18th Annual International Health Conference, Arlington, VA.

Wedderburn, Maxine. 1991. "Understanding the Childbirth Choices of Jamaican Women." Paper presented at the 18th Annual International Health Conference, Arlington, VA.

Whitney, Edson E., P.L. Coleman, J.G. Rimon, S.H. Yun, L. Kincaid, A. Silayan-Go, and W. Abejuela.1991. "Dial a Friend: Increasing Access to Counseling and Health Services for Young Women in Metro Manila." Paper presented at the 18th Annual International Health Conference, Arlington, VA.

Yacoob, May and Bill Brieger. 1991. "Putting a Face on the Numbers: The Uses of Anthropology and Epidemiology in Guinea Control among Women." Paper presented at the 18th Annual International Health Conference, Arlington, VA.

Zigirumugabe, Sixte. 1991. "Women's Perceptions of Their Health Needs: A Qualitative Study in Rwanda." Paper presented at the 18th Annual International Health Conference, Arlington, VA.

# About the Editors
# and Contributors

**Maggie Bangser** is the Asia Program Officer at the International Women's Health Coalition and has worked for ten years on public policy and public interest issues in the United States and the Third World including women's health, reproductive rights, and education.

**Carolyn M. Bloomer** is a Ph.D. candidate in anthropology at the University of North Carolina at Chapel Hill. Her area specialty is the People's Republic of China, where she did field work in 1988, 1989 and 1991. She is the author of *Principles of Visual Perception*, 2nd Rev. Ed., (1990).

**Susan J. Griffey Brechin** is currently a doctoral student at the Tulane University School of Public Health and Tropical Medicine, New Orleans, Louisiana, as well as an independent consultant in international public health.

**Susan Brems** is a medical anthropologist who specializes in women's reproductive health and has recently completed long-term fieldwork on this topic in northeast Brazil.

**Oona M.R. Campbell** is developing Methodologies for Measuring Maternal Health in Developing Countries as part of a collaborative program at The London School of Hygiene and Tropical Medicine. She is a reproductive epidemiologist with a background in demography.

**Francine M. Coeytaux** is a public health specialist with extensive experience in the development and evaluation of family planning and reproductive health programs in Africa and Latin America. An Associate of The Population Council, she has been responsible for the initiation of a new, worldwide program to address the problems of septic and incomplete abortion.

**Peggy Curlin** is the President of The Centre for Development and Population Activities (CEDPA). She has fifteen years of experience in reproductive health and development with a focus on women-to-women services.

**Andrea Eschen** is a Staff Associate at The Population Council working in reproductive health and family planning.

**Lynn P. Freedman** is Staff Attorney of the Development, Law and Policy Program at Columbia University's Center for Population and Family Health, and is also an assistant professor at Columbia's School of Public Health.

**Jill Gay,** currently a consultant with Bass & Howes, Washington, DC, consulted with the National Council for International Health on the 1991 Conference. Formerly with the Institute of Medicine of the National Academy of Sciences, she is a founder of Alt-WID.

**Marcia Griffiths** is a nutritional anthropologist, social marketing specialist and President of The Manoff Group. She has spent more than a decade working on creative research methods to make programs more responsive to client needs and is currently applying her experience to maternal health as the social marketing senior technical specialist on the MotherCare project.

**Siobán D. Harlow** is a reproductive epidemiologist who specializes in the menstrual cycle and in occupational health. She is currently on the faculty of the Escuala de Salud Publica de Mexico.

**Lori Heise** is a Project Associate with the Center for Women's Global Leadership at Rutgers University, New Brunswick, New Jersey. Ms. Heise directs the Center's Violence, Health and Development Program which seeks to raise awareness of gender violence in the international development community. Previously, Ms. Heise was a Senior Researcher with the Worldwatch Institute in Washington D.C.

**Jodi L. Jacobson** is a Senior Researcher at the Worldwatch Institute in Washington, D.C. Her work focuses on women and development, reproductive health and family planning, and the relationships between human population and the environment.

**Marge Koblinsky,** an international public health specialist, is presently Director of the MotherCare Project with John Snow, Inc. Her interest and work in women's reproductive health began with biochemical research and includes operations research with MCH and family planning programs, and programming and funding for international donors.

**Kathleen M. Kurz,** nutritionist at the International Center for Research on Women, currently heads a research program on the Nutrition of Adolescent Girls. She has authored research articles addressing issues of nutritional status and fertility.

**Ann H. Leonard,** Deputy Executive Director for International Programs of IPAS, has extensive experience in the design and evaluation of programs to reach women throughout the world with safe abortion care. Her work has focused primarily on efforts to decentralize care to make a full range of services more accessible.

**Deborah Maine** is an epidemiologist and Program Director of the Prevention of Maternal Mortality Program at Columbia University's Center for Population and Family Health.

**Jeanne McDermott** is a nurse-midwife with experience in maternal and child health and family planning in Africa. She is currently employed as an epidemiologist at the Centers for Disease Control.

**Diana M. Measham** specializes in issues related to women's health and health financing in developing countries and is currently a Senior Program Associate at Family Care International, New York.

**Barbara Mensch,** a sociologist and demographer, is an associate in the programs division of the Population Council, New York, New York.

**Kathleen M. Merchant** is currently a consultant to the International Nutrition Foundation for the United Nations World Health Organization. She has authored several research articles addressing issues of maternal nutritional depletion resulting from reproductive stresses.

**Elizabeth N. Ngugi** is a registered nurse, midwife, and lecturer at the University of Nairobi Department of Community Health. She has been educating and empowering prostitutes in Kenya regarding their reproductive health, specifically the prevention of sexually transmitted dieseases (including AIDS).

**Bisi Ogunleye** is National Coordinator and President of the Country Women Association of Nigeria.

**Freda L. Paltiel** is a policy adviser with extensive experience and many publications in the fields of health, social policy and public administration, and the Senior Adviser, Status of Women, Health and Welfare Canada. She was Canada's first Coordinator, Status of Women with leading responsibilities for the implementation of the Recommendations of the Royal Commission on the Status of Women; serves as an adviser to the World Health Organization; has chaired and is a member of the Executive Subcommittee on Women, Health and Development of the Pan American Health Organization; and represents Canada at many intergovernmental and expert meetings. She is the author of a number of publications on women and mental health and on violence against women.

**Irene Sandvold** is a public health nurse-midwife with experience in education and international health. She currently works in the Bureau of Health Professions of the U.S. Department of Health and Human Services and has served as an advisor for PAHO/WHO and AID.

**Judith Timyan,** Director of Health Programs at Population Services International, is an anthropologist who has spent 16 years living and working in West Africa in community development and health programs.

**Anne Tinker** is Health Specialist in the Population and Human Resources Department of the World Bank and has been involved in policy and program development in international public health and family planning for twenty years.

**Maxine Whittaker** is currently a consultant to the MCH-FP Extension Project of the International Centre for Diarrhoeal Disease Research in Bangladesh; the Woman, Children and Health Project of the Australian National University, and the National Centre for Epidemiology and Population Health in Australia.

# Index

Abortion
  access to care, 140-142
  contraceptive services following,
    118-120
  family planning and, 139-140
  morbidity and mortality due to,
    133-134, 136
  prevalence, 135
  recommendations for safety, 142,
    161
  technologies, 137-138
  unsafe, 133-134, 136
Abuse. *See* Alcohol abuse; Substance
  abuse; Violence against women
Access to care. *See also* Quality of care
  recommendations, 229-232
  required elements, 217-218
  service factors, 218-225, 229
  user factors, 226-229, 231
Acquired immunodeficiency syndrome, 27. *See also* Human
  immunodeficiency virus
  education campaigns, 188
  fear of sexual violence and, 185
  rape victims, 177
  services by family planning
    institutions, 116-118
Adamson, Peter, 184
Adolescents
  family planning program, 122-123
  nutrition, 69-70
  pregnancies, 75-76
Africa. *See also specific countries*
  early pregnancy statistics, 75
  empowerment of women, 24
  female circumcision, 95, 179-180
  female school enrollment, 11
  food production, 13
  gender bias, 18-19

impact of poverty, 7
Inter-African Committee on
  Traditional Practices Affecting
  the Health of Women and
  Children, 180
literacy, 11
maternal mortality, 153, 161
prenatal care, 20, 22
sexually transmitted diseases, 92-94
suicide attempts, 174
wage gap, 14
African American women
  prenatal care, 4-5
  suicide attempts, 174
Aging policies, 53-54. *See also* Elderly
  women
Agriculture
  access to technical support, 85
  production, 13, 151
AIDS. *See* Acquired immunodeficiency
  syndrome
AIDSCOM research grant program, 98
Alcohol abuse, 208-209
Alisjahbana, maternal morbidity
  studies, 36, 39
Alma-Alta Conference, 236
American Medical Association,
  Council on Ethical and Judicial
  Affairs, 165-166
American Psychological Association,
  Task Force on Women's Depres-
  sion, 205
Anemia, 38-39, 76-77, 95
Anthropologists, medical, 236-237
Anthropometric indicators
  arm circumference, 86
  Body Mass Index, 86
  criteria for use, 85-86
  height, 86